D0906206

PUBLIC ADMINISTRATION AND PUBLIC POLICY
A Comprehensive Publication Program

EDITOR-IN-CHIEF

EVAN M. BERMAN
Distinguished University Professor
J. William Fulbright Distinguished Scholar
National Chengchi University
Taipei, Taiwan

Founding Editor

JACK RABIN

RECENTLY PUBLISHED BOOKS

Government Performance and Results: An Evaluation of GPRA's First Decade, Jerry Ellig, Maurice McTigue, and Henry Wray

Practical Human Resources for Public Managers: A Case Study Approach, Nicolas A. Valcik and Teodoro J. Benavides

Globalism and Comparative Public Administration, Jamil Jreisat

Government Budgeting and Financial Management in Practice: Logics to Make Sense of Ambiguity, Gerald J. Miller

Globalism and Comparative Public Administration, Jamil Jreisat

Energy Policy in the U.S.: Politics, Challenges, and Prospects for Change, Laurance R. Geri and David E. McNabb

Public Administration in Southeast Asia: Thailand, Philippines, Malaysia, Hong Kong and Macao, edited by Evan M. Berman

Governance Networks in Public Administration and Public Policy, Christopher Koliba, Jack W. Meek, and Asim Zia

Public Administration and Law: Third Edition, David H. Rosenbloom, Rosemary O'Leary, and Joshua Chanin

Public Administration in East Asia: Mainland China, Japan, South Korea, and Taiwan, edited by Evan M. Berman, M. Jae Moon, and Heungsuk Choi

Handbook of Public Information Systems, Third Edition, edited by Christopher M. Shea and G. David Garson

Science and Technology of Terrorism and Counterterrorism, Second Edition, edited by Tushar K. Ghosh, Mark A. Prelas, Dabir S. Viswanath, and Sudarshan K. Loyalka

Bureaucracy and Administration, edited by Ali Farazmand

Performance-Based Management Systems: Effective Implementation and Maintenance, Patria de Lancer Julnes

Handbook of Governmental Accounting, edited by Frederic B. Bogui

Labor Relations in the Public Sector, Fourth Edition, Richard Kearney

Available Electronically
PublicADMINISTRATION*netBASE*

American Society for Public Administration
Series in Public Administration and Public Policy

GOVERNMENT PERFORMANCE AND RESULTS

An Evaluation of GPRA's First Decade

JERRY ELLIG

MAURICE MCTIGUE

HENRY WRAY

CRC Press
Taylor & Francis Group
Boca Raton   London   New York

CRC Press is an imprint of the
Taylor & Francis Group, an **informa** business

CRC Press
Taylor & Francis Group
6000 Broken Sound Parkway NW, Suite 300
Boca Raton, FL 33487-2742

© 2012 by Taylor & Francis Group, LLC
CRC Press is an imprint of Taylor & Francis Group, an Informa business

No claim to original U.S. Government works

Printed in the United States of America on acid-free paper
Version Date: 20110728

International Standard Book Number: 978-1-4398-4464-9 (Hardback)

Visit the Taylor & Francis Web site at
http://www.taylorandfrancis.com

and the CRC Press Web site at
http://www.crcpress.com

Contents

PART I GPRA AND THE QUALITY OF PERFORMANCE INFORMATION

PART II GPRA AND THE QUALITY OF GOVERNMENT

Acknowledgments

An evaluation project of federal performance reports spanning ten years must necessarily involve scores of dedicated people. In Appendix I, we list the members of the research teams who evaluated the reports or provided other critical research assistance during each year the Mercatus Center produced its *Performance Report Scorecard*. We also gratefully acknowledge the help of external advisors who reviewed our evaluations of agency reports and offered comments on the report that summarized the results each year; they too are listed in the appendix. Of course, the usual academic caveats apply. The fact that someone gave us advice doesn't mean we took it, and we remain responsible for any remaining errors in the project or this book.

Several individuals involved in this project over the years deserve special mention. Our colleague Steve Richardson developed the initial approach to the *Scorecard*, oversaw the research team, and coauthored the annual *Scorecard* report for the first three years. Other colleagues pitched in as *Scorecard* coauthors in various years; they include Jay Cochran, Sarah E. Nutter, and Jennifer Zambone. We have benefited greatly from the efforts of excellent project managers who also served as outreach liaisons to federal agencies: Heather Hambleton, Lisa Korsak, and Jen Wekelo. Numerous colleagues at the Mercatus Center have contributed indirectly to this volume via stimulating and challenging conversations about government performance management; they include Jerry Brito, Susan Dudley, Jason Fichtner, Eileen Norcross, Frederic Sautet, Veronique de Rugy, and Richard Williams. (Apologies to any friends we left out!) Evan Berman, editor of this book series, deserves thanks both for his encouragement of this project and for a number of significant improvements to the manuscript sparked by his comments. We also thank four research assistants whose work contributed directly to this book: Christina Forsberg, Stefanie Haeffele-Balch, John Pulito, and Nick Tuszynski.

Finally, we thank our employer, the Mercatus Center at George Mason University, for supporting this project for ten years. Key individuals include David Nott, the CEO who authorized the first *Scorecard* as an experiment in 2000; his successors Paul Edwards, Tony Woodlief, and Brian Hooks; and Tyler Cowen, the center's general director. Their support ensured that we could pursue this project with maximal academic freedom, calling 'em as we saw 'em.

About the Authors

Dr. Jerry Ellig (jellig@gmu.edu), has been a senior research fellow at the Mercatus Center at George Mason University since 1996. Between August 2001 and August 2003, he served as deputy director of the Office of Policy Planning at the Federal Trade Commission. Dr. Ellig has also served as a senior economist for the Joint Economic Committee of the U.S. Congress and as an assistant professor of economics at George Mason University. Dr. Ellig has published numerous articles on government management and regulation in both scholarly and popular periodicals.

The Honorable Maurice P. McTigue, QSO (mmctigue@gmu.edu), has been a distinguished visiting scholar at the Mercatus Center at George Mason University since 1997. Originally a farmer from New Zealand, he served as a member of the New Zealand Parliament, held eight different Cabinet portfolios, and served as New Zealand's ambassador to Canada and the Caribbean. In 1999, in recognition of his public service, Her Majesty Queen Elizabeth II bestowed upon Mr. McTigue the prestigious Queen's Service Order during a ceremony at Buckingham Palace.

Henry Wray, J.D. (henrywray@verizon.net), is a visiting fellow at the Mercatus Center at George Mason University. He served for more than 30 years on the staff of the U.S. Government Accountability Office (GAO) and the U.S. Congress. At GAO he served as an associate general counsel, ethics counselor, and head of the audit group responsible for evaluations of the U.S. Department of Justice, the law enforcement components of the U.S. Department of Treasury, and the federal judiciary. Mr. Wray has served on the professional staff of the House Budget Committee, the House Committee on Government Reform, and the Senate Governmental Affairs Committee. After retiring from GAO, he served as counsel for the Senate Governmental Affairs Committee and senior counsel to the House Subcommittee on Government Efficiency, Financial Management and Intergovernmental Relations.

Introduction

Public and transparent performance reporting in the United States is at least as old as the first permanent English-speaking settlement. In September 1608, Captain John Smith became president of the struggling colony in Jamestown, Virginia. The colonists nearly perished because many refused to work. The numerous "gentlemen" (sons of the nobility) believed physical labor was beneath their dignity. The less gentle preferred to pilfer tools, guns, and other items to barter with the natives for food. Neither group was held accountable for the negative consequences of their behavior. All food went into a common storehouse, from which everyone was fed.

Smith is famous in American history books for the rule he instituted: "He that will not worke shall not eate (except by sickness he be disabled)." Less well known is that Smith pioneered transparent and public performance reporting: "He made also a Table, as a publicke memorial of every mans deserts, to incourage the good, and with shame to spurre on the rest to amendment. By this many became industrious ... for all were so tasked, that there was no excuse could prevaile to deceive him." Positive outcomes quickly ensued: "This order many murmured was very cruell, but it caused the most part so well to bestirre themselves, that of 200 (except they were drowned) there died not past seven" (Barbour 1986, 208–14). With all due respect to Light (1997), Smith's initiative to bail out the colony in swampy Jamestown may truly be the first "tide of reform" in American public administration.

Though predating the Government Performance and Results Act (GPRA) by 385 years, Smith's initiative satisfies most of the prerequisites for open and honest government management. Beneficial outcomes for the public were well defined, performance measures were clear, causation was well understood, and performance was transparently linked to consequences. Performance reporting was public, accessible, jargon-free (except for the archaic spelling), and verifiable.

Today's governments are rather more complex than the original Jamestown settlement. That makes effective accountability more difficult, but the same basic principles apply: define outcomes, define measures, understand how activities affect outcomes, and link outcomes to costs and consequences.

Those concepts underlie GPRA. Enacted in 1993, this legislation directs U.S. federal agencies to define the outcomes their agencies seek to produce, identify measures that show whether they are making progress on these outcomes, and disclose the results to Congress and the public. GPRA requires agencies to produce periodic strategic plans with goals that include outcomes, annual performance plans with performance measures, and annual performance reports. Strategic plans must explain the outcomes agencies seek to produce for citizens. Annual performance reports must report on the measures and explain the agency's plans to improve performance in the future.

Congress enacted GPRA in part because "waste and inefficiency in federal programs undermine the confidence of the American people in the government." GPRA also noted, "Federal managers are seriously disadvantaged in their efforts to improve program efficiency and effectiveness, because of insufficient articulation of program goals and inadequate information on program performance." The legislation also states that "congressional policymaking, spending decisions and program oversight are seriously handicapped by insufficient attention to program performance and results" (GPRA Sec. 2a). The legislation sought to improve public confidence, program management, and congressional decision making by making better information available about the effectiveness and efficiency of federal programs and spending.

When federal agencies issued their first performance reports for fiscal year 1999, the Mercatus Center at George Mason University embarked on what became a ten-year research program to evaluate the quality of disclosure and offer suggestions for improvement. The Mercatus *Performance Report Scorecard* assessed the reports from 24 agencies covered by the Chief Financial Officers Act, which account for the vast majority of all federal spending.* Over the course of ten years, the *Scorecard* project evaluated approximately 240 GPRA reports. About 25 different individuals served on the research teams that evaluated these reports. Twenty-six different men and women served on the advisory boards that reviewed and commented on our draft evaluations and annual *Scorecard* publication. (A full list of research teams and advisors appears in Appendix I. The usual academic caveat applies: responsibility for any remaining errors in the reports or this book rests solely with us, the authors.)

No specific grants or contracts underwrote this research. The Mercatus Center funded this project out of its general operating budget. We undertook this project largely because one of this book's coauthors, Maurice McTigue, experienced first-hand the power of performance management to improve government's effectiveness and reduce its cost when he held seven different cabinet posts and served as a member of New Zealand's parliament from 1985 to 1994. New Zealand, of course, is widely regarded as a pioneer of outcome-oriented, market-based reforms often referred to as the new public management (Kettl 1997, Scott et al. 1997). By the

---

* The principal parts of government not included in these 24 agencies are the judiciary, the legislative branch, the executive office of the president, and the independent agencies not among the 24 CFO Act agencies. See OMB (2007a, 78). Outlays for these agencies actually exceed the "total outlays" figure, but they total 99% of total outlays plus undistributed offsetting receipts.

mid-1990s, it appeared that GPRA would be the principal legislative vehicle for implementation of new public management ideas in the United States. This created an exciting research opportunity that neither the scholars nor the policy practitioners at the Mercatus Center could afford to miss.

From the start, the *Scorecard* project had both positive and normative goals that were linked to the purposes of GPRA. As scholars, our positive goal was to create a "publicke memorial" of both quantitative and qualitative data that would document the strengths and weaknesses of agency GPRA reports and show how they changed over time. As concerned citizens and former government officials, our normative goals were to "spurre on" federal agencies to produce more accurate and useful disclosure, disseminate knowledge about best practices to "incourage" them in this task, and ultimately "bestirre" decision makers in the administration and Congress to use performance information to make program and budget decisions.

The results of this project can help answer a wide variety of questions in political economy and public administration, such as:

- What factors make performance reports relevant and informative?
- Has the quality of information disclosed to the public improved?
- Why do some agencies produce better reports than others?
- Has GPRA led to greater availability and use of performance information by federal managers?
- Has GPRA led to greater use of performance information in budget decisions?
- What steps would make federal management and budget decisions more performance oriented?

This book is our attempt to answer those questions. All ten editions of the *Performance Report Scorecard* are available on the Mercatus Center's web site, www. mercatus.org, for the benefit of researchers who might want to use our data to further pursue these or other questions.

Intellectual Foundations of the Book

This book falls firmly in the tradition of the new public management and rationalist approaches to decision making and policy. GPRA has been the major factor driving strategic planning and performance reporting in the U.S. government since the mid-1990s. But it is just one example of a performance-oriented revolution that has also occurred on the state level and internationally. Budget shortfalls and new debt burdens will likely increase interest in public management and budgeting techniques that allow governments to "do more with less," so this is an appropriate time to take stock of what GPRA has accomplished and what remains to be done.

We believe citizens are better off when government management and budget decisions are based on actual outcomes produced by programs and policies.

Outcome measurement is imperative because government entities are too large and complex to be centrally planned. Improved effectiveness and efficiency require that government managers and employees be permitted to exercise their creativity and judgment in implementing policies and programs. But if lawmakers do not hold public agencies accountable by providing detailed rules and directions, they must hold them accountable for the results produced with public resources. The new public management bargain, which offers public managers and employees increased flexibility in return for accountability for results (Richardson 2010), strikes us as an eminently sensible one.

In that sense, we are proponents of performance measurement, performance management, and performance budgeting. We would like to see government decision making become more rational, with articulated ends achieved using the most cost-effective means. However, we are not starry-eyed idealists who believe that government decisions will always be rational (if we could just get the right people in charge), nor are we cheerleaders who believe our enthusiastic exhortations are sufficient to overcome real institutional obstacles (if we just cheer loudly enough). Rather, we believe that any movement toward greater outcome focus in government must be tempered with an appreciation of what is realistically possible. Our expectations of what GPRA might realistically achieve, and our suggestions for improvement, are rooted in analysis of how institutions and incentives constrain the actions of government decision makers.

Institutions

Performance reporting may make government more businesslike, but government is not business. Diverse authors note that we should not expect government performance reporting to produce a financial "bottom line" comparable to the profit-and-loss statements of businesses, because there is no common denominator that allows policymakers to directly compare the value produced by programs that aim to achieve diverse outcomes (Key 1940, Wildavsky 1992, von Mises 1946). Of course, policymakers can more directly compare the results of programs that seek to achieve the same objectives (Lewis 1952). The best results we are likely to achieve through performance measurement therefore are: (1) a reduction in inefficiency through reallocation of resources among programs that seek to achieve similar outcomes, and (2) somewhat more satisfactory decisions among programs that achieve very different types of outcomes, because performance measurement at least gives decision makers a clearer understanding about the size of the trade-offs involved.

Not all outcomes, however, are equally measurable. The diversity of federal agency missions, structures, history, and program types suggests it is unrealistic to expect all agencies to do equally well at defining and measuring outcomes (Wilson 1989, Radin 2000, 2006). Policymakers may ultimately have to choose between some outcomes that are reasonably well defined and measured, and others that are not. Still, we think the effort to specify outcomes and identify indicators of success—even if those indicators are not always quantitative—should lead to better decisions than those that will occur if policymakers are vague about the outcomes they seek and do not know whether objectives have been achieved.

Finally, we do not expect performance reporting to automate policy or budget decisions; performance information is just another input into decisions. Over time, effective use of outcome information by policymakers could lead to reallocation of expenditures away from programs that do not produce the desired results. As several scholars note, though, this is not a mechanical process. Some programs may fail to produce results because they are poorly structured, have vague goals, or receive insufficient funding (Moynihan 2008, 127–29, Joyce 2007). Fixing those problems could transform some ineffective programs into effective ones. And performance, of course, is not the only reason policymakers might choose to grow, shrink, or terminate programs. Different decision makers with different values or priorities can be expected to make different budgeting decisions when faced with the same performance information. Nevertheless, we would expect that better outcome information would lead legislators to terminate or shrink at least some of the less effective programs in order to reallocate resources to more effective ones, reduce budget deficits, or reduce taxes. This is one observable change in behavior that might tell us whether performance information is making a difference in budgeting.

Incentives

Our expectations of what is possible are also heavily tempered by public choice economics. Numerous scholars emphasize that federal managers' actions depend heavily on the incentives they face. Classic works by Tullock (2005) and Downs (1967) note that individuals in a bureaucracy achieve career advancement by performing their roles to the satisfaction of their superiors. It follows from this that agency managers can be expected to adopt and use performance measures if they believe that is what their superiors (the political appointees and, ultimately, Congress and the president) want them to do. Tullock (2005, 205–9) notes that measurement of results, where possible, improves the likelihood that bureaucracies will accomplish the tasks that policymakers intend them to accomplish. Even in cases where measurement of outcomes is difficult or impossible, his theory suggests that officials will do their best to implement it as well as they can, or at least create the appearance of implementation, if they believe that is what their superiors want. Tullock's theory implies that top federal managers will develop and implement performance measurement and management if it is clear that Congress and the president want them to. Managers further down the ranks will take their cues from top management.

This theory of bureaucracy explains the widely recognized phenomenon that managers are more likely to use performance information when their leadership credibly commits to performance management (Dull 2009, GAO 2008, 9, Melkers and Willoughby 2007, 74, 94–95, Perrin 2007, 116–117, Ingraham et al. 2003, 131). It also suggests that one way to improve the quality and use of performance information is to alter public managers' financial and career advancement incentives to reward performance. Thus, it is no surprise that extensive civil service reform accompanied the performance measurement initiatives in the Westminster countries (Kettl 1997, Scott 1996). Government pay scales and lifetime job security were eliminated; pay and retention depend on performance. Two years before U.S. agencies issued their first GPRA reports, Scott, Ball, and Dale (1997, 375) noted:

> The New Zealand reforms tackled all parts of the public sector and all subsystems (personal, budgeting, reporting, and the like)…. The same degree of comprehensiveness is not evident in the United States.

Performance management reforms will be more effective when managers have incentives to improve performance. Conversely, when managers fail to implement GPRA-like reforms, we're inclined to seek an explanation in terms of managers' incentives, rather than blaming the managers and assuming that they are simply ignorant or bad people.

Similar logic applies to elected leaders. Politicians can garner political support by concentrating benefits on well-organized groups and dispersing costs among the general, unorganized populace (Olson 1965). In this context, "benefits" may consist either of outcomes produced by programs, or simply expenditures that transfer wealth even if they are not the most effective means of producing desirable outcomes. (Military bases that no longer serve any legitimate defense purpose and the infamous "bridge to nowhere" are two recent examples.) To the extent that they focus merely on transferring wealth to political supporters, politicians have less reason to concern themselves with monitoring programs to ensure that they produce outcomes effectively and efficiently. As the architect of a multi-billion-dollar program once told us, "Members of Congress don't want to measure what outcomes this program achieves. They just want to be able to show how much money it spends in their districts." In other words, sometimes the expenditure, rather than the result, is the primary "outcome" elected officials care about.

The U.S. Constitution's separation of powers complicates the picture further. Congress and the president may have systematically different political incentives to care about performance management. Legislators represent specific geographic constituencies and can gain politically by steering expenditures to their states or congressional districts while dispersing the costs across the entire nation. A constituency receives the benefits of the expenditure but does not bear the full costs. "An example from everyday life is the tendency of restaurant bills that are split equally among diners (by previous agreement or norm) to be larger in total than separate checks would have been" (Primo 2007, 44). The president, on the other hand, has to appeal to the nation's median voters, which may give the president stronger political incentives to monitor programs for efficiency and balance costs with benefits (Niskanen 1994a). In short, politicians' interest in and use of performance information ultimately depends on the strength of their incentives to monitor program effectiveness and efficiency instead of merely delivering expenditures to recipients who desire them. Elected leaders will care about performance information only if they first care about performance.

The *Scorecard* Research Protocol

The *Performance Report Scorecard* evaluated how well agency performance reports disclose to the public the outcomes they produce. The *Scorecard* did not offer an opinion on the quality of agencies' performance, nor did it express views on what activities the government should or should not undertake. It assessed the quality of disclosure, not the quality of results.

Reports were evaluated according to 12 criteria grouped into three categories:

1. Transparency: How easily can a nonspecialist find and understand the report?
   Reports should be accessible, readable, and usable by a wide variety of audiences, including Congress, the administration, the public, news media, and other stakeholders. If a report fails to disclose significant achievements and problems to stakeholders, benefits or failures arising from agency activities will remain secret to all but a few insiders, and citizens will have no real opportunity to indicate their approval or disapproval.
2. Public benefits: How well does the report document the outcomes the agency produces for the public and compare them with costs?
   An agency's value to the public becomes clear only when its goals and measures are expressed in terms of the benefit produced or harm avoided for a particular set of clients or the public at large. To demonstrate openly how agency activities produce meaningful results for the community, reports should focus on outcomes (i.e., tangible benefits that matter in the lives of citizens), rather than on programs or activities as such. The reports should also clearly present the costs of achieving those results. These costs include both the agency's expenditures and other costs borne by the public at large. For regulatory agencies, much of this information should come from rigorous retrospective analysis of the actual effects of regulation, analogous to the information they are supposed to produce when conducting a regulatory impact analysis prior to issuing a regulation. The ultimate objective of such reporting is to match outcomes with costs, so that policymakers and the public understand what citizens are paying to achieve various outcomes.
   Goals and measures that merely document agency activities, such as counts of checks processed or number of people enrolled in a program, assume that

such activities automatically provide public benefits. Such an assumption can be incorrect for a wide variety of reasons. An agency report must highlight achievement of results; otherwise, it will not inform the public of the success or failure of its programs. Budget decisions that rely on such flawed information will fail to reflect realistic assessments of what agencies can accomplish with appropriations.

3. Leadership: How well does the report demonstrate that agency managers use performance information to make decisions?

    Agencies should use the performance information produced by their organizations to identify solutions to problems and to change future plans accordingly. The report should inspire confidence in an agency's ability to enhance citizens' quality of life commensurate with the resources they have entrusted to the agency. Among the factors that give such confidence is tangible evidence that the agency is using performance and financial data to improve management of its programs.

Table 1 lists the evaluation criteria. On each of the 12 criteria, a report could achieve a score ranging from 1 point (no useful content) to 5 points (potential best practice). A report that adequately meets all requirements would receive the middle score of 3 on each factor, resulting in a total score of 36. A 2 indicates that the report accomplishes some but not all of the objectives under a given criterion. A 1 indicates failure to provide much relevant information. A 4 indicates unusually good practices that are better than most, and a 5 indicates an especially superior presentation.

To report the scoring results as transparently as possible, we weighted each criterion equally in calculating each agency's total score and rankings. In theory, total report scores could range from 12 to 60 points. The highest score any report actually earned was 56 points, which the Labor Department's report achieved in fiscal year 2008. The lowest score ever was 17 points, which the Defense Department's report received in fiscal year 2007.

Even when a report received a 5 on a particular criterion, that does not mean there was no room for improvement. A 5 indicates a relative best practice, but best practices should not be confused with perfection. One of the goals of the *Scorecard* was to aid in the diffusion of best practices across agencies. Therefore, a practice that earned a 5 in one year might only receive a 4 or 3 in future years as it becomes standard for most agencies and new best practices emerge. Over time, the research team tightened its scoring standards to reflect the development of new best practices.

The *Scorecard* has been a useful tool for addressing both the positive and the normative issues associate with GPRA. But we soon found that additional research was needed to provide satisfying answers to some of the nagging questions about GPRA's effects. As a result, this book draws extensively on scholarly research and Government Accountability Office (GAO) reports to help answer some of the questions that the *Scorecard* cannot answer on its own.

Table 1   Mercatus *Scorecard* Criteria

Transparency: How easily can a nonspecialist find and understand the report?
1. Accessibility: Is the report easily accessible via the Internet and easily identified?
2. Readability: Is the report easy for a layperson to read and understand?
3. Verification and validation: Are the performance data valid, verifiable, and timely?
4. Baseline and trend data: Did the agency provide baseline and trend data to put its performance measures in context?
Public benefits: How well does the report document the outcomes the agency produces for the public and compare them with costs?
5. Outcome goals: Are the goals and objectives stated as outcomes?
6. Outcome measures: Are the performance measures valid indicators of the agency's impact on its outcome goals?
7. Agency affected outcomes: Does the agency demonstrate that its actions have actually made a significant contribution toward its stated goals?
8. Linkage to costs: Did the agency link its goals and results to costs?
Leadership: How well does the report demonstrate that agency managers use performance information to make decisions?
9. Vision: Does the report show how the agency's results will make this country a better place to live?
10. Explain failures: Does the agency explain failures to achieve its goals?
11. Major management challenges: Does the report adequately address major management challenges?
12. Improvement plans: Does it describe changes in policies or procedures to do better next year?

Outline of the Book

This book consists of two parts. Part I, "GPRA and the Quality of Performance Information," focuses on the quality of presentation and information in GPRA performance reports. It discusses the results of the *Scorecard* extensively, then uses the same scoring framework to evaluate performance reports produced by U.S. states and agencies in other countries. Part I shows how the quality of GPRA reports changed over time and presents numerous examples practitioners can use to improve their own performance reporting.

Part II, "GPRA and the Quality of Government," evaluates the completeness of GPRA's coverage and the extent to which decision makers have used the performance information generated in response to GPRA. For scholars and practitioners alike, Part II helps answer a nagging question: Has any of this planning and reporting activity actually had an effect?

Part I: GPRA and the Quality of Performance Information

Chapter 1: The Evolution of GPRA Performance Reporting

This chapter chronicles the improvements we have observed in federal performance reporting through the lens of the Mercatus Center's annual *Performance Report Scorecard*. The chapter includes both a quantitative analysis of scoring trends and a high-level qualitative analysis of improvements in best practices from fiscal year 1999 through fiscal year 2008. It also uses *Scorecard* data to evaluate the effect of two significant format changes: the fiscal year 2002 merger of GPRA performance reports with agency financial reports to create performance and accountability reports, and the fiscal year 2007–2008 pilot format that allowed agencies to produce a summary report geared toward the average citizen and place more detailed performance and financial information in multiple other documents.

Chapter 2: Best Practices for Outcome-Oriented Reports

This chapter is the first of two that provide detailed discussion of best practices in U.S. federal performance reporting as of fiscal year 2008. We use the term *best practices* in a relative sense; each year's best practices are the best practices we found in that year's performance reports. Unless otherwise noted, the examples in this chapter (as well as Chapter 3) are taken from the fiscal year 2008 cycle of federal agency GPRA performance reports. Fiscal year 2008 was the tenth full cycle of GPRA reporting and the last round of reports we evaluated in detail.

These chapters should be especially useful for practitioners who seek specific ideas they could use to improve their own performance reports. Each practice includes a checklist that shows positive features of good reports and also identifies features that may indicate problems. Chapter 2 focuses specifically on reporting information about outcomes. It highlights examples of outcome-oriented goals and objectives, outcome-oriented measures, use of baseline and trend data, and use of narratives and vignettes to tell an outcome-oriented story.

Chapter 3: Other Essential Best Practices

Outcomes are key to the performance story, but they aren't the only thing that matters to have a solid, useful performance report. This chapter identifies best practices for providing other, substantive information that is critical to accurate evaluation of performance: ensuring that data are valid and verifiable, linking performance information with cost information, assessing failures and problems, and outlining plans for improvement. The chapter also addresses matters of style, such as accessibility and readability.

Chapter 4: The State Factor

Performance reporting is hardly a federal invention; several states have been known as leaders in this field. This chapter compares and contrasts the best practices we have identified in federal performance reports with the practices employed in the reports of several states. To do so, we apply the *Scorecard* evaluation criteria to performance reports from three states that face diverse transportation challenges: Colorado, Connecticut, and Florida. We evaluate reports from the transportation department in each state to maximize comparability. Transportation is of ubiquitous interest on the federal, state, and local levels. It is also an area where some outcomes, such as safety and congestion, are readily measurable, so we should be able to identify some best practices by examining reports from transportation departments. In addition, the U.S. Department of Transportation's GPRA report consistently ranked among the top three in our *Scorecard*. Thus, we will compare state reports with a quite good federal report. The chapter concludes by discussing best practices in federal performance reports that could improve state performance reporting, and practices in state reports that improve on federal practices.

Chapter 5: The International Context

The United States is not the first country to attempt to systematically report policy outcomes, and it may not even be the leader. Other nations, such as Australia, New Zealand, and the United Kingdom, are well known as innovators in performance evaluation, reporting, and budgeting. This chapter uses the *Scorecard*'s evaluation framework to compare performance reports from those three nations with U.S. federal performance reports. As on the state level, we compare reports from transportation departments, for the same reasons. Transportation is of wide interest not just in the United States, but worldwide. As in Chapter 4, we offer observations on practices in other countries' reports that could be used to improve U.S. reports, and vice versa.

Part II: GPRA and the Quality of Government

Transparent public disclosure of outcomes is merely a means to an end. The ultimate goal is improvements in the quality of government through increased use of performance information by federal managers, executive branch policymakers, and legislators. Part II of the book examines whether this has in fact occurred and suggests steps that could improve the use of performance information to deliver more effective government.

Chapter 6: Regulation—Where Transparency Falls Short

GPRA reporting has focused heavily on programs funded by federal expenditures. This chapter assesses the extent of GPRA reporting on federal activities that reflect another major way governments allocate resources: regulation. GPRA reporting has been applied inconsistently to regulation. Agencies that accomplish some of their strategic goals through regulation implicitly capture some of the results of regulation when they report on their performance. However, when agencies enact regulations, they rarely make provisions for retrospective analysis of the regulation's actual effects.

Without rigorous retrospective analysis, we doubt that agencies can truly know whether regulations have accomplished their intended outcomes, or at what cost. We offer several proposals for integrating GPRA considerations into existing regulatory review processes. Regulatory reform is a perennial, hotly debated topic in the United States and other countries. By refocusing the debate on performance measurement, we hope to turn down the heat and switch on the light.

Chapter 7: Tax Expenditures—The Silent Partner

The federal government allocates substantial resources through tax expenditures—reductions in tax liability taxpayers receive in exchange for spending money on activities the government seeks to encourage. The home mortgage interest deduction, deductibility of premiums for employer-provided health insurance, and tax credits for energy-efficient windows are all examples of tax expenditures. In many cases, tax expenditures are substitutes for direct spending programs. Yet in the United States, successive administrations have made little progress in applying GPRA to tax expenditures. We suggest how rigorous program evaluation could identify outcomes linked to tax expenditures and how responsibility for such analysis could be shared among federal agencies with the relevant expertise.

Chapter 8: GPRA and Performance Management within Agencies

One of GPRA's major purposes was to improve federal managers' ability to manage by providing them with information about results. Numerous scholars suggest that this could be one of GPRA's most important contributions (Frederickson and Frederickson 2006, 185, Hatry et al. 2005, 200, Joyce 2007). Scholarly studies and extensive GAO surveys have both sought to assess GPRA's effect on the availability and use of performance information, and Chapter 8 summarizes the results. This chapter outlines the pre-GPRA state of performance management, summarizes scholarly case studies that reveal how agencies use performance information, and shows overall trends in the availability and use of performance information revealed by periodic GAO surveys. The available evidence suggests that GPRA has indeed improved the availability and use of performance information in many federal agencies, but the effects are quite uneven across agencies.

Chapter 9: Toward Performance Budgeting?

GPRA authorized experiments in performance budgeting, which was supposed to link appropriations with outcomes. Performance budgeting has the potential to generate significant benefits as decision makers reallocate resources from programs that are less effective to those that are more effective. This chapter examines whether performance information has significantly affected budget decisions. While agencies and presidential administrations have devoted significant effort toward performance budgeting, the U.S. Congress has thus far shown little interest in using this information to make budget decisions. This differential interest makes sense when one understands the differing incentives Congress and the executive branch face to be concerned about efficient administration of programs.

More widespread use of performance information requires a change in political incentives that would prompt politicians to care more about performance. Consequently, we conclude by considering alternative proposals that would tighten the links between performance and budgeting by altering political incentives.

Chapter 10: Conclusions

The *Scorecard* project spanned fiscal years 1999 to 2008. The first nine chapters of the book focus on this time period. In this final chapter, we review several significant developments that make performance management a fiscal imperative for the future. The financial crisis and consequent explosion in government deficits and debt have raised public ire, but astute voices warned during the previous decade that known demographic trends would require a fundamental reexamination of the U.S. federal government's core functions. We believe reliable performance information should be a key ingredient in this reassessment of the federal budget. After all, if we are going to reassess "what Americans want from their government and how much they are willing to pay for those things" (Walker 2005, 2), the first step is knowing what we're getting now.

GPRA AND THE QUALITY OF PERFORMANCE INFORMATION

1

Chapter 1

The Evolution of GPRA Performance Reporting

Evaluating the same 24 agencies' Government Performance and Results Act (GPRA) reports over a ten-year period allows us to address a number of related topics. We can identify which agencies consistently produced good reports, which agencies consistently produced poor reports, and which agencies showed the most dramatic improvement. We can track how the overall quality of disclosure changed over time, using both quantitative scores and qualitative analysis of best practices. We can also examine how significant changes in reporting formats altered the quality of disclosure. In so doing, we provide helpful ideas and examples for professionals who produce agency strategic plans and performance reports. In addition, these topics are crucial to answering the broader question of whether GPRA has improved the quality of performance information available to decision makers and the public.

This chapter provides a high-level overview of scoring trends, improvements in best practices, and the effects of two big changes in the reporting format introduced during the ten years covered by our *Scorecard*. To gauge progress, it offers a summary snapshot of best practices in fiscal years 1999 and 2008. Chapters 2 and 3 contain a much more detailed discussion of current best reporting practices as of fiscal year 2008, including specific examples from different agencies' reports. Space constraints preclude us from tracing the year-by-year evolution of best practices on individual scoring criteria in this book. We urge readers who are interested in this to consult the annual editions of the *Scorecard,* which identify each year's best practices on each scoring criterion and name the reports that exemplify those practices. All ten annual editions of the *Scorecard* are available at www.mercatus.org. Most agency performance reports are available online via the agency's web site, though not all agencies make the first few years' reports available online.

Scoring Trends

The quality of GPRA reports improved substantially during the ten years of the *Scorecard* project. Table 1.1 shows the change in each report's score between fiscal year 1999 and fiscal year 2008. For the 17 reports whose scores improved, the average increase was 8.94 points, almost double the average increase of 4.84 points for all 24 reports. Nine reports achieved double-digit increases in their scores.

The Department of Labor produced the best report in fiscal year 2008. Previously, Labor's report had captured first place four years in a row, from fiscal year 2002 through fiscal year 2005. Labor also produced the most-improved report during the ten-year period. Other big improvers included the Nuclear Regulatory Commission (+15 points), the Departments of Homeland Security and Commerce (+13 points), the Departments of State and Health and Human Services (+12 points), and the National Science Foundation and Departments of Justice and Agriculture (+11 points).

Two other departments' reports showed relatively smaller improvements, but that's because they consistently scored high and ranked near the top in every year. The Department of Transportation's report was second only to Labor in the number of first-place finishes, topping the list four times. Transportation's report never ranked below third. The Department of Veterans Affairs finished in the top three every year except 2005, when it ranked fourth. One should not make too much of these differences between the best reports. In most years, the *Scorecard* virtually produced a three- or four-way tie for first place, with the best reports separated from each other by only a few points.

The Department of State provides perhaps the most intriguing "rise and fall" story. State's report ranked 17th in fiscal year 1999 and fell to 20th in fiscal year 2001. It then rose steadily, finishing in the top four from fiscal year 2003 through fiscal year 2006. State's report plummeted to 18th place in fiscal year 2007 and recovered to 6th place in fiscal year 2008.

A good deal of State's changing fortunes can be traced to changes in its strategic plan, which defines the department's goals and measures. Outcome-oriented goals and measures have a big influence on the scores a report receives on at least three of the evaluation criteria:

Criterion 5: Outcome goals: Are the goals and objectives stated as outcomes?
Criterion 6: Outcome measures:- Are the performance measures valid indicators of the agency's impact on its outcome goals?
Criterion 7: Agency affected outcomes: Does the agency demonstrate that its actions have actually made a significant contribution toward its stated goals?

Figure 1.1 shows how the State Department's scores on these three criteria changed over time. During the four years it achieved high scores on the outcome-oriented criteria, it ranked among the top four reports. Table 1.2 compares the State

Table 1.1   Fiscal Year 2008 Scores and Ranks vs. Fiscal Year 1999

	Fiscal Year 2008		Fiscal Year 1999		Change in Score	Change in Rank
	Total Score	Rank	Total Score	Rank		
Labor	56	1	36	5	+20	+4
Veterans	54	2	48	3	+6	+1
Transportation	53	3	51	2	+2	−1
DHS[a]	40	4	27	22	+13	+18
NRC	40	4	25	17	+15	+13
Education	37	6	37	4	0	−2
Interior	37	6	31	11	+6	+5
State	37	6	25	17	+12	+11
Treasury	37	6	36	5	+1	−1
Energy	36	10	27	14	+9	+4
EPA	36	10	31	11	+5	+1
HHS	36	10	24	20	+12	+10
USAID	36	10	52	1	−16	−9
Commerce	35	14	22	22	+13	+8
Justice	34	15	23	21	+11	+6
Agriculture	33	16	22	22	+11	+6
GSA	32	17	32	9	0	8
NSF	32	17	21	24	+11	+7
Social Security	32	17	33	8	−1	−9
NASA	31	20	27	14	+4	−6
OPM	28	21	27	14	+1	−7
HUD	27	22	28	13	−1	−9
Defense	26	23	34	7	−8	−16
SBA	22	24	32	9	−10	−15
Average	36.13		31.29		4.83	
Median	36.00		29.50		6.50	

Source: McTigue, Maurice, Henry Wray, and Jerry Ellig, *10th Annual Performance Report Scorecard: Which Federal Agencies Best Inform the Public?* Arlington, VA: Mercatus Center at George Mason University, 2009, 10, http://mercatus.org/publication/10th-annual-performance-report-scorecard-which-federal-agencies-best-inform-public.

Note: Highest rank = 1; lowest = 24. maximum possible score = 60; minimum = 12.

[a] Since DHS did not exist in 1999, the chart shows its score and rank from fiscal year 2004, the first year its report was included in the *Scorecard*.

Table 1.2   State Department's Goals and Measures, Fiscal Years 2006 and 2007

2006	2007
Strategic Goals	
• Regional stability: Avert and resolve local and regional conflicts to preserve peace and minimize harm to the national interests of the United States. • Counterterrorism: Prevent attacks against the United States, our allies, and our friends, and strengthen alliances and international arrangements to deter global terrorism. • Homeland security: Secure the homeland by strengthening arrangements that govern the flows of people, goods, and services between the United States and the rest of the world. • Weapons of mass destruction: Reduce the threat of weapons of mass destruction to the United States, our allies, and our friends. • International crime and drugs: Minimize the impact of international crime and illegal drugs on the United States and its citizens. • American citizens: Assist American citizens to travel, conduct business, and live abroad securely. • Democracy and human rights: Advance the growth of democracy and good governance, including civil society, the rule of law, respect for human rights, and religious freedom. • Economic prosperity and security: Strengthen world economic growth, development, and stability, while expanding opportunities for U.S. businesses and ensuring economic security for the nation. • Social and environmental issues: Improve health, education, environment, and other conditions for the global population. • Humanitarian response: Minimize the human costs of displacement, conflicts, and natural disasters. • Public diplomacy and public affairs: Increase understanding for American values, policies, and initiatives to create a receptive international environment.	• Achieving peace and security. • Governing justly and democratically. • Investing in people. • Promoting economic growth and prosperity. • Providing humanitarian assistance. • Promoting international understanding.

Table 1.2 *(Continued)*   **State Department's Goals and Measures, Fiscal Years 2006 and 2007**

2006	2007
Strategic Objectives	
None in the usual sense of strategic objectives used to elaborate on the strategic goals. The report designates broad descriptors above the strategic goals as "strategic objectives."	No strategic objectives as such. There is a list of "strategic priorities" for each goal, but they add little substance to the goals.
Performance Goals	
State has 32 programmatic annual performance goals, all of which are clearly stated as intermediate or end outcomes.	None.
Performance Measures	
State has 94 performance measures. They included many end outcomes or intermediate outcomes, but were less results-oriented than the goals. About half of the measures capture intermediate or end outcomes.	The highlights document describes 28 illustrative performance measures, of which about one-third capture intermediate or end outcomes. Most are numbers that relate to outputs or activities. Several would be more outcome-oriented if expressed as a percentage rather than a raw number. The rest of the 101 measures are listed without any accompanying narratives. Thus, it is difficult to assess their outcome orientation.

Source: McTigue, Maurice, Henry Wray, and Jerry Ellig, *9th Annual Performance Report Scorecard: Which Federal Agencies Best Inform the Public?* Arlington, VA: Mercatus Center at George Mason University, 2008, 38–39, http://mercatus.org/sites/default/files/publication/20080506_9th_Annual_ Performance_Report_Scorecard.pdf.

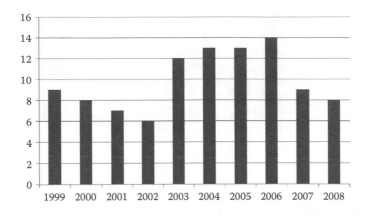

Figure 1.1   State Department's scores on outcome-oriented criteria.

Table 1.3   Department of Health and Human Services Goals and Measures

2006	2007
Strategic Goals	
• Reduce the major threats to the health and well-being of Americans. • Enhance the ability of the Nation's health care system to effectively respond to bioterrorism and other public health challenges. • Increase the percentage of the nation's children and adults who have access to health care services, and expand consumer choices. • Enhance the capacity and productivity of the nation's health science research enterprise. • Improve the quality of health care services. • Improve the economic and social well-being of individuals, families, and communities, especially those most in need. • Improve stability and healthy development of our nation's children and youth.	• Health care: Improve the safety, quality, affordability, and accessibility of health care, including behavioral health care and long-term care. • Public health promotion and protection, disease prevention, and emergency preparedness: Prevent and control disease, injury, illness, and disability across the life span, and protect the public from infectious, occupational, environmental, and terrorist threats. • Human services: Promote the economic and social well-being of individuals, families, and communities. • Scientific research and development: Advance the scientific and biomedical research and development related to health and human services.

Table 1.3 *(Continued)* **Department of Health and Human Services Goals and Measures**

2006	2007
Strategic Objectives	
None.	There are 16 strategic objectives, of which 10 capture measurable outcomes and another four are outcome-oriented but at a very high level.
Performance Goals	
None described in the report.	None.
Performance Measures	
Of the 35 performance measures covered by the report, about one-third are outcome-oriented.	About two-thirds of the 40 performance measures are stated as end outcomes or intermediate outcomes.

Source: McTigue, Maurice, Henry Wray, and Jerry Ellig, *9th Annual Performance Report Scorecard: Which Federal Agencies Best Inform the Public?* Arlington, VA: Mercatus Center at George Mason University, 2008, 36, http://mercatus.org/sites/default/files/publication/20080506_9th_Annual_Performance_Report_Scorecard.pdf.

Department's strategic goals, strategic objectives, performance goals, and performance measures in fiscal years 2006 and 2007. The department's goals and measures clearly became much less outcome-oriented in fiscal year 2007.

Several reports ranked consistently low for most of the ten-year period. Defense ranked 7th in fiscal year 1999, never finished higher than 16th subsequently, and usually ranked below 20th. The Office of Personnel Management never ranked higher than 12th and usually ranked 20th or lower.

Health and Human Services also ranked 20th or below in most years. Unlike Defense and OPM, however, HHS shot up to 5th place in fiscal year 2007 and finished 10th in fiscal year 2008. For HHS, these scores in the last two years might signify some lasting improvements. As with State, HHS surged on the strength of improved outcome-oriented goals and measures in its strategic plan. Table 1.3 compares the department's goals and measures in fiscal years 2006 and 2007.

Homeland Security shows a similar pattern. This department existed for only six of the ten years covered by the *Scorecard*. From fiscal year 2003 through fiscal year 2006, it never ranked better than 21st. Homeland Security climbed to 5th place in fiscal year 2007 and 4th place in fiscal year 2008. Improvements in

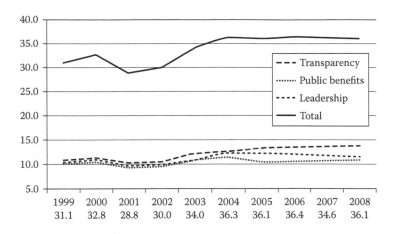

Figure 1.2 Average score changes.

Homeland Security's goals and measures are covered in Chapter 2. (Comprehensive score and ranking data for all agencies are available in McTigue et al. 2009).

Figure 1.2 shows that average total scores increased by about 15% between fiscal year 1999 and fiscal year 2008. Average total scores hit a plateau in fiscal year 2004. For the ten-year period, the largest increase came in the transparency criteria, which improved by 25%. Scores for the public benefits and leadership criteria each increased by about 10%.

All of these score data understate the full extent of improvement because the research team tightened the scoring criteria over time as new best practices emerged. To gain a better understanding of how the quality of disclosure improved, we performed both a quantitative and a qualitative evaluation. The quantitative evaluation reevaluated some fiscal year 1999 reports according to the standards used in fiscal year 2008. The qualitative evaluation assessed the progress in best practices during the ten-year period.

Quantitative Evaluation of Progress

The ideal way to control for tighter scoring standards over time would be to reevaluate all of the fiscal year 1999 reports using the more stringent fiscal year 2008 standards. Resource constraints precluded this. However, for the final *Scorecard* in 2008, the research team reexamined the top four reports from fiscal year 1999 using the same standards applied in fiscal year 2008. Table 1.4 shows the results. Evaluated by fiscal year 2008 standards, the best fiscal year 1999 report (from USAID) would have ranked 16th in fiscal year 2008, with just 33 points out of a possible 60. The other fiscal year 1999 reports would have ranked even lower.

Table 1.4 Top Four 1999 Reports Would Rank Low in 2008

	Transparency	Public Benefits	Leadership	Total	Rank
Labor	20	19	17	56	1
Veterans	19	16	19	54	2
Transportation	16	20	17	53	3
DHS	15	13	12	40	4
NRC	15	13	12	40	4
Education	14	12	11	37	6
Interior	16	10	11	37	6
State	15	10	12	37	6
Treasury	14	10	13	37	6
Energy	13	11	12	36	10
EPA	13	11	12	36	10
HHS	13	13	10	36	10
USAID	15	10	11	36	10
Commerce	15	10	10	35	14
Justice	15	8	11	34	15
Agriculture	12	10	11	33	16
USAID 1999	9	11	13	33	16
GSA	11	12	9	32	17
NSF	15	7	10	32	17
Social Security	12	8	12	32	17
NASA	11	8	12	31	20
Transportation 1999	9	12	10	31	20
Veterans 1999	11	10	10	31	20
OPM	11	8	9	28	21
HUD	11	8	8	27	22
Education 1999	10	8	9	27	22
Defense	11	7	8	26	23
SBA	8	8	6	22	24
Fiscal year 2008 average	13.8	10.9	11.5	36.1	
Fiscal year 2008 median	14.0	10.0	11.0	36.0	

Source: McTigue, Maurice, Henry Wray, and Jerry Ellig, *10th Annual Performance Report Scorecard: Which Federal Agencies Best Inform the Public?* Arlington, VA: Mercatus Center at George Mason University, 2009, 12, http://mercatus.org/publication/10th-annual-performance-report-scorecard-which-federal-agencies-best-inform-public.

Note: Highest rank = 1, lowest = 24, maximum possible score = 60, minimum = 12.

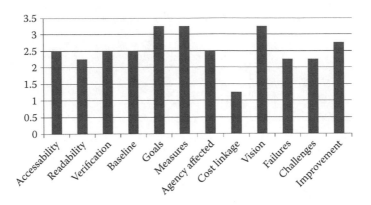

Figure 1.3   Average scores for reevaluated fiscal year 1999 reports.

We can gauge improvement in these agencies' reports by comparing the scores on their reevaluated fiscal year 1999 reports with the scores their reports received in fiscal year 2008. Using the scores reported in Table 1.4, USAID's report improved by about 9% over ten years (from 33 to 36 points), Education's report improved by 37% (from 27 to 37 points), Transportation's report improved by 71% (from 31 to 53 points), and Veterans Affairs report improved by 74% (from 31 to 54 points).

Extrapolating from these four reports, report quality may have improved by about 75% on average.* Of course, that means the quality of some agencies' reports increased by even more than that amount, and others by less.

Figure 1.3 shows how these four reports scored on individual criteria. Average scores on criterion 5 (outcome-oriented goals), criterion 6 (outcome-oriented measures), and criterion 9 (vision) all exceed the satisfactory score of 3—even when evaluated by fiscal year 2008 standards. This suggests that even in the early days of GPRA, the higher-ranking agencies got off to a good start in formulating a clear vision and outcome-oriented goals and measures. However, the average score on criterion 8 (linkage of results to costs) barely exceeds 1. This indicates that, compared to fiscal year 2008 practice, even the top scorers had little cost-related content in fiscal year 1999.

---

* Scores for the four reevaluated fiscal year 1999 reports averaged one-third lower under the fiscal year 2008 standards than under the fiscal year 1999 standards. If we assume that using the fiscal year 2008 scoring standards would have reduced all fiscal year 1999 scores by one-third, the average fiscal year 1999 score using fiscal year 2008 standards would have been 20.65 instead of the 31.29 shown in Table 1.2. An increase from 20.65 to the average fiscal year 2008 score of 36.13 implies that the average quality of performance reports improved by at least 75%. If the average fiscal year 1999 score using fiscal year 2008 scoring standards would have been 20.65, the percentage improvement is calculated by subtracting this score from the actual fiscal year 2008 score (36.13), then dividing this difference by 20.65.

Evolution of Best Practices

Qualitative analysis of best practices also reveals substantial improvements since fiscal year 1999. For fiscal year 1999, one agency's GPRA report consisted of a copier paper box full of separate reports from individual components of the agency; no agency would try to get away with that now. An agency could receive the highest possible score for accessibility of its report in fiscal year 1999 simply by posting the report on its web page and making it easy to find. In 2008, that was a minimal requirement. Best practices included making the report available on time, downloadable as a single document or individual sections, with clear information about whom to contact with comments or questions. Similarly, in fiscal year 1999, a report received the top score on linking results to costs because it broke down costs and personnel by program area. In 2008, the best reports broke costs down by individual performance measure and presented the information for multiple years.

The list below summarizes how the state of the art advanced during the decade. Except for criterion 1 (accessibility), the best practices in the list below are not usually typical. In most cases, only a few reports in each year used the best practices. Many reports could still improve greatly simply by adopting best practices used by other agencies. This list provides just short summaries that indicate the extent of progress. For readers seeking specific improvement ideas, Chapters 2 and 3 explore recent best practices in depth.

Criterion 1: Accessibility

Fiscal Year 1999

Labor and OPM had their reports available online with obvious links from their home pages. Sixteen agencies made their reports available online, but only four earned a score of 5 for clearly labeling the report as the annual performance report and making it easy to find.

Fiscal Year 2008

Thirteen agencies earned a score of 5 because they posted their reports on time, created a direct link on the home page, permitted downloads as both single and multiple files, and provided contact information for questions or comments.

Criterion 2: Readability

Fiscal Year 1999

USAID produced a lengthy report with a massive amount of detail, but the organization, headings, sidebars, tables, and charts made the report easy to scan and digest. Relative lack of jargon made the report understandable to readers who are not specialists in foreign aid.

Fiscal Year 2008

Justice and Labor were the only reports to score a 5. The "Management's Discussion and Analysis" section and the "Performance" section of Justice's report are much shorter than in most agency performance and accountability reports. Justice's report includes 25 key measures, and presents goals, measures, and results in convenient tables. Labor's report is visually appealing with helpful tables and graphics. The secretary's letter describes key achievements over time as well as fiscal year 2008 results for each strategic goal. Both reports are complemented by excellent, brief "citizens' reports" that include two-page performance snapshots, concise summaries of results, and reader-friendly links to additional information.

Criterion 3: Verification and Validation

Fiscal Year 1999

The Department of Education's report presented a thorough discussion of validation procedures and data limitations. The report acknowledged data deficiencies and outlined plans to develop new databases, improve data quality, and ensure the accuracy of financial statements.

Fiscal Year 2008

Labor's report assessed the quality of its data for each performance goal and provided data sources for each measure. Tables in the Veterans Affairs report provided data definitions, verification and validation information, and data limitations.

Criterion 4: Baseline and Trend Data

Fiscal Year 1999

Transportation's report presented trend data for as far back as five or ten years. Defense juxtaposed three years of actual data with the goals for each program for the next three years. Veterans Affairs, Education, and USAID also provided useful baseline data.

Fiscal Year 2008

Labor and Veterans Affairs both presented four years' worth of baseline data for key measures. Data included targets, actual results, and (in Labor's case) costs. Labor and Treasury used graphics to show performance trends. Veterans Affairs showed long-range targets for each measure, and Transportation presented a fiscal year 2009 forecast for each measure.

Criterion 5: Outcome-Oriented Goals

Fiscal Year 1999

All five of Transportation's strategic goals were outcome-oriented. Most of Veterans Affairs' and USAID's were too.

Fiscal Year 2008

The vast majority of Labor's and Transportation's goals and objectives were clear, measurable outcomes that the general public can appreciate and understand, such as safer workplaces, employment of people who were in job training programs, reduced highway congestion, and reduced transportation accidents and fatalities.

Criterion 6: Outcome Measures

Fiscal Year 1999

Most measures in the Veterans Affairs and Transportation reports were outcomes or closely related to outcomes.

Fiscal Year 2008

Labor's measures for three of its four strategic goals were outcomes; the fourth had a mix of outcome, activity, output, and efficiency measures. Transportation's measures for three of five strategic goals were all outcomes; for two other goals, about half the measures were end or intermediate outcomes.

Criterion 7: Agency Affected Outcomes

Fiscal Year 1999

USAID explained how its activities contributed to results in specific cases, and also acknowledged other factors that may have contributed to the results.

Fiscal Year 2008

Four agencies consistently described how their activities led to observed results on highly outcome-oriented performance metrics.

Criterion 8: Results Linked to Costs

Fiscal Year 1999

The Veterans Affairs report included charts that juxtaposed personnel and costs by program area with performance measures for each program area.

Fiscal Year 2008

Labor and Transportation both assigned costs to strategic goals and most individual performance measures. Labor's report contained this information for several years.

Criterion 9: Vision

Fiscal Year 1999

Transportation made a case for how it affects Americans' quality of life by writing each strategic goal so that it identifies a broad result of interest to citizens and then explained the means by which the department hopes to accomplish the result.

Fiscal Year 2008

Narratives in both the Transportation and Veterans Affairs reports cited specific, major accomplishments that affect citizens' quality of life. Narratives and vignettes were linked to outcome-oriented performance metrics, and performance metrics demonstrated that the narratives describe general results rather than isolated, anecdotal successes.

Criterion 10: Explanation of Failures

Fiscal Year 1999

USAID's report provided explanations when targets were not met and described planned remedies for unmet targets.

Fiscal Year 2008

The Veterans Affairs report included a performance shortfall analysis, which described reasons for shortfalls and outlined steps and a timeline to remedy them. The report even offered performance improvement steps in cases where targets were met. NASA, Transportation, and Treasury also identified shortfalls on performance measures, explained reasons for the shortfalls, and outlined plans to improve.

Criterion 11: Major Management Challenges

Fiscal Year 1999

Transportation, USAID, and Veterans Affairs all included thorough discussions of management challenges identified by the agency inspector general and the GAO.

Fiscal Year 2008

Best practices included an insightful inspector general report that lists major management challenges and assesses the agency's progress toward resolving them, an agency self-assessment of progress, a description of actions taken, a timeline for resolving each challenge, and an explanation of how each challenge is related to the agency's strategic goals. No agency did all of these things, but various combinations can be found in the reports from Labor, EPA, Transportation, and Veterans Affairs. The best example of an insightful inspector general report was for SBA. Unfortunately, the SBA citizens' report did not reference this very useful document, which appeared in the agency's financial report.

Criterion 12: Improvement Plans

Fiscal Year 1999

Discussion of each measure in Transportation's report included fiscal year 1999 results, projected performance in fiscal year 2000, and actions planned to achieve goals in fiscal year 2001.

Fiscal Year 2008

Reports from Labor, Veterans Affairs, and Transportation presented improvement strategies for performance shortfalls and major management challenges. They also described broader challenges the agencies expect to face in the future and offered plans for addressing them. This qualitative description of best practices is consistent with the quantitative score assessment: performance reporting made significant progress between 1999 and 2008.

Improvements in scores and best practices on the Mercatus *Scorecard* are of course just rough indicators of improvements in the quality of useful performance information. As agencies became more familiar with the *Scorecard* criteria, some may have sought to "game" the scoring system by searching for the easiest ways to improve their scores rather than the most useful ways to improve their performance information. By the end of the project, approximately half of the 24 agencies each year were seeking more detailed advice and feedback from the Mercatus Center research team. This we provided free of charge, as the *Scorecard* was never intended to be a "loss leader" for paid consulting. Though some gaming surely occurred, the size of the score improvements and the nature of the improvement in best practices suggest that agencies also accomplished some genuine improvements in the quality of performance disclosure.

Effects of Major Format Changes

During the course of the *Scorecard* project, agency GPRA reports experienced two significant format changes. In fiscal year 2002, agencies issued combined performance and accountability reports that included both GPRA performance information and audited financial statements. In fiscal year 2007, OMB adopted a pilot reporting format that allowed agencies to put GPRA performance information in their congressional budget justifications, produce a shorted highlights document summarizing key performance information, and produce a separate financial report. Scorecard data allow us to evaluate the effects of both changes on the quality of GPRA reporting.

Performance and Accountability Reports

GPRA called for each agency to produce an annual performance report. Beginning in fiscal year 2002, the Reports Consolidation Act allowed agencies to combine their GPRA performance reports with financial statements and related information previously published as the agency's accountability report. The legislation required agency heads to include a transmittal letter assessing the completeness and reliability of both the performance and financial data. OMB guidance specified that a performance and accountability report must include three sections: (1) "Management's Discussion and Analysis," which serves as an overview of both the performance and the financial information, (2) a performance section that supplies all the information required by GPRA, and (3) a financial section that includes financial statements, auditors' reports, the agency inspector general's discussion of major management challenges, and the chief financial officer's explanation of how the agency plans to deal with concerns raised by auditors and the inspector general (OMB 2002b).

All agencies evaluated in the *Scorecard* produced performance and accountability reports in fiscal year 2002. The greatest potential benefit of combining the two reports is that it creates opportunities to match cost information with information about outcomes. For agencies that previously had no cost information at all in their performance reports, the financial statements at least provide something. More importantly, the requirement that management provide an overview of performance and financial information created opportunities to integrate the two, or at least brought that possibility to management's attention.

Score data for criterion 8 (linkage of results to costs) suggest that the combined performance and accountability report may have improved the linkage of outcomes and costs. Between fiscal year 2001 and fiscal year 2002, the average score on this criterion increased by 23%—by far the largest increase before or since.

The mandatory transmittal letter from the agency head created a new opportunity for agencies to explain how they serve citizens. Many departments habitually use this letter as an opportunity to explain the principal outcomes the agency seeks to achieve and highlight key accomplishments. As Chapter 3 notes, three of the strongest have been from the Departments of Labor, Veterans Affairs, and Transportation. Some agencies, however, treat the transmittal letter as nothing more than a perfunctory recitation of the assurances required by law. The Defense Department never even had the secretary of defense sign the letter.

Highlights and Citizens' Reports

For fiscal years 2007 and 2008, OMB allowed agencies to use an alternative reporting format under a pilot program. Instead of producing a performance and accountability report that combined performance and financial information, agencies had the option of publishing detailed performance information along with their congressional budget justifications, producing a separate financial report, and producing a shorter highlights document intended to summarize both the performance and financial results. For fiscal year 2008, the highlights document was renamed the "citizens' report." Also in that year, all agencies were required to produce a two-page snapshot that highlighted key performance and financial information. The citizens' reports included these snapshots, and agencies not producing citizens' reports were free to utilize them in their PARs. OMB (2009c) also combined all of the snapshots into the fiscal year 2008, Performance Report of the Federal Government.

Table 1.5 lists which agencies used which format in fiscal years 2007 and 2008. Nine agencies opted for the pilot approach each year. In addition, eight agencies that produced traditional performance and accountability reports also produced a highlights document or citizens' report, even though they were not required to do so. Both of these phenomena raised a novel issue: Exactly what would count as a report for our evaluation purposes?

To answer this question, we started with the premise that our evaluation was intended to gauge the usefulness of these reports to the general public. The pilot format did not in any way absolve agencies of the responsibility to produce meaningful information for the public. In Circular A-136, OMB stated:

> Using an alternative format should not in any way reduce the public's access to the detailed financial and performance information available in a consolidated PAR and should aim to make the presentation of performance information more meaningful.... The goals of the pilot are to allow agencies to explore different formats to enhance the presentation of financial and performance information and make this information more meaningful and transparent to the public. (OMB 2007c, 11–12)

Table 1.5 Reporting Formats in Fiscal Years 2007 and 2008

Traditional PAR Format	Pilot Format
Department of Transportation (2007, 2008)	Department of Health and Human Services (2007, 2008)
Department of Labor (2007, 2008)	Department of Homeland Security (2007, 2008)
Department of Veterans Affairs (2007, 2008)	Agency for International Development (2007, 2008)
Nuclear Regulatory Commission (2007, 2008)	National Aeronautics and Space Administration (2007)
Department of Commerce (2007, 2008)	Department of Energy (2007, 2008)
Department of Justice (2007, 2008)	National Science Foundation (2007, 2008)
Department of the Treasury (2007, 2008)	Department of State (2007, 2008)
General Services Administration (2007, 2008)	Small Business Administration (2007, 2008)
Department of Agriculture (2007, 2008)	Department of Defense (2007, 2008)
Environmental Protection Agency (2007, 2008)	Office of Personnel Management (2008)
Social Security Administration (2007, 2008)	
Department of Education (2007, 2008)	
Department of the Interior (2007, 2008)	
Department of Housing and Urban Development (2007, 2008)	
Office of Personnel Management (2007)	
National Aeronautics and Space Administration (2008)	

For agencies participating in the pilot program, the highlights document is the primary one available and accessible to the public that explains performance and financial information. We recognized, however, that the highlights document might not contain as much detailed information as a traditional performance and accountability report. Therefore, for pilot agencies we started our evaluation with the highlights document. We then included information from other documents if the highlights document clearly indicated where and how the reader could find this information and presented it in an accessible and understandable form. The most common example of this was agency inspector general discussions of major management challenges. Pilot agencies included these in their financial reports, but usually informed the reader about this in the highlights document. Some also noted that more detailed performance information was available in a separate performance report. We did not consider information published in congressional budget justifications, because these documents are lengthy and difficult for non-specialists to navigate. None of the highlights documents specifically referenced or directly linked to a specific place in the budget justifications for the reader to find a particular type of information. By fiscal year 2008, most pilot agencies produced freestanding performance reports.

We treated the highlights document differently for agencies that produced traditional performance and accountability reports. For those agencies, the performance and accountability report should still be the primary means of communication with the public. After evaluating this report, we then examined the agency's highlights document to see if anything in that document merited a higher score. The principal way a highlights document might supplement a traditional performance and accountability report would be by improving readability. In fact, several agencies did receive extra points on our readability criterion due to the quality of their highlights documents.

One way to assess the effects of the pilot format is to compare the fiscal year 2007 and 2008 scores of reports using that format with the scores of traditional performance and accountability reports. Table 1.6 shows that the quality of the 15 traditional performance and accountability reports exceeded the quality of the nine pilot reports by a wide margin. In fiscal year 2007, the average score for traditional performance and accountability reports was 24% higher than the average score for pilot reports. In fiscal year 2008, the average score for traditional performance and accountability reports was 18% higher. Traditional reports did much better on all three categories (transparency, public benefits, and leadership). In fact, the only individual criteria with little scoring difference were criterion 1 (availability) and criterion 5 (outcome-oriented goals). One might expect little difference in these scores related to reporting format, since criterion 1 largely depends on how the agency presents its report on the web, and criterion 5 depends on the quality of the goals established in the agency's strategic plan.

Comparing scores of the traditional and pilot formats might not provide an unambiguous evaluation of the pilot program if there are systematic differences

Table 1.6 Regular PARs Outscore Pilot Format

	Transparency	Public Benefits	Leadership	Total Score
PAR 2007 average	14.07	11.27	12.00	37.33
Pilot 2007 average	10.78	9.44	9.78	30.00
Difference	3.29	1.82	2.22	7.33
% Difference	31%	19%	23%	24%
PAR 2008 average	14.27	11.67	12.33	38.27
Pilot 2008 average	12.89	9.67	10.00	32.56
Difference	1.38	2.00	2.33	5.71
% Difference	11%	21%	23%	18%

Source: McTigue, Maurice, Henry Wray, and Jerry Ellig, *9th Annual Performance Report Scorecard: Which Federal Agencies Best Inform the Public?* Arlington, VA: Mercatus Center at George Mason University, 2008, 24, http://mercatus.org/sites/default/files/publication/20080506_9th_Annual_Performance_Report_Scorecard.pdf; McTigue, Maurice, Henry Wray, and Jerry Ellig, *10th Annual Performance Report Scorecard: Which Federal Agencies Best Inform the Public?* Arlington, VA: Mercatus Center at George Mason University, 2009, 18, http://mercatus.org/publication/10th-annual-performance-report-scorecard-which-federal-agencies-best-inform-public.

between the agencies that chose each reporting format. We noticed one obvious difference: reports from most of the agencies choosing the pilot format did not rank highly on our fiscal 2006 *Scorecard*. To the extent that scores and rank show some inertia from year to year, average scores for agencies choosing the pilot format might have been lower even if they had produced their reports in the traditional format.

Figure 1.4 controls for this difference by showing the average scores for the two different reporting formats in fiscal years 2006, 2007, and 2008. The average total score for agencies producing traditional performance and accountability reports was virtually identical in all three years. Scores for reports using the pilot format, however, fell noticeably in fiscal year 2007. The average total score fell by more than 4 points, or 12%. Scores fell in all three categories and on most individual criteria. Especially noteworthy were drops of 25% or more for criterion 3 (verification and validation of data), criterion 4 (baseline and trend data), criterion 8 (linkage of results to costs), and criterion 12 (plans to remedy performance deficiencies). These scores fell mainly because this information was significantly abbreviated—or disappeared from public view altogether—in the pilot format in fiscal year 2007.

Agencies using the pilot format largely remedied these deficiencies in fiscal year 2008. Reports using the pilot format in fiscal year 2008 had scores averaging

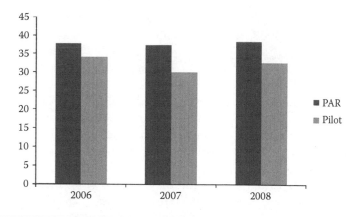

Figure 1.4 Pilot scores dipped, then rose.

1.5 points lower than those same agencies' traditional reports for fiscal year 2006. Most of this difference can be attributed to lower scores on two criteria: criterion 8 (linkage of results to costs) and criterion 12 (discussion of plans for improvement). The 20% drop on criterion 8 likely happened due to the tightening of the research team's standards on this question between fiscal year 2006 and fiscal year 2008, and not for any reason unique to the pilot format. Scores on criterion 12 also dropped by 16% between fiscal year 2006 and fiscal year 2008. However, just three reports account for this drop: State and Defense each fell 1 point, and SBA lost 2 points because no useful content could be found for fiscal year 2008. All the other pilot agencies achieved the same score on this criterion in both years.

Between fiscal years 2007 and 2008, pilot agencies' scores improved on 11 out of 12 criteria. Huge increases occurred on two criteria that saw huge drops in fiscal year 2007: criterion 3 (verification and validation of data) and criterion 4 (baseline and trend data). The much improved pilot scores for criteria 3 and 4 resulted mainly because there were more and clearer links to source documents in fiscal year 2008 than in fiscal year 2007—particularly the freestanding performance reports, which usually contained details on data quality and prior year results.

Despite some shortcomings, pilot agencies in fiscal year 2008 regained most of the ground they lost in fiscal year 2007. Most of the fiscal year 2007 drop in pilot agencies' scores reflects the inevitable difficulties of adjusting to a new reporting format, rather than a problem inherent in the pilot format.

Which Format Is Better?

Two years of experience with the pilot revealed that it is a workable format that can produce good reports. This still leaves the issue of which format is better: the PAR, the pilot, or the stand-alone performance report? Or, are there better alternatives to all of these formats?

The PAR reports scored better than pilot reports in both fiscal years 2007 and 2008. For fiscal year 2008, seven of the nine reports scoring above satisfactory (36 points) were PARs. The highest-scoring format was a PAR accompanied by a citizens' report. The top two reports, as well as six of the nine reports scoring above average, used this format. However, the pilot reports narrowed the gap in fiscal year 2008. Since most agencies participating in the pilot tended to score lower over the years than the nonpilot agencies, the differences in PAR and pilot agency scores can be attributed at least in part to factors other than the reporting format.

Thus, the score data suggest that either a traditional PAR or the pilot format can produce a good report. Over the years, our reviews identified both high- and low-quality reports in the PAR, pilot, and stand-alone performance report formats. The quality of the report depends much more on its content and effective execution of the format than it depends on just the choice of format. We return to this topic in greater depth when we discuss best practices for readability in Chapter 3.

Conclusion

The quality of disclosure in GPRA performance reports improved greatly between fiscal years 1999 and 2008. The improvement shows up in the aggregate *Scorecard* scoring data, especially once those data are adjusted to reflect the fact that the research team tightened the scoring criteria to reflect new best practices. The improvement also shows up in the qualitative evaluation of best practices.

The experiences of numerous individual reports show that agencies could improve their reports substantially regardless of where they started. Two of the best reports in fiscal year 1999—from Transportation and Veterans Affairs—improved by about 75% after adjusting for tightened scoring standards in later years. The most improved report, from Labor, started out in 5th place in fiscal year 1999. Yet even some reports that started with low scores and rankings made large gains. Homeland Security, for example, rose 18 spots in the rankings, from 22nd place in fiscal year 2003 (its first year) to 4th place in fiscal year 2008. HHS looked like it would be a perpetual cellar dweller until it rocketed to 5th place in fiscal year 2007. Nine reports achieved double-digit score increases over the ten years covered by our study.

The combination of performance and financial information to create a single performance and accountability report likely improved linkage of results with costs at a time when few agencies were thinking about this issue. This innovation, however, further increased the length of reports that were often already too long. Individual agencies sought to remedy this problem by turning the management's discussion and analysis section into an effective summary of the entire report, or by issuing a separate, shorter highlights document. OMB institutionalized the latter practice in fiscal year 2007 with the pilot reporting format. Even many agencies that did not use the pilot format took advantage of the opportunity to issue a shorter highlights document aimed at the general public.

Informative performance reporting starts with solid strategic planning. If an agency's strategic plan has a clear mission, plus outcome-oriented strategic goals and measures, then its performance report can show how it achieved those outcomes and offer a solid picture of how the agency's activities improve citizens' welfare. Over the years, we have seen numerous examples of good performance reports that were preceded by solid strategic plans. We have never seen the reverse—an informative performance report that is based on a poor strategic plan.

Our evaluations of these ever-changing documents suggest that an effective performance report must include three features, regardless of its specific format: (1) solid substantive content that documents the agency's goals, outcomes, shortcomings, and future plans; (2) a summary document or section that presents the "big picture"; and (3) easy access to more detailed performance and financial information, regardless of whether this information is in a single report or multiple documents. Chapters 2 and 3 provide more detail on the best practices that accomplish these goals.

Chapter 2

Best Practices
for Outcome-Oriented
Reports

Governmental (as well as nongovernmental) organizations develop many different kinds of goals and measures in order to satisfy the needs of a variety of users,
or stakeholders. For example, they typically need detailed activity and efficiency
goals and measures to support internal program administration as well as human
resource and financial management. They also need to inform external executive
branch and legislative overseers and policymakers, along with other sophisticated
stakeholders who have a high degree of expertise in the organization's programs.

While all these needs are important, our focus here is on the ultimate stakeholders for government organizations at all levels: the citizens who pay the bills and
rely on their services. Citizen stakeholders generally are not interested in internal
organizational processes, procedures, and practices. Nor do they seek the kind of
detailed performance data important to legislative committees with jurisdiction
over the organization or other "insiders" who deal with the organization on a regular basis. Instead, average citizens want to know the bottom line: What results is the
organization achieving that benefit the public and justify their investment in it as
taxpayers. And they want this information presented in a way that they can readily
access, digest, and understand.

In order to meet the general public's needs, governmental performance reporting systems must contain certain key elements: a strong set of outcome-oriented
goals that align with the organization's core mission(s), measures that credibly track

progress toward meeting the outcome goals, and periodic reporting that clearly and candidly explains the organization's performance results against its measures and provides a basis for assessing the extent of progress toward achieving mission outcomes.

Although we focus on the general public, a reporting system built around the foregoing key elements provides an essential foundation for serving the needs of an organization's other stakeholders as well. These other stakeholders usually require more detailed or specialized information, but all of them share with the general public an interest in knowing the organization's key goals, measures, and results. For example, legislative and executive branch policymakers want to ensure that the organization's stated goals are both consistent with and best designed to advance its statutory mandates and functions. Specific users of the organization's programs want to ensure that those programs are achieving their intended results. And, of course, the organization's own managers want to ensure that their internal operations and processes flow from and effectively implement its mission and goals. Indeed, many important stakeholders and their representatives, such as congressional staff who do not work for committees or employees of other agencies, may be similar to the general public in that they lack detailed knowledge of a given agency's history and inner workings. These stakeholders can benefit from a clear and simple explanation of the agency's mission, goals, and achievements, even if they seek more detailed information after they have digested the basics.

An outcome goal can be defined as the intended benefit (or harm avoided) that results from an organization's programs and activities. It should be articulated in clear terms that describe specific benefits to the community rather than the means and methods the organization uses to achieve those benefits. Goals that track things an organization does or how it does them have their place for internal management and oversight purposes. However, they are not the same as mission-related outcome goals that explain to the public what results the organization exists to achieve and how successfully it achieves these results.

Good public performance reporting systems come in many shapes and sizes. There is no one-size-fits-all format as long as the system contains the core elements noted above: mission-related outcome goals, credible measures, and periodic public reporting on performance results. One statutory system that has these elements is the Government Performance and Results Act of 1993 (GPRA), which applies to virtually all executive agencies of the federal government. GPRA requires each agency to develop (1) long-term strategic goals that extend at least five years into the future, (2) annual performance goals that break down the strategic goals into annual increments, and (3) performance measures that set specific annual targets for the annual performance goals. Under GPRA, agencies issue annual performance reports to Congress and the public that cover, among other things, their performance results against their annual goals and measures. Since GPRA provides a good model, and the one we have worked with extensively, we will use it as our focal point here. GPRA also has been in full operation for over a decade, thus providing a wealth of examples. Likewise, GPRA reporting has become sufficiently advanced to offer a number of best practices.

Our evaluations of federal agency reports under GPRA should be translatable to most other public performance accountability and reporting systems. A clear mission, outcome-oriented goals, and performance measures are universal aspects of strategic planning and reporting; they are hardly unique to GPRA.

Strategic goals, annual performance goals, and annual performance measures are, of course, interrelated and must complement each other. All must be strong in order to provide a solid foundation for performance accountability and reporting. We discuss them in turn below.

Outcome-Oriented Goals and Objectives

Why Are Outcome Goals Important?

Performance goals can address many different aspects of an organization's work, such as activities, outputs, and processes (e.g., number of job safety regulations issued). By contrast, outcome goals focus on the end results of those activities, outputs, and processes (e.g., safer workplaces). Outcomes are the ultimate test of an organization's value and the effectiveness of its programs and activities.

Ignoring bottom-line outcomes has serious adverse consequences for all concerned. For example, studies found that federal job training programs invested millions (perhaps billions) of dollars training many more individuals for particular jobs than the number of positions available in the job market. One Government Accountability Office (GAO) study found that in fiscal year 1995, the federal government spent $273 million to train over 112,000 students in fields with projected labor supply surpluses. The GAO study referred to an inspector general estimate that the government spent over $1 billion in fiscal year 1990 for cosmetology training, although the national supply of cosmetologists exceeded demand by over 1 million (GAO 1997b, 1–4). This not only wastes tax dollars but also disadvantages the intended program beneficiaries, who were trained for nonexistent jobs. A focus on outcomes, such as placements in sustainable jobs, would have served both the programs' beneficiaries and the taxpaying public much more effectively.

What Constitutes a Good Outcome Goal?

Ideally, an outcome goal should capture a public benefit conferred (or harm avoided) in a way that is (1) clear and important to ordinary citizens, (2) objectively measurable, (3) directly related to the organization's mission, and (4) within its span of influence.

The following are examples of good strategic outcome goals taken from recent federal agency performance reports:

- Department of Education: Improve student achievement, with a focus on bringing all students to grade level in reading and mathematics by 2014 (Education 2008, 7).
- Department of Health and Human Services: Improve the safety, quality, affordability, and accessibility of health care; prevent and control disease, injury, illness, and disability across the life span (HHS 2009, 7, 11).
- Department of Homeland Security: Reduce the risks of potential terrorists, instruments of terrorism, or other unlawful activities from entering the United States through our borders (DHS 2009, 9).
- Department of Labor: Safe, healthful, and fair workplaces (DOL 2008, 13).
- Department of Transportation: Enhance the public health and safety by working toward elimination of transportation-related deaths and injuries (DOT 2008, 98).
- Nuclear Regulatory Commission: Prevent the occurrence of any nuclear reactor accidents; prevent the occurrence of any releases of radioactive materials that result in significant radiation exposure or that cause adverse environmental impacts (NRC 2009, 8).

In each example, the goal is clearly stated, measurable, and of obvious public importance. Likewise, each goal relates directly to the agency's core mission.

Crafting good outcome goals is more challenging for some organizations than others given the nature of their missions, the availability of credible measurement data, and a host of other factors. Organizations with scientific and research and development missions typically find it more difficult to articulate measurable outcomes (particularly in annual increments) than organizations whose missions relate to such self-evident and readily measurable public benefits as transportation, workplace, and food safety. However, all public organizations should be able to explain to the public, at least at the strategic goal level, the fundamental outcomes they exist to achieve. For example, one federal agency with broad research and development missions, the Department of Energy, has successfully articulated outcomes that capture obvious public benefits under its "energy diversity" strategic goal:

- Increase energy options and reduce dependence on oil.
- Improve the quality of the environment by reducing greenhouse gas emissions and their impacts to land, water, and air from energy production and use.
- Create a more flexible, more reliable, and higher-capacity U.S. energy infrastructure.
- Cost-effectively improve the energy efficiency of the U.S. economy (DOE 2009, 6).

Table 2.1   Intermediate Outcome Examples

Intermediate Outcome	End Outcome	Source
Provide accurate and timely weather information, particularly for severe weather warnings	Increased public safety	(Commerce 2008, 133–134)
Improve teacher quality and increase the proportion of high school students taking a rigorous curriculum	Higher student achievement	(Education 2008, 7)
Achieve effective control of our borders	Reduced risk of terrorism and other illegal activities	(DHS 2009, 9)

Intermediate versus End Outcomes

While strategic goals focus on long-term end outcomes, it is often challenging for organizations to develop performance goals that convert end outcomes into annual measurable increments. One approach that organizations frequently use to address this challenge is setting intermediate outcome performance goals. An intermediate outcome goal is one that does not directly achieve the ultimate public benefit but represents an obvious or documented step toward reaching the ultimate benefit. For example, increased use of seat belts is an intermediate outcome toward the end outcome of fewer highway deaths and injuries. Table 2.1 provides further examples of intermediate outcome goals taken from federal agency performance reports.

Outcomes Vary in Relation to Organizational Mission

What constitutes an outcome goal may differ by organization depending on its mission. Economy, efficiency, and other process-related goals, while important in their own right, usually do not constitute public benefit outcomes. However, they can rise to this level for organizations whose core functions involve the delivery of services and benefits directly to the public. For example, the Social Security Administration's first strategic goal is "to deliver high-quality, citizen-centered service," and the first objective under that goal is to "make the right decision in the eligibility process as early as possible" (SSA 2008a, 17). Likewise, the Department of Veterans Affairs has key goals and measures relating to the timeliness and accuracy of claims and benefit determinations (VA 2008, 8). For these agencies, prompt and accurate claims processing goes to the heart of their missions.

Organizations that do not have direct contact with the public (such as those with internal government management, personnel, and procurement missions) often find it challenging to articulate outcomes that resonate with the general public. However, they too can capture outcomes of clear benefit and interest to most citizens. For example, the U.S. General Services Administration, which performs intragovernmental procurement and property management functions, has developed goals that emphasize getting the best value for the American taxpayers. These include:

■ Economical and efficient management of federal assets
■ Develop and deliver timely, accurate, and cost-effective acquisition services and business solutions (GSA 2008, 18)

Outcomes Need to Be Objectively Measurable

Outcome goals should lend themselves to quantifiable measurement by credible data. Goals that are stated at such a high level of generality as to defy objective measurement do nothing to inform the public. Examples given previously deal with specific, measurable public health and safety outcomes such as safer transportation modes and workplaces and improved public health. By contrast, vague and high-level goals such as the following are difficult to break down into concrete measures that tie to the agency's role:

■ Maximize U.S. competitiveness and enable economic growth for American industries, workers, and consumers (Commerce 2008, 12)
■ Expand America's ownership society, particularly in underserved markets (SBA, 2009, 1)
■ U.S. and world economies perform at full economic potential (Treasury 2008, 7)

Also to be avoided are goal statements that read more like marketing slogans than measurable performance outcomes. The Office of Personnel Management (OPM) fiscal year 2008 performance report was one of the worst offenders in this regard. Among its strategic goals: federal agencies will be "employers of choice" and will have "exemplary" human resources management practices; OPM will be "a model of performance for other Federal agencies" and a "leader in the human resources professional community" with "positive name recognition" and "constructive and productive relationships with external stakeholders" (OPM 2009, 4).

Outcomes Should Credibly Reflect the Organization's Missions and Sphere of Influence

Outcomes should cover all of the organization's core missions and be consistent with its statutory charter. The performance report should show whether things improved because of what an organization did, and if so, how much of the improvement can be attributed to its actions. Attribution often is challenging because of the many external factors that come into play. However, every organization should be able to mount a credible case supporting the nexus between its programs and activities and their results. The organization should neither understate nor overstate its role. Claims of impact should be supported by program evaluations or other empirical evidence of a cause-and-effect relationship. A less desirable alternative would be to logically connect outcome measures, output measures, and anecdotal evidence. A case that rests on merely assumed cause-and-effect relationships is less credible. The report should explain how organization outputs create or enhance outcomes for the public and describe the nature and extent of influence so that outcomes can be attributed (at least in part) to specific organization actions. Discussion of the operating environment and the extent of the organization's influence is helpful in keeping expectations ambitious, yet realistic.

For example, the Department of Housing and Urban Development (HUD) 2008 report contains a separate section captioned "Risks, Trends, and Factors Affecting Goals" that addresses in detail external factors affecting the department's missions. As the report states:

> Understanding external factors enables more successful programs by allowing HUD to plan for contingencies, form strategic partnerships, and better focus and leverage resources to accomplish its strategic goals. (HUD 2008, 50)

External factors, however, should be treated as influences that must be controlled in order to identify the organization's contribution—not excuses for a failure to demonstrate performance.

Wording Matters

Outcomes should be expressed in clear, specific terms that a lay reader can readily understand and relate to public benefits. Avoid vague terms such as *support*, *facilitate*, and *promote* to describe what the organization will do since they make measurement difficult and obscure the organization's role. Table 2.2, which compares the Department of Homeland Security's strategic goals for fiscal years 2006 and 2007, demonstrates the difference that wording can make.

While the department's missions did not change from 2006 to 2007, its 2007 goal statements are significantly more specific and outcome-oriented.

Elaborate on Goals as Necessary

Where strategic goals must be stated at a high level of generality, organizations often use subsidiary strategic objectives to provide more specific and measurable intended outcomes. For example, the Department of Veterans Affairs report uses

Table 2.2   DHS Strategic Goals, 2006 and 2007

2006 Strategic Goals	2007 Strategic Goals
Awareness—Identify and understand threats, assess vulnerabilities, determine potential impacts, and disseminate timely information to our homeland security partners and the American public. **Prevention**—Detect, deter, and mitigate threats to our homeland. **Protection**—Safeguard our people and their freedoms, critical infrastructure, property, and the economy of our nation from acts of terrorism, natural disasters, or other emergencies. **Response**—Lead, manage, and coordinate the national response to acts of terrorism, natural disasters, or other emergencies. **Recovery**—Lead national, state, local, and private sector efforts to restore services and rebuild communities after acts of terrorism, natural disasters, or other emergencies. **Service**—Serve the public effectively by facilitating lawful trade, travel, and immigration.	**Protect our nation from dangerous people.** Achieves the outcomes of (1) reducing the risk of potential terrorists, instruments of terrorism, or other unlawful activities from entering the United States through our borders; (2) ensuring lawful immigrants and visitors are welcomed and they receive timely and correct immigration information and benefits; and (3) reducing the risk of potential terrorists, instruments of terrorism, or other unlawful activities from threatening our transportation systems. **Protect our nation from dangerous goods.** Achieves the outcomes of (1) reducing the risk of a nuclear or radiological attack in the United States; and (2) reducing the risk of a biological attack in the United States. **Protect critical infrastructure.** Achieves the outcomes of (1) ensuring the protection and resiliency of the nation's fixed critical infrastructure and key assets; and (2) ensuring the protection of all transportation modes. **Build a nimble, effective emergency response system and a culture of preparedness.** Achieves the outcomes of (1) ensuring Americans and their governments at all levels can respond to and recover from catastrophic incidents; and (2) ensuring Americans are prepared, capable, and ready to respond to adverse incidents.

Source: U.S. Department of Homeland Security, *Performance and Accountability Report, FY 2006*, 2006, 10 www.dhs.gov/xlibrary/assets/cfo_par2006_fullreport.pdf; U.S. Department of Homeland Security, *Highlights Report, FY 2007*, 2007, 9, www.dhs.gov/xlibrary/assets/cfo_highlightsfy2007.pdf.

the following strategic objectives to add specificity to its first strategic goal, "restoration and improved quality of life for disabled veterans":

■ Strategic objective 1.1—Specialized health care services: Maximize the physical, mental, and social functioning of veterans with disabilities and be a leader in providing specialized health care services.
■ Strategic objective 1.2—Decisions on disability claims: Provide timely and accurate decisions on disability compensation claims to improve the economic status and quality of life of service-disabled veterans.
■ Strategic objective 1.3—Suitable employment and special support: Provide eligible service-connected disabled veterans with the opportunity to become employable and obtain and maintain employment, while delivering special support to veterans with serious employment handicaps.
■ Strategic objective 1.4—Improved standard of living for eligible survivors: Improve the standard of living and income status of eligible survivors of service-disabled veterans through compensation, education, and insurance benefits (VA 2008, 27–29).

Quality Counts More Than Quantity

To avoid overwhelming the reader or losing focus on what really matters, goals included in public reports should be few in number and concentrated on key organizational outcomes. While there is no magic number, most major federal agencies, including cabinet departments, limit their reports to a handful of strategic goals. For example, the Department of Health and Human Services is able to capture its vast and varied missions within four strategic goals:

■ Health care: Improve the safety, quality, affordability, and accessibility of health care, including behavioral health care.
■ Public health promotion and protection, disease prevention, and emergency preparedness: Prevent and control disease, injury, and disability across the life span, and protect the public from occupational, environmental, and terrorist threats.
■ Human services: Protect the economic and social well-being of individuals, families, and communities.
■ Scientific research and development: Advance scientific and biomedical research and development related to health and human services (HHS 2009, 4).

Annual performance goals also should be limited in number for public reporting purposes. Another large federal agency, the Department of Labor, uses only 24 performance goals in its report (Labor 2008, 12). Some federal agencies have a large number of performance goals to meet the needs of various stakeholders but focus their public reports on a smaller universe of key or representative goals that capture their core mission outcomes. (See Chapter 3 for more detail on techniques to limit the number of goals in performance reports.)

Many federal agencies now include strategic and performance goals focused on management improvement, but these should not be confused with mission outcome goals.

Management goals (financial, human resources, information technology, etc.) exist only to support the achievement of mission outcome goals.

Don't Let Desire for Perfection Be the Enemy of the Good

Public organizations face many conceptual, practical, and sometimes political challenges in developing credible outcome-oriented performance goals and measures. Their missions often are complex and subject to numerous external factors beyond their exclusive control. Also, challenges over the availability, reliability, and timeliness of data abound. An organization that sets out to get its performance metrics completely right the first time is probably doomed to failure. Moreover, concern over potential vulnerabilities can cause managers to "dumb down" their goals and measures to things that are easily attainable and readily verifiable through available data. This is especially so in an environment where managers feel, rightly or wrongly, that they will be held personally and unconditionally responsible for achieving the organization's outcomes.

Good outcome goals and measures are far more likely to result from an environment where developing performance metrics is viewed as an iterative process that will require trial and error and improve through experience. It is also important that the performance metrics be viewed (and used) primarily as a diagnostic to analyze and improve performance rather than to automatically punish managers or programs. Of course, poor performance may ultimately lead to termination of a program if it cannot improve, especially if other programs that seek to accomplish similar outcomes deliver superior performance. But the first reaction to poor performance should be to ask "Why?" Such an environment should strongly encourage innovation and reasonable risk taking.

Outcome-Oriented Measures

Performance measures track progress toward achieving outcome goals. Under GPRA, performance goals and measures are usually broken down into annual increments.

Not all programs and activities lend themselves to annual measurement; thus the annual framework does not fit all situations. GPRA permits an agency, with permission of the Office of Management and Budget, to develop an alternative reporting format that does not use quantitative annual measures. Nevertheless, we will focus on annual measurement here since it is the predominant model.

Each annual performance goal should be subject to one or more annual performance measures. Measures typically are expressed as quantifiable performance targets to be achieved for the applicable year. Not all performance measures need to be outcome-oriented; different types of measures may be important for different organization stakeholders. However, in order to persuasively demonstrate an organization's value to the general public, its report should have a core set of specific and understandable outcome measures to implement a set of specific and understandable outcome goals.

Outcome-Oriented Goals Need Outcome-Oriented Measures

Since the fundamental purpose of performance measures is to track progress toward the organization's performance goals, the measures must provide a credible basis for assessing progress toward the goal outcomes they implement. Ideally, they do this by being expressed as outcomes themselves that mirror the outcome goal. For example, measures for the Transportation Department's safety goal track statistics directly related to transportation-related fatalities and injuries, as Figure 2.1 shows.

For measures that do not directly track goal outcomes, the relationship between the measure and outcome goal achievement must be made clear. If this relationship is not self-evident, measures should be accompanied by narratives that explain their relevance to the applicable outcomes. Figure 2.2 demonstrates how the Treasury Department report elaborates on one such measure.

Activity Levels Do Not Measure Outcomes

Activities, such as number of grants made, participants trained, regulations issued, facilities built, projects funded, etc., may contribute to achieving outcomes. However, they do not provide a basis to measure progress toward the outcome itself. Indeed, as noted previously, reliance on activity or output measures may actually *detract* from outcome achievement, e.g., training individuals for jobs in excess of demand in the job market. These observations state the obvious. Nevertheless, one of the most common shortcomings we find in federal performance reports is a tendency to use activity or output performance measures to implement outcome goals. Table 2.3 illustrates the disconnect between some 2008 State Department outcome strategic goals and their representative measures, which are activities that do not track progress toward the outcome goals.

Raw Number versus Percentage Measures

Measures expressed as raw numbers may relate to outcomes, but they usually do not demonstrate whether progress is being made toward the outcome, i.e., whether the overall condition is getting better or worse. For example, one highlighted measure

Reduction in Transportation-Related Deaths Reduction in Transportation-Related Injuries	
Highway Safety	**Rail Safety**
✓ Passenger vehicle occupant highway fatality rate per 100 million passenger vehicle-miles traveled (VMT) ✓ Large truck and bus fatality rate per 100 million total VMT ✗ Rate of motorcyclist fatalities per 100,000 motorcycle registrations (CY) ✓ Rate of nonoccupant fatalities per 100 million VMT (CY)	✓ Rail-related accidents and incidents per million train-miles **Transit Safety** ✓ Transit fatalities per 100 million passenger-miles traveled
Aviation Safety	**Pipeline Safety**
✓ Number of commercial air carrier fatalities per 100 million persons onboard ✓ Number of fatal general aviation accidents	✗ Number of serious incidents for natural gas and hazardous liquid pipelines **Hazardous Materials Safety** ✓ Number of serious hazardous materials transportation incidents

Figure 2.1 Transportation Department safety goals. CY = current year. (Source: U.S. Department of Transportation, Performance and Accountability Report, FY 2008, 2008, 99, www.dot.gov/par/2008/pdf/DOT_PAR_2008.pdf.)

used by the Department of Homeland Security is the number of border miles under effective control (DHS 2009, 9). Border security certainly is an outcome. However, simply reporting the number of border miles under control gives the reader little sense of progress toward that outcome. The same is true of the Interior Department's measure of the number of land and surface water acres reclaimed from the effects of past coal mining (Interior 2008, 27). These measures would be more meaningful and outcome-oriented if expressed as percentages, i.e., the percentage of border miles under control or the percentage of total acres to be reclaimed, respectively.

There are many opportunities, particularly in law enforcement areas, to convert raw number measures into percentages or other forms that capture progress toward the desired outcome. Justice Department measures such as the number of organized criminal enterprises dismantled or number of child pornography websites shut down (Justice 2008, I-11) do not tell the reader whether the overall conditions

Office of the Comptroller of the Currency

Measure: Percent of National Banks with Composite CAMELS Rating 1 or 2 (Oe)

	FY 2005	FY 2006	FY 2007	FY 2008	FY 2009
Target	90	90	90	90	90
Actual	94	95	96	92	
Target met?	Y	Y	Y	Y	

Definition: This measure reflects the overall condition of the national banking system at fiscal year-end. Bank regulatory agencies use the Uniform Financial Institutions Rating System, CAMELS, to provide a general framework for assimilating and evaluating all significant financial, operational, and compliance factors inherent in a bank. Evaluations are made on capital adequacy, asset quality, management, earnings, liquidity, and sensitivity to market risk. The rating scale is 1 through 5, where 1 is the highest rating granted.

Indicator type: Indicator.

Data capture and source: The Supervisory Information Office identifies the current composite ratings from examiner view (EV) and supervisory information system (SIS) at fiscal year-end. The number of national banks at fiscal year-end is obtained from the Federal Reserved Board's National Information Center database. The percentage is determined by comparing the number of national banks with current composite CAMELS ratings of 1 or 2 to the total number of national banks at fiscal year-end.

Date verification and validation: Either quarterly or semiannually, an independent reviewer compares a sample reports of examination to the examiner view (EV) and supervisory information system (SIS) data to ensure the accuracy of the recorded composite ratings. Any discrepancies between the supporting documentation and the systems data are reported to the respective assistant deputy comptroller or deputy comptroller for corrective action.

Data accuracy: Reasonable.

Data frequency: Quarterly.

Future plans/explanation for shortfall: To sustain this level of achievement, the OCC will execute its bank supervision operating plan that focuses on credit quality, allowance of loan and lease losses (ALLL) adequacy, off-balance-sheet activities, liquidity and interest rate risk management, consumer protection, and Bank Secrecy Act/antimoney laundering compliance. The OCC also will continue its recruiting of entry-level examiners, aligning supervision resources to the areas of greatest risk, training the examiner staff, and enhancing examination guidance.

Figure 2.2 Treasury Department CAMELS measure. (Source: U.S. Department of the Treasury, Performance and Accountability Report, FY 2008, 2008, 340, www.ustreas.gov/offices/management/dcfo/accountability-reports/2008-par/ Full_Version.pdf.)

Table 2.3 Measures That Don't Track Outcomes

Strategic Goal	Representative Measure
Achieving peace and security	Number of foreign people trained in counterterrorism by U.S. government programs
Governing justly and democratically	Number of domestic election observers trained with U.S. government assistance

Source: State, 2009.

they address (prevalence of criminal gangs or child pornography websites) are getting better or worse. Percentage measures, if they could be developed on the basis of estimates of the magnitude of the overall problem, would be more informative. In this regard, Justice is developing baseline measures of the supply of illegal drugs available in the United States to improve on existing raw number measures of amounts of illegal drugs seized (Justice 2008, II-14).

Overreliance on End Outcome Measures Should Be Avoided

Some organizations rely exclusively on bottom-line measures that focus only on end outcomes. For example, the Justice Department's measures for its goal to prevent terrorism are zero terrorist acts committed by foreigners within the United States and zero catastrophic acts of domestic terrorism (Justice 2008, I-11). These certainly are appropriate outcome measures. However, *exclusive* reliance on all-or-nothing pass/fail or zero tolerance measures does not provide a basis for assessing gradations of performance or progress from year to year. By contrast, while the Nuclear Regulatory Commission uses end outcome zero tolerance measures (e.g., no nuclear reactor accidents), it combines them with more nuanced intermediate outcome measures that allow analysis of performance trends. The additional measures include:

- Significant accident sequence precursors of a nuclear reactor accident
- New conditions evaluated at a specified risk level
- Events with radiation exposure levels that exceed a certain criterion (NRC 2009, 3)

Measures Must Provide a Credible Means for Tracking Progress over Time

The purpose of performance measures, of course, is to serve as a basis for assessing progress toward achieving performance goals. Notwithstanding this obvious fact, we have found recurring problems in this regard. Some of these problems should be avoidable, such as a logical disconnect between a measure and its goal or the use of measures that lack credible data sources. Another avoidable problem is overreliance on nonquantifiable measures. For example, many of the National Aeronautics and Space Administration's performance measures are not quantifiable and are applied on a judgmental basis. The prior year entries state whether or not the agency was judged to have been successful with respect to individual measures but generally do not provide specifics to put its performance in context (NASA 2008, 33). Thus, the report offers little baseline or trend data to assist the reader in assessing progress from year to year.

Lack of consistency in measures from year to year also poses a challenge, although it is a double-edged sword. Performance measures should not be set in stone. As an organization gains experience, it can be expected to refine its performance measures. Measures also can and should vary with changes in priorities and a variety of other circumstances. Thus, good performance measures that have limited prior year data due to newness or revision may still convey more information than inferior measures with more data points that are not clearly linked to an organization's results. However, assuming that its core missions remain largely the same, an organization should strive to maintain some consistency and comparability in its performance measures over the years.

Performance Targets Should Be Realistic but Challenging

Target selection is an important part of developing and implementing performance measures. Performance targets should be quantified and directly relevant to the measures and goals to which they apply. Ideally, the relevance and significance of the targets will be self-evident to a lay reader. Targets also should convey a sense that the organization is challenging itself rather than settling for low-ball performance levels that can easily be met. As discussed in more detail below, there are several likely indicators that performance targets are not sufficiently ambitious:

- Current year performance results far exceed their targets.
- Current year targets are set below prior year performance results.
- An organization reports 100% success for all or almost all of its measures, particularly over a period of several years.

Conversely, the fact that an organization raises the bar by regularly increasing its performance targets from year to year suggests that it is challenging itself.

Use Clear, Comprehensible Language to Define Measures and Targets

As with goals, performance measures do little to inform the public if a lay reader cannot understand them. In this regard, the Environmental Protection Agency uses outcome-oriented but highly technical measures and targets dealing with reductions in various forms of air pollutants (EPA 2008, 87–90). However, the report does not clearly explain in layman's terms how significant these measures are in relation to the intermediate goal of air quality or the ultimate goal of improved human health outcomes.

To the greatest extent practical, measures and targets should be written in plain language. Where measures must be stated in technical or arcane terms, the report should at least include accompanying narratives to explain their significance and relevance to mission outcomes.

Focus on a Manageable Number of Measures

As with goals, measures should be limited in number in order to avoid overwhelming the reader and obscuring what really matters the most. Where an organization feels the need to use a large number of measures, focusing its performance report on a smaller set of key or representative measures is a good technique. This point is discussed further in Chapter 3.

Eliminate Measures That Lack External Significance

One way to limit the number of performance measures is to omit from public reporting measures that have little if any relevance to the public. Workload, productivity, and other process-related measures generally fall into this category since they are relevant primarily, if not exclusively, to internal management. The Office of Personnel Management's report for fiscal year 2006 provides striking examples of this. The report listed as key performance measures that the agency would join two human resource management professional organizations and that it would acknowledge receipt of congressional inquiries within 24 hours (OPM 2006, 15). Such measures are so prosaic that it is hard to understand how they would qualify for inclusion in a public report at all, much less rise to the level of key performance indicators. They contributed only to the size of the report. Customer satisfaction measures fall into this category as well. Indeed, they are sometimes treated as a substitute for true outcome-oriented measures that get more directly at whether an organization is meeting the public's needs.

Providing Context: Baselines and Trends

The bottom-line question for citizens is whether an organization's actions are making a given situation better or worse. To answer this question, the organization needs strong performance metrics that feature a core set of outcome goals and measures. It also needs to present those metrics in a way that facilitates analysis of trends over time. Data should be displayed in a way that allows readers to absorb and understand their significance easily. Both quantity of data (years of data included) and presentation matter.

There can be practical constraints on the quantity and quality of prior year data. As noted previously, one potential constraint is that performance measures evolve over time as the organization gains experience and circumstances change. Another potential constraint is lagging data. Many organizations deal with complex outcomes that do have readily available information sources capable of producing timely annual results data. For example, the Environmental Protection Agency's fiscal year 2008 performance report lacked current results for about one-third of its measures (EPA 2008, 11–12). The Department of Education reported current results for less than 20% of its key 2008 measures (Education 2008, 26–30). One way of ameliorating this problem is to report current year results on an estimated basis, if possible, rather than simply reporting nothing. Chapter 3 discusses the subject of data and data lags in more detail.

Multiple years of data help identify trends, but they do not by themselves show how close the organization is to achieving its goals, or explain why the organization will produce a significant level of public benefits if it hits its targets. Performance reports should explain rationales behind the selection and revision of quantitative targets, so the reader can understand the magnitude of the organization's goals in relation to the size of the problem.

The More Comparable Prior Year Trend Data, the Better

Federal government performance reports generally include prior year results for performance measures going back at least three years immediately preceding the year covered by the report. The better reports include baseline and prior year results data for consistent (or at least comparable) measures going back even more years, often to the baseline for the applicable measure. Good reports also display prior year data in a way that enables the reader to readily grasp performance trends. Here are some examples.

The Transportation Department report provides a number of years of results for its measures, including a key safety performance measure illustrated in Figure 2.3.

Performance Measure	2002	2003	2004	2005	2006	2007	2008 Actual	2008 Target	Met/Not Met
Passenger vehicle occupant highway fatality rate per 100 million passenger vehicle-miles traveled (VMT)		1.21	1.17	1.15 (r)	1.11 (r)	1.05[a]	1.03[b]	1.06	✓

Figure 2.3 Transportation Department highway fatality measure results. (Source: U.S. Department of Transportation, Performance and Accountability Report, FY 2008, 2008, 93, www.dot.gov/par/2008/pdf/DOT_PAR_2008.pdf.)

Performance Measure				
Passenger Vehicle Occupant Highway Fatality Rate per 100 Million Passenger Vehicle Miles Traveled (VMT)				
	2005	*2006*	*2007*	*2008*
Target	1.15	1.12	1.10	1.06
Actual	1.15 (r)	1.11 (r)	1.05[a]	1.03[b]

Note: (r), revised.

[a] Estimate based on projected 2007 VMT.
[b] Projection based on trends from historical data. Actual number will be different, depending on external factors, such as the economy, price of fuel, actual miles driven, vehicle mix, etc.

Figure 2.4 Transportation Department highway fatality targets. (Source: U.S. Department of Transportation, Performance and Accountability Report, FY 2008, 2008, 101, www.dot.gov/par/2008/pdf/DOT_PAR_2008.pdf.)

As Figure 2.4 demonstrates, the report also shows several years' worth of prior year targets as well as results for its measures.

The Labor Department report likewise is rich in prior year data, showing prior year targets as well as results in Figure 2.5.

The Department of Veterans Affairs report shows multiple prior year results and targets for its measures. It also includes the long-term (strategic) target for each measure, which further assists the reader in assessing the extent of progress (Figure 2.6).

Include External Trend Data Where Available

Another helpful feature is to provide trend data relevant to an organization's performance from sources outside the organization, even if these data are not specifically incorporated into the organization's own annual performance measures. Such data can be particularly useful for organizations that have difficulty demonstrating outcome achievement in annual increments. Figure 2.7, from the Environmental Protection Agency's 2008 report, offers an example.

Another example comes from the Department of Housing and Urban Development's report, shown in Figure 2.8.

Explain Targets and Trends

Reports should at least briefly describe the rationale for individual performance measures and targets as well as the significance of performance trends. Figure 2.9,

Increase the employment, retention, and earnings of individuals registered under the Workforce Investment Act Adult Program.

Performance Goal 07-2A (ETA)
Indicators, Targets, and Results

		PY 2002 Goal Not Achieved	PY 2003 Goal Achieved	PY 2004 Goal Achieved	PY 2005 Goal Achieved	PY 2006 Goal Not Achieved	PY 2007 Goal Not Achieved
Percent of participants employed in the first quarter after exit	Target	70%	71%	75%	76%	76%	71%
	Result	74%	74%	77%	77%	70%	68%
	•	Y	Y	Y	Y	N	N
Percent of participants employed in the first quarter after exit still employed in the second and third quarters after exit	Target	80%	82%	85%	81%	82%	83%
	Result	84%	85%	86%	82%	82%	84%
	•	Y	Y	Y	Y	Y	Y

Indicator target reached (Y), improved (I), or not reached (N).

Figure 2.5 Labor Department Workforce Investment Act Adult Program trend data. (Source: U.S. Department of Labor, Performance and Accountability Report, FY 2008, 2008, 91, www.dol.gov/_sec/media/reports/annual2008/2008annualreport.pdf.)

Organization/Program/Measure	Past Results				FY 2008		Strategic Target
	FY 2004	FY 2005	FY 2006	FY 2007	Results	Targets	
Veterans Benefits Administration							
Performance Measures							
National accuracy rate (core rating work) % (compensation) (through July)	87%	84%	88%	88%	86% Y	90%	98%
Compensation and pension rating—related actions—average days to process	166	167	177	183	179 R	169	125
Rating-related compensation actions—average days pending (a) corrected	120	122	130	(a) 132	121 Y	120	100
Average days to process—DIC actions (compensation)	125	124	136	132	121 Y	118	90

Figure 2.6 Veterans Affairs Department results and strategic targets. (Source: U.S. Department of Veterans Affairs, Performance and Accountability Report, FY 2008, 2008, 240, www4.va.gov/budget/report/.)

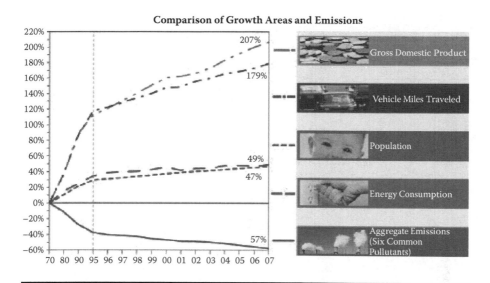

Figure 2.7   Environmental trend data. (Source: U.S. Environmental Protection Agency, *Performance and Accountability Report, FY 2008,* 2008, 58, www.epa. gov/ocfo/par/2008par/par08report.pdf.)

for example, shows how the Agriculture Department report includes narratives for each performance measure that briefly explain target selection and results.

The Education Department report uses a specific target context description to accompany its performance measures. For example, the report (Education 2008, 63) explains measures and targets dealing with Education's research agency, the Institute of Education Sciences (IES), and its What Works Clearinghouse as follows:

> Target Context. The Department's measures for evaluating progress towards the goal of transforming education into an evidence-based field are tied to the Clearinghouse. The measures assess the productivity of IES's investments in producing scientifically valid research on teaching and instruction with respect to the core academic competencies of reading/writing and mathematics or science. The measure that is tracked is the number of programs and practices on these topics that have been developed with IES funding and that have shown to be effective in raising student achievement under the research quality standards of the Clearinghouse. As shown by Clearinghouse reviews of existing research on program effectiveness in reading/writing and mathematics, few older studies meet the Clearinghouse quality standards. Thus, the targets under the measure are ambitious and will, if met, result in a doubling, or more, of the existing base of research-proven programs and practices.

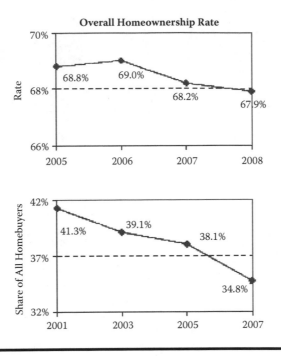

Figure 2.8 Homeownership trend data. (Source: U.S. Department of Housing and Urban Development, *Performance and Accountability Report, FY 2008,* **2008, 131, www.hud.gov/offices/cfo/reports/hudpar-fy2008.pdf.)**

Similarly, the Labor Department report (DOL 2008, 91) uses narratives captioned "program perspective and logic" to explain briefly the program or function to which measures apply, as well as the nature of the measures:

Program Perspective and Logic

The WIA [Workforce Investment Act] Adult Program helps adult workers (unemployed and employed) acquire the skills they need to compete in a global economy. Funds are distributed by formula to States, which operate networks of One-Stop Career Centers that provide comprehensive services to workers and employers. Services include assessments of skills needs, individual career planning, occupational skills training, on-the-job training, skills upgrading, entrepreneurial training, and adult literacy activities. States also use the WIA Adult Program to leverage additional Federal and non-Federal resources to increase the quality and variety of assistance. Through collaboration with its program partners, the WIA Adult Program assists individuals in their career goals, reduces welfare dependency, and improves the quality, productivity and competitiveness of the nation's workforce.

Exhibit 32: Pathogen Reduction (Food Inspection)

Annual Performance Goals, Indicators, and Trends	2004	2005	2006	2007	Fiscal Year 2008		
					Target	Actual	Result
4.1.1 Reduce overall public exposure to generic *Salmonella* from broiler carcasses using existing scientific standards	n/a	n/a	45% of category 1 Industry	71% of category 1 Industry	80% of category 1 Industry	80% of category 1 Industry	Met
4.1.2 Reduce the overall public exposure to *Listeria monocytogenes* in ready-to-eat products	n/a	0.28%	0.24%	0.23%	0.27%	0.19%	Met
4.1.3 Reduce the overall public exposure to *E. coli* O157:H7 in ground beef	0.04%	0.21%	0.40%	0.28%	0.23%	0.48%	Unmet

Note: FY 2008 data reflect the volume-adjusted percent rate, better estimate population exposure to pathogens, which may differ from the non-volume-adjusted percent positive rates reported in prior years.

Rationale for met range: This measure targets reducing human foodborne illness rates from *E. coli* O157:H7 in ground beef. USDA's FY 2013 goal is 0.17 cases per 100,000. USDA met its Healthy People 2010 goal for *E. coli* illnesses from ground beef as of FY 2007. The department aggressively set its FY 2013 goal at 50% under the goal. To reach its FY 2013 goal, USDA has set its FY 2008 performance objective at 0.27 cases per 100,000 or a volume-adjusted percent positive rate of 0.23. A lower number of cases indicates better performance.

- 4.1.1: Data assessment metrics to meet the target range is 80% of industry in category 1.
- 4.1.2: Data assessment metrics to meet the target range is 0.27 cases per 100,000.
- 4.1.3: Data assessment metrics to meet the target range is 0.23 cases per 100,000.

Figure 2.9   Agriculture Department selected measures. (Source: U.S. Department of Agriculture, Performance and Accountability Report, FY 2008, 2008, 81, www.ocfo.usda.gov/usdarpt/par2008/pdf/par2008.pdf.)

DOL measures the success of this program with the Federal jobs training program common measures. The common measures enable comparisons to be made to government-wide education, employment and job training programs that share similar core purposes. The common measures are entered employment, employment retention, and average earnings. A high entered employment rate indicates success in placing individuals in jobs. A high retention rate indicates employment stability. Increased average earnings indicate that participants are getting better jobs at better wages.

What's Wrong With This Picture?

Unexplained major disparities between targets and current or prior year results raise a red flag for the reader about the credibility of the targets or the performance data. For example, actual results that far exceed their targets suggest that the organization set the performance bar too low. Figure 2.10, from a Small Business Administration performance report, illustrates this problem.

The report shows that the agency far exceeded its fiscal year 2008 targets for each of the three listed measures. However, each fiscal year 2008 target was set below the agency's actual performance results during the preceding year. Indeed, the agency's fiscal year 2008 performance for each measure actually deteriorated from the prior year! The report offers little explanation for any of this, essentially stating that the targets are "best estimates" and results are hard to predict.

Another example is a measure by the Economic Development Administration (EDA), Department of Commerce, for which the fiscal year 2008 target is less than actual performance results for each of the previous five years, as Figure 2.11 demonstrates.

There may be valid reasons for setting current year targets below prior year performance levels. However, in the absence of a specific explanation, the reader cannot be blamed for inferring that the organization is not challenging itself.

In contrast to the above examples, the Department of Veterans Affairs report provides strong evidence that the organization does not hesitate to raise the performance bar by setting challenging targets from year to year. According to a table in its report, the department's performance for seven of the 11 fiscal year 2008 key measure targets it missed actually improved over fiscal year 2007 performance levels. Indeed, the department's fiscal year 2008 performance improved over the prior year for all but four of the 23 key measures that had targets (VA 2008, 8–9).

Anticipate and Explain Obvious Red Flags

Many organizations could help themselves by reviewing their performance results before they are reported publicly in order to identify obvious incongruities. Where such incongruities exist, the organization would be wise to explain them in the

Drug-Free Workplace

Performance Indicator	Type of Measure	FY 2005 Actual	FY 2006 Actual	FY 2006 Actual	FY 2007 Actual	FY 2008 Actual	FY 2008 Variance
SB educated (#)	Output	5,150	531	2,731	2,280	1,450	57%
Programs implemented (#)	Output	1,029	62	453	363	165	120%
Cost per SB educated ($)	Efficiency	$201	2,194%	$311	$476	$1,023	53%

Figure 2.10 Small Business Administration drug free workplace measure data. (Source: U.S. Small Business Administration, Annual Performance Report, FY 2008, 2009, 21, www.sba.gov/idc/groups/public/documents/sba_homepage/serv_abtsba_2008_apr_001-040.pdf.)

EDA Performance Measure			
Measure: Private investment leveraged—6-year totals (in millions)[a]			
Year	Status	Actual	Target
FY 2008	Exceeded	$1,393	$970
Year	Status	Historical Results	Historical Target
FY 2007	Exceeded	$2,118	$1,200
FY 2006	Met	$1,059	$1,020
FY 2005	Exceeded	$1,781	$1,040
FY 2004	Exceeded	$1,740	$650
FY 2003	Exceeded	$2,475	$581

[a] This is the six-year result measure. FY 2008 actuals are the result of investments made in FY 2002. FY 2007 actuals are of investments made in FY 2001, and so on.

Figure 2.11 Commerce Department private investment leveraged measure. (Source: U.S. Department of Commerce, Performance and Accountability Report, FY 2008, 2008, 285, www.osec.doc.gov/bmi/BUDGET/FY08PAR/DOC_PAR_FY08_508version.pdf.)

report both for its own benefit and to better inform the reader. As noted previously, wide fluctuations in results from year to year and between targets and results cry out for explanations.

Tell an Outcome-Oriented Story

Credible outcome-oriented performance metrics lie at the heart of effective public performance reporting. An organization cannot have credible outcome-oriented reporting without strong outcome-oriented performance metrics. At the same time, the performance metrics are not all that counts. The narrative portions of performance reports bring the data to life, showing how the organization's results affect real people.

As discussed previously, narratives should be used to flesh out and clarify goals and measures whose significance and public benefits are not self-evident to a lay reader. Narratives also should be used to address obvious red flags, such as wide variations in performance results from year to year and performance targets that appear nonchallenging in relation to current or prior year results. However, report narratives have important uses in addition to explaining specific performance metrics and results. They offer an opportunity for the organization to "tell its story" to the public in a free-form and conversational way that highlights its major accomplishments.

The narrative portions of a performance report, whose formats tend to be less constrained than those portions dealing with the detailed performance metrics, offer many opportunities to address the general public. Good reports find ways to take advantage of these opportunities. They use the organization head's transmittal letter as more than a perfunctory document that recites the necessary legalisms. The best transmittal letters highlight important outcome-oriented accomplishments. Other narrative portions in the better reports describe performance highlights in a way that the general public can understand and appreciate. They frequently include "vignettes" that illustrate how the organization's programs have benefited specific individuals. The narratives can be particularly useful for agencies that have difficulty translating their performance accomplishments into clear and specific annual outcomes. This includes research and development agencies, agencies with highly technical missions, and agencies whose broad outcome accomplishments take years to mature. Of course, even the best narratives cannot serve as a substitute for credible performance metrics.

The report should speak directly to the public about how the organization produces benefits that are important to citizens. Politics have no place in this report. The public's interests are paramount, not individual or partisan credit or blame. Just as the best corporate reports feature communication directly from the chief executive, public organization reports should demonstrate accountability of organization heads for their organization's performance. Lofty ideals should be supported by an outcome orientation, sound strategies, and successful achievement discussions. The report should create confidence in the organization's ability to improve America's future. Anecdotes and success stories can be important communication strategies in this regard, but their value is limited if not backed up by solid performance data

Take Advantage of the Transmittal Letter

Public performance reports typically begin with a transmittal letter from the organization head that need only cover a few formalities, such as assurances of compliance with certain legal and accounting requirements. However, the transmittal letter offers a unique opportunity to communicate to the public since it is the first thing (perhaps the only thing) the reader sees. Good transmittal letters go beyond the boilerplate content and highlight specific organization accomplishments for the applicable year. For example, the Secretary of Labor's transmittal letter (Labor 2008, 5–6) notes the following accomplishments, among others:

> For Veterans ... Entered employment and employment retention rates increased by one or two percentage points for all veterans and for disabled veterans participating in DOL's programs.

> For Keeping Workers Safe ... Between 2006 and 2007—the most recent year for which data are available—the workplace injury and illness incidence rate declined to its lowest level ever among private

employers since the changes in OSHA recordkeeping in 2002; declining by 21 percent over the past six years. The rate declined in 5 of 19 private industry sectors and was statistically unchanged in the remaining 14 industry sectors.

Likewise, the Secretary of Transportation states in her transmittal letter (DOT 2008, 3):

> I am proud to report that 83 percent of vehicle occupants used seat-belts during daylight hours this year, up from 82 percent in 2007. This was, in large part, due to high visibility enforcement campaigns, such as Click It or Ticket, and effective enforcement laws in 26 States. We estimate that approximately 270 lives are saved for every one percent increase in belt use.
>
> I am also proud to report that child safety restraint use for children is at an all-time high—more than 98 percent for those less than 1 year old and 96 percent for 1 to 3 year-olds—due to the network of more than 30,000 dedicated child passenger safety technicians that DOT has helped to develop over the past 10 years. When properly used, child safety restraint systems reduce fatalities by 71 percent in infants and 54 percent in toddlers. I was disappointed to learn, however, that 7 of 10 child safety seats are installed improperly, so we launched a new campaign this year that educates parents on proper installation and provides a new 5-star rating system that tells consumers which child-safety seats are easiest to install.

The following are just two of many specific accomplishments listed at length in the transmittal letter from the Secretary of Veterans Affairs (VA 2008, 1):

> Patient Access: In 2006, 94 percent of primary care appointments were scheduled within 30 days of the patient's desired appointment date. In 2008, 98.7 percent of primary care appointments were scheduled within 30 days of the desired appointment date.
>
> Quality of Health Care: VA attained scores of 84 percent and 88 percent for the Clinical Practice Guidelines and Prevention Index, respectively. These indices are nationally recognized industry standards used to measure quality of health care.

Highlight Specific Outcome-Oriented Accomplishments throughout the Report

The transmittal letter is not the only place to highlight accomplishments. Many reports include specific achievements throughout the portions dealing with performance. Here is an example from the Environmental Protection Agency report (EPA 2008, 79):

> ENERGY STAR Saves Billions in Energy Consumption: In 2007, Americans, with the help of ENERGY STAR saved $16 billion on their energy bills and avoided greenhouse gas emissions equivalent to those of 27 million vehicles.... EPA introduced ENERGY STAR in 1992 as a voluntary market-based partnership to reduce greenhouse gas emissions through increased energy efficiency. Today, in partnership with the U.S. Department of Energy, ENERGY STAR offers businesses and consumers energy-efficient solutions to conserve energy, save money, and help protect the environment for future generations. More than 12,000 organizations are ENERGY STAR partners, committed to improving the energy efficiency of products, homes, buildings, and businesses.

The Interior Department provides another example (Figure 2.12).

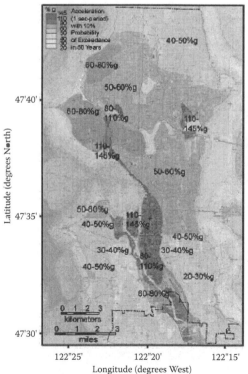

Earthquake Hazard Maps for Seattle

Seattle sits atop a sedimentary basin that strongly affects the patterns of earthquake ground shaking. The City has completed a study of the unreinforced masonry buildings which failed during the 1949, 1965, and 2001 earthquakes in Puget Sound. The study identified nearly 1,000 unreinforced masonry buildings, including a public high school, that are at very high risk in the next earthquake.

The Seattle Urban Seismic Hazard maps, developed by USGS, are being used to provide the basis for a major local policy decision. Because only about 15 percent of masonry buildings have been seismically retrofitted, the City is using the new study to prioritize the work that needs to be done to ensure public safety.

The maps are *probabilistic*—that is, they portray the ground shaking with a certain probability of occurring—and provide a much higher-resolution view of the potential for strong earthquake shaking than previously available. The maps supply critical information for our cities with high earthquake hazards and risks.

Figure 2.12 Interior Department earthquake graphic. (Source: U.S. Department of the Interior, *Performance and Accountability Report, FY 2008,* 2008, 65, www. doi.gov/pfm/par/par2008/par08_final.pdf.)

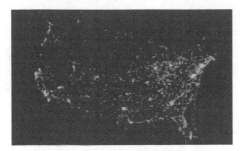

Thousands of aircraft cross the United States on a weekday afternoon in this snapshot of air traffic using NASA's Future Air Traffic Management Concepts Evaluation (FACET) tool. Keeping this multitude of aircraft safely separated is the focus of advanced concepts and technology being developed by NASA and its partners. The technology also helps aircraft avoid other hazards such as weather and terrain by automatically detecting hazards and providing resolutions. (Credit: NASA)

Figure 2.13   Air traffic snapshot. (Source: U.S. National Aeronautics and Space Administration, *Performance and Accountability Report, FY 2008,* **2008, 11, www. nasa.gov/pdf/291255main_NASA_FY08_Performance_and_Accountability_ Report.pdf.)**

Including specific accomplishments such as these is particularly useful to convey an understanding of public benefits for organizations that find it challenging to break down their performance into annual goals and measures, such as those with basic scientific research missions. The National Aeronautics and Space Administration is a case in point, using a number of examples like those in Figure 2.13.

Use Personal Vignettes That Demonstrate the Organization's Direct Impact on Individuals

Another related technique is to include examples of how an organization and its programs have improved the lives of real people. The Labor report does this throughout; Figure 2.14 provides one example.

The Department of Veterans Affairs also uses this technique, highlighting, for example, the first liver transplant at one of its hospitals (Figure 2.15).

While vignettes can enrich a report, they should not be cherry-picked to highlight atypical success stories. In order to be credible, vignettes need to be representative of the organization's actions and their impacts.

At 17, Maira came to the Wisconsin's Waukesha County Workforce Development Center in 2003 for help with school. She was behind in class and getting poor grades—due in part to major family difficulties. After enrollment in the WIA Youth program, Maira earned a High School Equivalency Diploma (HSED) and prepared for college. A summer work experience with the Waukesha Police Department convinced Maira to pursue a career in police science. While attending Waukesha County Technical College, Maira gave birth to a baby girl (Isabella) and still completed that semester with good grades. In May 2007, Maira graduated with a criminal justice degree and was selected to attend the Recruit Academy at Milwaukee Area Technical College for a 13-week training program. After completing the training program, she accepted an officer position with the Fond du Lac Police Department with a starting wage of $19.00/hour. Photo credit: DOL/ETA

Figure 2.14   Labor Department vignette. (Source: U.S. Department of Labor, *Citizens' Report, FY 2008,* **2009, 76, www.dol.gov/_sec/media/reports/Citizens2008/ CitizensReport.pdf.)**

Conclusion

As noted at the outset of this chapter, there is no one-size-fits-all model for successful public performance reporting. However, we believe that any effective system of reporting, whatever its particular form or format, must be built on a foundation of credible, outcome-oriented performance metrics. We hope that the principles and specific examples set out in this chapter will assist in laying that foundation.

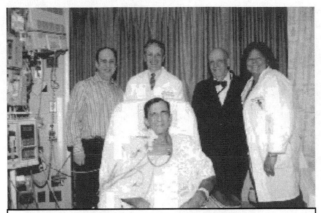

Liver transplant patient Michael Abshire, a 63 year-old, U.S. Navy veteran from Webster, Texas was released to go home in early December. Abshire poses with (from left) David H. Berger, M.D., MEDVAMC Operative Care Line Executive; John A. Goss, M.D., Chief, Division of Abdominal Transplantation at Baylor College of Medicine; Ralph G. Depalma, M.D., VA National Director of Surgery; and Donna Jackson, R.N.-C., Liver Transplant Clinical Coordinator.

Figure 2.15 Veterans Affairs Department vignette. (Source: U.S. Department of Veterans Affairs, *Performance and Accountability Report, FY 2008,* **2008, 36, www4.va.gov/budget/report/.)**

Chapter 3

Other Essential
Best Practices

Overview

The guts of a performance report consist of its performance metrics—the goals and measures. A report that falls short here will have little value no matter how good its additional content. At the same time, however, good performance metrics alone do not guarantee a good report. This chapter describes other attributes that are important to achieving effective performance reporting.

Two of these are self-evident: accessibility and readability. Since we are dealing with reporting to the public, it is essential that members of the public can easily locate, navigate, and understand the report. A report with outstanding substantive content is wasted in terms of the general public if ordinary citizens cannot find it or make sense of it. Equally important, the report must be supported by adequate, credible data. Additionally, reports should go beyond simply reciting performance results. The better reports candidly analyze the organization's results, particularly performance shortfalls, and explain improvement strategies. Doing so indicates that the organization is not just reporting for reporting's sake but actually uses the report's data to influence and improve its performance.

Reports also should link budget costs to performance results. The ultimate objective of such linkages is to provide a solid basis for performance-based budgeting. In other words, what level of performance results can be achieved for what level of investment? While performance–cost linkage is still in its early stages at the federal level, some agencies have begun to develop potential best practices in this area.

Finally, analyzing performance results and developing improvement strategies are not limited to an organization's program performance. Large public organizations face significant management challenges that can adversely affect their ability to accomplish their missions or leave them vulnerable to fraud, waste, and abuse. This is certainly true of federal government agencies. For example, the U.S. Government Accountability Office (GAO) has identified 30 high-risk areas across the federal government that present major economy, efficiency, or effectiveness challenges (GAO 2009a, 1–3). Some of these areas represent government-wide problems such as human capital management and information systems security; others are agency specific. Additionally, federal agency inspectors general identify serious management challenges at their agencies each year. Given the importance of such problems, federal agency performance reports are required by law to address major management challenges (31 USC 3516(d)).

This chapter discusses each of the aspects of performance reporting mentioned above.

Accessibility

Access to performance information is critical because public accountability can only be achieved if members of the public are actually able find out what benefits an organization provides. The organization's performance report should be easily available to the public, other stakeholders, and the media. Ideally, this means that the home page of the organization's web site displays a link clearly guiding the reader to the most recent report. If one has to be an expert on performance management, the organization's internal structure, or the structure of the organization's web site to locate the report, the spirit of accountability to the public is not satisfied. If the report is lengthy (as most federal agency reports are), it should be divided into sections for more convenient reading and downloading. Making the report available in multiple formats is also desirable since readers' needs vary and each format has its advantages and disadvantages (e.g., ease of printing, searching, etc.). Finally, the organization should include contact information so that people can mail, phone, or email questions, comments, or requests for a hard copy of the report.

Over the ten years that we reviewed federal agency performance reports, accessibility proved to be one of the areas of greatest improvement. For the first round of reports we reviewed, covering fiscal year 1999, only four of the 24 agencies posted their reports online in a way that clearly identified the document as the annual performance report and made it easy to find. For fiscal year 2008 (and indeed for several preceding years), almost all agencies posted reports in a timely fashion online, creating a direct home page link to the report, permitting downloads in both single and multiple files, and providing at least some contact information. All but one of the reports were posted either on the same day the hard copy report was formally transmitted to the president and Congress or within a few days thereafter. While accessibility improved greatly over the years, opportunities for further improvement remained.

More Prominent Home Page Links

While almost all agencies had direct home page links to their 2008 reports, the prominence of the links varied considerably. Some agencies (e.g., the Interior, Justice, and Labor Departments) highlighted the report via a prominent home page link. However, others had a relatively obscure link in small print at the bottom of their home pages. In a new feature for 2008, the web page containing the reports for two agencies (the Nuclear Regulatory Commission and the U.S. Agency for International Development) included an introductory video by the organization head.

More Specific Contact Information

It is important that an organization provide contact information for readers who wish to obtain a copy of the report or who have questions or comments about it. While most federal agencies had some type of contact information, the usefulness of the information varied. Some agencies had no contact information online, thus forcing the reader to peruse the body of the report for such information. Contact information in some instances (both online and in the body of reports) was limited to a general telephone number or mailing address for the agency, thus placing the burden on the reader to navigate through the agency bureaucracy in order to find someone knowledgeable about the report.

The most useful approach is to post contact information online that puts the reader directly in touch with organization officials who have specific knowledge of the report, and therefore can respond directly to their inquiries. Examples of agencies having such online, report-specific contact information are the Departments of Education, Energy, Labor, and Treasury. The Environmental Protection Agency had particularly good contact information in its report. The report's table of contents page and the inside back cover identified extensive report-specific contacts, and an email address for submitting comments appeared at the bottom of each page of the report. In addition, Figure 3.1, from the report's final page, contained an explicit invitation for public comments.

Greater Use of Hyperlinks and Other Interactive Features

As we emphasize in various contexts and portions of this book, one major challenge that organizations face is tailoring their reports to meet the needs of diverse

We Welcome Your Comments!

Performance and Accountability Report. We welcome your comments on how we can make this report a more informative document for our readers. We are particularly interested in your comments on the usefulness of the information and the manner in which it is presented. Please send your comments to:

Office of the Chief Financial Officer
Office of Planning, Analysis, and Accountability
Environmental Protection Agency
1200 Pennsylvania Ave., NW
Washington, D.C. 20460
www.epa.gov/ocfo/par/2008par/index.htm

Figure 3.1 EPA comment invitation. (Source: U.S. Environmental Protection Agency, Performance and Accountability Report, FY 2008, 2008, 440, www.epa. gov/ocfo/par/2008par/par08report.pdf.)

audiences without producing documents of unmanageable volume. Stakeholders ranging from governmental officials and other "insiders" intensely concerned with the organization's work to ordinary citizens having a more generalized interest will seek information in far different levels of detail. Organizations can significantly enhance the usefulness of their reports to readers of all levels, and at the same time reduce volume, by incorporating interactive features such as drop-down menus and hyperlinks into the online versions of their reports. This is an excellent way to convey basic information to all readers while enabling those interested in more specifics to find it in detailed source files.

For example, federal agency reports must address the completeness and reliability of their underlying financial and performance data. Conveying a general sense of data quality may be sufficient for many readers. However, others will want to know chapter and verse about data sources as well as steps taken to verify and validate the data. The needs of both audiences can be met by a brief data assessment from the agency head hyperlinked to a more detailed description in another source file.

Liberal use of reader-friendly hyperlinks or similar techniques is particularly important when the organization's performance report actually consists of several different documents, such as separate reports on performance and financial matters. For example, the citizens' reports produced by the Justice and Labor Departments contain direct links to the descriptions of major management challenges in the full performance and accountability reports (Justice 2009, 6; Labor

2009, 24). Hyperlinks or cross-references also can be useful in helping readers navigate through lengthy single reports. For example, the "Performance Scorecard" table in the Department of Veterans Affairs report summarizes performance results for the department's 25 key measures and usefully includes page references to the more detailed discussion of each key measure in the report's performance section (VA 2008, 8–9).

Better Links to Prior Year Reports

A current report tells the organization's performance story for a limited time period—one year or whatever the reporting cycle happens to be. Many readers may wish to review prior year reports as well in order to gain additional perspective. Prior year performance reports for most federal agencies are retained online, but the ease of locating and accessing them varies greatly. Sometimes we had to conduct a series of searches to access the prior year federal reports. Usually this was because searches on the agency web sites produced the reports randomly and, occasionally, only in bits and pieces. For a number of agencies, however, the web page link to the current report also produced the prior year versions or at least provided a direct link to them. Examples are the Department of Energy (www.energy.gov/about/budget.htm) and the Social Security Administration (www.ssa.gov/finance). This is a best practice that all organizations can easily emulate.

Readability and Ease of Use

The performance report is fundamentally a communications device that must address different audiences with different needs. Some readers are subject matter experts in an organization's work who seek an in-depth understanding of the organization's performance and may be willing to plough through a lengthy, detailed, and technical report (or series of reports) to get it. From our perspective, however, the most important readers are the ordinary citizens who pay the bills. They have a right to know in clear and concise language how well the organization is accomplishing the important public outcomes it seeks to achieve on their behalf and in return for their tax dollars.

From this perspective, it is essential that the report's style, language, and subject matter reflect the central purpose of communicating to the public. Reports that do this well communicate important performance results in a way that lay readers can readily comprehend and appreciate. This means, for example, that a reasonably intelligent lay reader can understand what the organization's stated performance goals and measures mean and how achieving them will produce important public benefits. It also means that the lay reader can read and digest the report without undue burden.

The report should focus on the organization's mission, how it marshals its efforts toward that end, and how much progress it made during the covered reporting period. The report's contents should be clear, logical, easy to navigate, and presented in such a way that the structure aids understanding. Consistent format, clarity of text, absence of jargon, and effective use of visual techniques like headings, graphs, tables, and photos are helpful. Acronyms can be helpful if they substitute for lengthy proper names. However, use of acronyms to refer to documents, processes, systems, nouns other than proper names, verbs, short names, or names of things known only to insiders inhibits understanding, even if the report provides a list of acronyms. Details can either inform or confuse, depending on how they are presented. Anecdotes can promote effective communication if they complement and illustrate, rather than substitute for, outcome-based measures.

What Reporting Format Works Best?

Performance reports can come in many formats. Even within the general framework of the Government Performance and Results Act, federal agencies have experimented with a number of different formats to implement the act's core requirements. As detailed in Chapter 1, the basic formats have included separate annual performance and financial reports, a combined annual performance and financial report (known as a performance and accountability report (PAR)), and a pilot reporting format featuring a performance overview report (first called a highlights document and later a citizens' report) with more detailed performance and financial information incorporated into separate documents. In one variation on these themes, some agencies opted to submit a citizens' report in addition to a full PAR report. In another variation for 2008, the Office of Management and Budget required all agencies to prepare a two-page snapshot document in addition to whatever format their performance reporting took. The snapshots provided a high-level overview of each agency's mission as well as representative performance and financial results.

Having reviewed many reports in each of the formats mentioned above, our bottom-line conclusion is that there is no single format that works best or worst. The intrinsic advantage of the PAR format is that it combines all performance and accountability information into a single document; the intrinsic disadvantage is the length of the resulting document. The average length of the 15 PAR reports we reviewed for 2008 was 318 pages. Of course, coupling the PAR with a briefer (well-done) citizens' report can compensate for its length.

There are also ways to reduce the size of the PARs substantially. One alternative would be to discontinue the PAR format and revert to the pre-PAR practice of separate performance and financial reporting. To some extent, this is precisely what most of the pilot agencies have done by producing stand-alone performance reports and financial reports. Dropping the detailed financial data from the performance document would eliminate about 100 pages (on average) of content that holds little interest for the general public. Transparency would not suffer as long as the report contains direct links to the complete financial data for readers who want more detail.

The main advantages of the pilot format are brevity (average length about 30 pages) and flexibility. The premise is that the citizens' report provides the general public with a concise overview of an agency's performance, which is probably all most members of the general public need or want. At the same time, the citizens' report format enables readers with more in-depth or specialized interests to access the other source documents for the additional information they need. Of course, these potential advantages depend on the citizens' report being a substantive, stand-alone document and one that has user-friendly links to other source information.

We also found that the snapshots generally were a useful addition to both PARs and pilot reports since they provided certain basic background, financial, and performance information in a concise and consistent format. However, the quality of the performance-related snapshot content was uneven. Not surprisingly, the content was far better for those agencies that had stronger performance metrics and produced better overall reports.

In the final analysis, however, any report's value to the public depends much more on the quality of its content (understandable outcome-oriented performance metrics, good organization, concise and insightful narratives, and so forth) than on its format. We strongly suspect that considerations of content would outweigh the potential advantages of other formats for performance reporting. Consistent with this conclusion, the remainder of this section focuses on ways to improve the presentational features and substantive content of performance reports irrespective of what form the report takes.

Be Concise

A basic performance reporting challenge for large and complex organizations is to convey information to the general public as concisely as possible through a document that has much required (and often highly technical) content and that must serve stakeholders with different needs. Size certainly can be a barrier to readability. Given its scope, requirements, and diverse audiences, the performance report for a major public organization will likely need to be a fairly large document. However, the fact that federal agencies' reports varied greatly in size indicates that even the most complex organizations have considerable flexibility and that the reports need not be oppressively long. For example, the length of PAR reports that we reviewed for 2008 ranged from a high of 567 pages (EPA 2008) to a low of 172 pages (NRC 2008). Organizations can use many techniques to kill fewer trees and package information more concisely. The following are some of the most effective techniques we have identified from federal performance reports.

Focus on a Limited Set of Performance Metrics

Performance reports that feature a multitude of goals and measures (sometimes literally hundreds) present serious readability and comprehension challenges.

Simply wading through the voluminous pages required to cover them is a major burden. Moreover, extensive performance metrics make it difficult for the reader to determine and focus on what really matters. By contrast, many federal agencies have successfully presented their results through a limited set of performance metrics that home in on important public outcomes. For example, the Justice Department used a total of 25 performance measures (Justice 2008, I-11–13), and the Department of Agriculture got by with 33 measures (Agriculture 2008, 7–9).

Even agencies that find it necessary to use many measures can focus their reports on the most important. For example, the Department of Veterans Affairs report stated that the department has a total of 138 performance measures, but the report concentrated on 25 key measures (VA 2008, 7–8, 19). While the Department of Health and Human Services used more than 1,000 performance measures, its citizens' report focused on 40 measures from the department's strategic plan (HHS 2009, 6). The main body of the report dealt primarily with 16 of these 40 as spotlight measures. There was one spotlight measure for each of the department's 16 strategic objectives; they seemed broadly and reasonably representative of what the department accomplished. The remaining 24 measures were mentioned briefly in the main body and covered more fully in an appendix to the report.

Minimize Lengthy, Text-Heavy Narratives and Maximize Tables and Graphics

Many reports make effective use of tables, graphs, and similar features to highlight aspects of their performance or to drive home key points. This saves space and enhances readability. One particularly helpful feature is a report card or scorecard table that summarizes the organization's overall performance results at a glance. For example, Figure 3.2 shows a table that the Social Security Administration used to summarize its performance results. The Department of Veterans Affairs used a similar performance scorecard table, shown in Figure 3.3.

The snapshots that agencies prepared for 2008 also included useful tables and graphics that presented performance results at a glance. Figure 3.4 shows an example from the Labor Department citizens' report.

Place Lengthy, Technical Presentations Outside the Main Body of the Report

Another way to reduce the length and complexity of reports is to omit some technical content in favor of providing a hyperlink to it for those readers who are interested. This technique is well suited, for example, as a means of dealing with the details of performance data validation and verification as well as performance measurement sources and methodologies. For example, the Education Department report links to other sources for additional detail on its data quality methods (Education 2008,

Strategic Objective 1.1: Make the Right Decision in the Disability Process as Early as Possible

Performance Indicator		FY 2008 Goal	FY 2008 Actual	Goal Achieved?	See Page #
1.1a	Percent of initial disability claims receipts processed by the Disability Determination Services up to the budgeted level[2]	100%	101%	←	45
1.1b PART	Minimize average processing time for initial disability claims to provide timely decisions	107 days	106 days	←	46
1.1c PART	Disability Determination Services net accuracy rate for combined initial disability allowances and denials	97%	Data available January 2009	TBD	47
1.1d	Achieve the budgeted goal for SSA hearings processed (at or above the FY 2008 goal)	559,000	575,380	←	48
1.1e	Maintain the number of SSA hearings pending (at or below the FY 2008 goal)	752,000	760,813	→	49
1.1f PART	Achieve target percentage of hearing level cases pending over 365 days	56%	37%	←	50
1.1g	Achieve target percentage of hearing level cases pending 900 days or more	Less than 1% of universe of over 900-day cases pending	0.2%	←	51
1.1h PART	Achieve the budgeted goal for average processing time for hearings	535 days	514 days	←	51
1.1i	Achieve the budgeted goal for average processing time for requests for review (appeals of hearing decisions)	242 days	238 days	←	52
1.1j	Decrease the number of pending requests for review (appeals of hearing decisions) over 365 days	28%	22%	←	53

Figure 3.2 Social Security Administration indicators and goals. (Source: U.S. Social Security Administration, Performance and Accountability Report, FY 2008, 17, www.ssa.gov/finance/2008/Full%20PAR.pdf.)

Performance Scorecard

Strategic Goals	Key Performance Measures (page references in full PAR)	FY 2007 Recap		FY 2008 Recap					Measure Type
		Targets	Results	Targets	Results	Target Achieved? Yes	No	Improved from FY 2007? Yes/No/Same	
Strategic Goal 1 — Restoration and Improved Quality of Life for Disabled Veterans	National accuracy rate for compensation core rating work (pp. 121, 228)	89%	88%	90%	86%		No	No	Output
	Compensation and pension rating-related actions—average days to process (pp. 119, 228)	160	183	169	179		No	Yes	Output
	Rating-related compensation actions—average days pending (pp. 120, 228)	127	132	120	121		No	Yes	Output
	Vocational rehabilitation and employment rehabilitation rate (pp. 126, 228)	73%	73%	75%	76%	Yes		Yes	Outcome
	Average days to process Dependency and Indemnity Compensation actions (pp. 130, 228)	125	132	118	121		No	Yes	Output

Figure 3.3 Veterans Affairs goals and measures. (Source: U.S. Department of Veterans Affairs, Performance and Accountability Report, FY 2008, 2008, 8, www4.va.gov/budget/report/.)

24). Similarly, the Environmental Protection Agency report provides links to other sources for data background on some performance measures (EPA 2008, 59).

An alternative approach is to shift detailed background information from the main body of the report to an appendix, although this does not reduce the total report volume.

Use Fewer Words

In addition to the foregoing specific suggestions and perhaps above all else, report drafters should strive to be less verbose. We frequently encountered reports with long text narratives that would discourage even the most persistent reader. Also, we have encountered examples of reports or portions of reports that cannot possibly need to be as long as they are. An example is EPA's 2008 performance and accountability report of 567 pages, which exceeded the second longest report by a full 100 pages. Furthermore, it is hard to believe that the "Management's Discussion and Analysis" sections of performance and accountability reports, which are supposed to be an overview, need to consume an average of more than 50 pages, as they did in 2008. It also is hard to believe that descriptions of major management challenges, important as they are, need to consume more than 90 pages, or almost 25% of the entire report, as one agency's did (Transportation 2008, 43–83, 318–370).

Another way to reduce verbiage and save trees is to exercise restraint in describing the organization's structure and operations. While some background along these lines is important, it should be limited to providing a concise overview of the organization's mission, structure, and program activities. This background should not go beyond information directly relevant and necessary to convey an essential understanding of why the organization exists and how it goes about achieving its intended performance results. The Housing and Urban Development Department's 2008 report (HUD 2008) offers an example of telling readers much more than they needed to know in this regard. Its 90-page "Management's Discussion and Analysis" section and 175-page performance section contain lengthy recitations concerning the department's structure and components, their history, and their programs and activities. Unfortunately, all of this text obscures rather than illuminates the department's core missions and actual results.

Keep the General Public in Mind

Organizations face many challenges in crafting their performance reports, but writing a report that ordinary citizens can read and understand should not be one of them. Report writers should affirmatively consider how well their product will communicate to lay readers. It is easy to tell which reports were (or were not) written from this perspective.

Summary of Department of Labor Ratings for Fiscal Year 2008

FY 2008 Performance: Results per Strategic Goal

Strategic Goal: A Prepared Workforce

Develop a prepared workforce by providing effective training and support services to new and incumbent workers and supplying high-quality information on the economy and labor market.

Budget per Strategic Goal ($ in millions): 2008 Actual = $3,872

Performance Measure(s)*	2006 Results	2007 Results	2008 Target	2008 Results	2009 Target
Job Corps Entered Employment—Percent of participants entering employment or enrolling in postsecondary education or advanced training/occupational skills training in the first quarter after exit.	80%	74%	82%	73% (not met)	73%

Strategic Goal: A Competitive Workforce

Meet the competitive labor demands of the worldwide economy by enhancing the effectiveness and efficiency of the workforce development and regulatory systems that assist workers and employers in meeting the challenges of global competition.

Budget per Strategic Goal ($ in millions): 2008 Actual = $4,503

Performance Measure(s)*	2006 Results	2007 Results	2008 Target	2008 Results	2009 Target
Workforce Investment Act Adult Program Employment Retention—Percent of participants employed in the first quarter after exit still employed in the second and third quarters after exit.	83%	82%	83%	84% (met)	83%

Strategic Goal: Safe and Secure Workplaces

Promote workplaces that are safe, healthful, and fair; guarantee workers receive the wages due them; foster equal opportunity in employment; and protect veterans' employment and reemployment rights.

Performance Measure(s)*	2006 Results	2007 Results	2008 Target	2008 Results	2008 Actual = $1,415
Mine industry injuries per 200,000 hours worked.	3.72	3.50	3.41	3.24 (met)	2009 Target
					3.08

Strategic Goal: Strengthened Economic Protections

Protect and strengthen worker economic security through effective and efficient provision of unemployment insurance and workers' compensation, ensuring union transparency, and securing pension and health benefits.

Performance Measure(s)*	2006 Results	2007 Results	2008 Target	2008 Results	2008 Actual = $51,460
Unemployment Insurance—Percent of intrastate first payments made within 21 days.	87.6%	88.2%	88.4%	86.8% (not met)	2009 Target
					87.7%

* This measure was selected from a number of performance measures aimed at the specific strategic goal.

Figure 3.4 Labor Department targets and results. (Source: U.S. Department of Labor, Citizens' Report, FY 2008, 2009, 3, www.dol.gov/_sec/media/reports/Citizens2008/CitizensReport.pdf.)

Keep It Simple

Reports may need technical content to satisfy legal requirements and the legitimate interests of specialized audiences. However, there are ample opportunities to reach the general public as well. Good venues for this include the citizens' report and the organization head's transmittal letter. The Justice Department citizens' report for 2008 provided an excellent example of a document written with the general public in mind. Its sections had captions such as "the Department of Justice at a glance" and "How do we serve you?" It had excellent user-friendly links to other source information. It included the department's snapshot as well as summaries of performance results by strategic goal that were concise and well suited to a lay audience. The summaries featured representative performance measures that, while not consistently outcome-oriented, were clear and focused on subjects of obvious importance to the public. The report highlighted accomplishments in each strategic goal area and included vignettes to illustrate some of them.

Avoid Acronyms

Government agencies are famous for coining acronyms. Indeed, one acquaintance in a federal agency told us he worked in the agency's Bureau of Acronyms. In the vast majority of cases, acronyms are merely another form of insider-speak that obscures rather than enlightens.

Table 3.1 lists some of the more noteworthy acronyms our research team encountered in ten years of reading federal performance reports. Some are tongue twisters; many are confusing. Some seem completely unnecessary, such as abbreviating citizens' report (CR), insecticide-treated nets (ITNs), or top officials (TOPOFF). We understand the Justice Department may want to avoid using the word *Mafia*, but *La Cosa Nostra* is almost as easy to say, and easier to understand, as *LCN*. A large number of acronyms refer to such obscure concepts, internal systems, or processes that they probably signify the agency is providing far too much detailed description of activities that are of interest only to insiders. And if it's really important to mention the National Intellectual Property Law Enforcement Coordination Council in a performance report, surely it should be sufficient to call it "the council" in the (hopefully) small number of subsequent references. Ditto for other internal organizations, such as the Identity and Access Management Working Group. We will see in Chapter 5 that in some countries, government employees actually manage to write performance reports with nary an acronym!

Data Quality

A report can be no better than the data it contains. Data quality has several dimensions in the context of performance reporting. First, performance data need to be

Table 3.1 TMA (Too Many Acronyms)

Acronym	Apparent Meaning	Perpetrator
GWOT	Global war on terrorism	Defense
LUST	Leaking underground storage tank	Environmental Protection Agency
NIPLECC	National Intellectual Property Law Enforcement Coordination Council	Commerce
IDAMWIG	Identity and Access Management Working Group	General Services Administration
SPITS	Service's Permit Issuance and Tracking System	Interior
CR	Citizens' report	Office of Personnel Management
HSPD-9	Homeland Security Presidential Directive 9	Agriculture
IAQTfS	Indoor Air Quality Tools for Schools	Environmental Protection Agency
MANPADS	Man Portable Air Defense System	Several
CHUMS	Computerized Homes Underwriting Management System	Housing and Urban Development
LCN	La Cosa Nostra	Justice
SBUV/2	Solar backscatter ultraviolet	NASA
ITNs	Insecticide-treated nets	Agency for International Development
EPOXY	Earnings Posted Overall Cross Total/Year-to-Date System	Social Security
TOPOFF	Top officials	Homeland Security
WAU	Whereabouts unknown	Interior
WYC	Watch your car	Justice
ABC	Abstinence, Being Faithful and Using Condom Approach	Agency for International Development
RIRIP	Risk-Informed Regulation Implementation Plan	Nuclear Regulatory Commission
PERSTEMPO	Personnel tempo	Defense
FBU	Funds can be put to better use	Interior
Daily Double (Acronym with two different meanings in the same year)		
SAR	Search and rescue	Homeland Security
	Selected acquisition report	Defense
Trifecta (Acronym with three different meanings in the same year)		
IP	Intellectual property	Commerce
	Internet protocol	Commerce
	Improper payment	Health and Human Services

accurate and reliable, e.g., verifiable through credible sources. Second, the data must be valid, i.e., relevant to their intended purpose and persuasive. For example, data used to measure a particular goal must logically relate to and demonstrate progress toward achievement of that goal. Third, performance data should be as timely and complete as possible.

Data quality is so important that a federal law, the Reports Consolidation Act of 2000, specifically requires the transmittal letter for federal agency performance reports to include "an assessment by the agency head of the completeness and reliability of the performance and financial data used in the report" and provides that the assessment must "describe any material inadequacies in the completeness and reliability of the data" as well as what the agency can do and is doing to resolve them (Pub. L. 106-531, 31 USC 3516(e)). The purpose of these requirements is to emphasize that ensuring the quality of the underlying data is a management priority and that deficiencies are acknowledged and corrected as quickly as possible. More generally, the report should indicate the organization's confidence in the quality of the data used to document its results. For example, data sources and descriptions should be provided for all performance measures.

Public organizations often face serious challenges in developing timely, complete, and reliable performance data. This is certainly true of major federal agencies, particularly those that seek to achieve broad national outcomes that are difficult to measure and attribute to specific causes. Indeed, the more outcome-oriented an organization's performance metrics, the more difficult the measurement challenges may be. Another challenge confronting many organizations, including federal agencies, is the need to rely on third-party data sources. This can affect both the timeliness and reliability of data. The data challenges for federal agencies are compounded by the Government Performance and Results Act's annual reporting cycle, which often results in severe data lags. For example, the Department of Health and Human Services reported current results for only 40% of its 2008 performance targets (HHS 2009, 6), and the Department of Education's 2008 report listed results for only 15 of its 81 key performance measures (Education 2008, 26–30).

Recognizing the inherent challenges, it is unrealistic to expect large organizations to be entirely free of data issues. On the other hand, one should expect organizations to disclose data weaknesses up front and to describe remedial steps in a way that instills confidence that they are doing their best to resolve or at least minimize the impact of data weaknesses. Based on our reviews, there are a number of specific steps organizations can take in this regard.

More Candid Data Assessments

Candid acknowledgment of data challenges, particularly on the part of the organization head, is the first step toward addressing them. Unfortunately, however, many federal agency heads respond to the Report Consolidation Act's data assessment requirements with a perfunctory statement that glosses over weaknesses that are evident from the body of the report. The EPA administrator's transmittal letter for the agency's 2008 report was one of the few that provided a concise yet straightforward data assessment:

> Data used to report progress are reliable and as complete as possible. Inherent to the nature of our work is a time lag between when we take action to protect human health or the environment and when we can measure a result from that action. Therefore, for the reporting year, we cannot provide results data for several of our performance measures; however, we portray trend data, when possible, to show progress toward results over time, and we present final results for prior years when data have become available in FY 2008. (EPA 2008, vii)

Similarly, employing a best practice, the Labor Department report systematically assessed and numerically rated the quality of its data for each performance goal (Labor 2008, 59–61).

Fuller Data Disclosure

Many reports simply do not provide enough information to give the reader a sense of how reliable the data are or even what data the organization uses. The credibility and usefulness of a report can be enhanced by providing data definitions and sources for individual measures. It is also helpful to describe what the organization does to verify and validate performance data. The 2008 reports for the Departments of Labor and Veterans Affairs are examples. The performance section of the Labor report elaborates on data quality for each goal and provides data sources for each measure. The Veterans Affairs report provides a detailed discussion of data quality, which includes specifics on verification techniques. Tables in the performance section provide detailed background on the data supporting the key measures, including data definitions, data validation and verification, and any data limitations. Additional data definitions and background appear later in the report.

At the same time, it is not necessary to burden the main body of a report with exhaustive detail on data sources and methods. For example, the performance section of the EPA report highlights data support for some measures and provides an online link to detailed data background for all measures (EPA 2008, 59).

Minimize the Impact of Data Lags

Data lags prevent many organizations from reporting current performance results for all of their measures. Nevertheless, federal agencies have found several ways to ameliorate this problem. One widely used practice is to report tentative performance results on the basis of projections or estimates, with updated information provided later (either in the next report or in a separate document) once the final results become available. Reporting estimates is certainly preferable to simply leaving blank spaces for performance results. At the same time, two important caveats apply to the use of estimates. First, of course, this practice is only appropriate to the extent that enough data exist to support reasonable estimates or projections. Second, the report should clearly indicate when they are being used in lieu of final results.

Even when current year results cannot be projected or estimated, there may be alternatives to simply providing no information. Agencies whose performance goals do not readily lend themselves to annual measurement can at least provide trend data extending over multiple years in order to convey some sense of progress. The Education Department report, for example, provides data on long-term trends in reading and mathematics achievement based on prior year results (Education 2008, 12–16). This helps to make up for the gap caused by the fact that current year data for these and other key education measures invariably lag behind the GPRA annual reporting cycle.

Don't Let Data Issues Dictate Performance Metrics

While data challenges can be daunting, organizations should resist the temptation to "dumb down" their performance metrics by limiting them to things that can be easily measured within the reporting timeframe. Doing so will tend to shift the metrics from outcomes to outputs and activities. In our view, strong outcome-oriented performance goals and measures that carry data challenges are preferable to goals and measures that make for easy reporting but tell little about the organization's value in achieving public benefits.

Explanation of Results and Improvement Strategies

While performance reports are an important source for public disclosure and accountability, performance reporting is not an end in itself. Performance reports should also serve as a diagnostic, assisting internal managers and external policy-makers to assess the organization's current progress toward achieving its mission outcomes and chart the course to improvements. The idea is to gather information on performance results and then to use that information in a strategic manner to guide future management actions and policy decisions. Thus, it is essential that the reports clearly disclose performance results, including performance shortfalls (i.e., missed targets), candidly explain the reasons for them, and describe improvement strategies. If an organization cannot identify reasons for shortcomings, its ability to claim credit for success is suspect. Moreover, failure to acknowledge or explain shortcomings stifles improvement efforts. The effects of unexpected events or barriers—both internal and external—should be explained, and solutions revealed or suggested. Special care should be taken with resource explanations to indicate precisely how more or different resources would fix the problem and why reallocations were not made internally.

Clear and Candid Disclosure of Results

Over the years of our reviews, we occasionally encountered reports that obscured performance results or presented them in a misleading manner. Rather than clearly disclosing results by simple terms (e.g., *met* or *not met*), checkmarks, or other symbols, some agencies buried their results in lengthy narratives. This required the reader to parse through the text (and sometimes interpret ambiguous passages) in order to determine whether performance measures were actually met or missed. Other agencies developed incongruous categories to describe their results. For example, a few reports categorized performance goals as "significantly met" if the agency met 75 to 99% of the applicable measures. In other words, performance could fall short of expectations by up to 25% and still qualify as significantly meeting the goal. Occasionally a report would highlight which goals were achieved or not achieved, while downplaying or failing to disclose the actual performance data that led to this determination. Fortunately, these problems had largely disappeared by the 2008 round of reports. However, they serve as a reminder that organizations need to report their results in a straightforward way or risk creating credibility issues.

Reporting Perfect or Near-Perfect Performance Is Cause for Skepticism, Not Celebration

No reasonable person would expect a major federal organization (or any organization with complex and difficult missions) to meet all of its performance targets. On the contrary, the best organizations set challenging performance targets that will inevitably result in some shortfalls, and they use the shortfalls as a springboard to improve. Therefore, we suspect that readers are skeptical rather than impressed when an organization reports no performance shortfalls or very few. Rather than assuming that the organization is performing flawlessly, the reader would more likely suspect that it either was not reporting candidly or was not challenging itself in its performance metrics. The National Science Foundation serves as an example. The agency reported no performance shortfalls with respect to its three programmatic strategic goals for fiscal year 2008, nor had it reported any such shortfalls at least as far back as fiscal year 2004 (NSF 2009, 9–10).

Explanations, Not Excuses

Explanations for performance shortfalls are most valuable when they serve a diagnostic purpose by identifying the causes of the shortfall and how it can be remedied. Too often, however, the explanations amount to no more than excuses that provide no useful insight. Common examples are statements to the effect that the target was challenging or too ambitious; or that the agency came close and will try harder next year; or that the shortfall was attributable to factors beyond the agency's control. Such statements provide no specifics that point the way to future improvement. Occasionally, an agency excuses shortfalls by challenging its own performance metrics. For example, the Office of Personnel Management report for 2008 attributed one shortfall to the fact that the performance data used did not align with the measure; another shortfall explanation called into question the validity of the measure (OPM 2008, 36, 42–43).

Model Reports

The following 2008 reports contain good explanations of performance results and serve as models in this regard.

The Department of Veterans Affairs had a specific section entitled "Performance Shortfall Analysis" that described causes and resolution strategies for significant performance shortfalls. Figure 3.5 shows an extract from the section.

Under the heading "How VA Leadership Uses Results Data" in the detailed performance section, the report briefly described performance improvement steps even where targets were met (e.g., VA 2008, 142).

Strategic Goal 1		
Restoration and Improved Quality of Life for Disabled Veterans		
Measure	*Target*	*Result*
Compensation and pension rating-related actions— average days to process	169	179 (r)
Causes	• The number of claims received continues to increase. VA received 891,547 claims in 2008, over 53,000 more than the 838,141 received in 2007.	
Resolution Strategies	• VA hired nearly 2,000 additional employees to process claims in 2008. • In May 2008, VA began to consolidate original and reopened disability and death pension claims to the three existing pension management centers and completed the consolidation in September 2008. • Through this consolidation, VA has already begun to realize efficiencies and greater effectiveness through specialization. The consolidation is expected to improve claims processing timeliness.	

Figure 3.5 VA performance shortfall analysis. (Source: U.S. Department of Veterans Affairs, Performance and Accountability Report, FY 2008, 2008, 84, www4.va.gov/budget/report/.)

In a table captioned "FY 2008 Performance Improvement Plan," excerpted in Figure 3.6, the National Aeronautics and Space Administration report listed each measure that was not fully achieved, explained why, and outlined plans for achieving the measure in the future.

As Figure 3.7 illustrates, the Treasury Department report specified gradations of performance results, both in the percentage of achievement for individual targets and the level of success.

Where targets were missed, an appendix consistently provided an explanation under the heading "Future Plans/Explanation for Shortfall" (Treasury 2008, 290–375). The explanations were brief but informative, and they were usually accompanied by a general description of remedial steps.

Linking Costs to Performance Results

Linking budget costs to results helps decision makers know how much they have to pay per successful program outcome. Armed with this information, they can assess the opportunities forgone when resources are allocated to less effective programs, and they can estimate how much more could be accomplished if resources were reallocated to the most effective programs. Comprehensive and accurate linking of costs to performance metrics lays the foundation for performance-based budgeting, a subject described more fully in Chapter 9.

Performance-cost linkages are still in the formative stage with respect to federal performance reporting. When we began our scoring in 1999, few reports linked budget costs even to strategic goals, the highest level of an agency's performance metrics. Over the years, performance–cost linkages became more widespread and sophisticated. This occurred as more agencies carried down the linkages to their strategic objectives, individual performance goals, and ultimately, individual performance measures—usually the level at which performance-based budgeting can be implemented. However, progress has been gradual and sporadic. For the 2008 round of federal performance reports we reviewed, we found that agencies could be divided into two camps: those that were making serious efforts to link costs to performance metrics in a meaningful way and those that were not. The agencies falling into the former camp made good faith efforts at performance–cost linkages with varying degrees of success. In the latter camp were 11 agencies that either failed to link budget resources to their performance metrics at any level or provided a linkage only to their strategic goals.

Developing linkages to the point of permitting meaningful performance–cost analysis presents methodological challenges. It probably is impractical or even impossible for some organizations to allocate costs to every individual performance measure. For example, a program funded from a single budget item may have multiple performance measures for which costs cannot be isolated, such as separate outcome, efficiency, and customer service measures. The goal should be to find the

Performance Measure	Description	Rating	Why the Measure Was Not Met or Was Canceled	Plans for Achieving the Measure (If Not Canceled)
8CS06 (Outcome 4.1)	Complete the Preliminary Design Review (PDR) for the Extravehicular Activity (EVA) Systems.	Yellow	NASA established these metrics when the EVA Systems project was still in early formulation. Since then, the project found it necessary to refine its schedule during the reporting period by shifting the PDR to align with new program milestones. In addition, in response to several protests filed by the Exploration Systems and Technology LLC (EST)—the unsuccessful offeror—with the GAO between contract award on June 12 and September 29, 2008, NASA notified the GAO that it determined that "corrective action" was appropriate and, as part of the corrective action, NASA terminated the original CSSS contract awarded to Oceaneering International, Inc. (OII) for the convenience of the government. The GAO then dismissed the original EST protest and all supplemental protests as "academic," given NASA's decision to take corrective action.	NASA is implementing a corrective action plan and will update its key project milestones accordingly to accommodate that plan. NASA is replanning the EVA Systems project preliminary design efforts to accommodate the delay. Although the GAO protests have been dismissed, federal acquisition regulations still prohibit NASA from discussing details about a pending procurement matter.

Figure 3.6 NASA performance shortfall analysis. (Source: U.S. National Aeronautics and Space Administration, Performance and Accountability Report, FY 2008, 2008, 102, www.nasa.gov/pdf/291255main_NASA_FY08_Performance_and_Accountability_Report.pdf.)

Cash Resources Are Available to Operate the Government

Performance Measure	Bureau	FY 2008 Target	FY 2008 Actual	Percent of Target Achieved	Performance Rating	FY 2009 Target	Target Trend	Actual Trend
Examination coverage—business corporations > $10 million	IRS	6.6%	6.1%	92%	Unmet	5.8%	→	→
Examination coverage—individual (%)	IRS	1%	1%	100%	Met	1%	←	←
Examination efficiency—individual (1040 form)	IRS	133	138	104%	Exceeded	140	←	←
Examination quality (LMSB)—coordinated industry	IRS	96%	97%	101%	Exceeded	96%	←	←
Examination quality (LMSB)—industry	IRS	88%	88%	100%	Met	88%	←	←
Field collection embedded quality	IRS	86%	79%	92%	Unmet	80%	→	→
Field examination embedded quality	IRS	87%	86%	99%	Improved	87%	↖	←
Health Care Tax Credit cost per taxpayer served	IRS	$14.25	$16.94	81%	Unmet	$17.00	←	←
Number of convictions	IRS	2,135	2,144	100.4%	Exceeded	2,135	↑	↑
Office examination embedded quality	IRS	90%	90%	100%	Met	90%	←	←
Percent of business returns processed electronically	IRS	20.8%	19.4%	93%	Improved	22.9%	←	←

Figure 3.7 Treasury performance results. (Source: U.S. Department of the Treasury, **Performance and Accountability Report, FY 2008,** 2008, 282, www.ustreas.gov/offices/management/dcfo/accountability-reports/2008-par/Full_Version.pdf.)

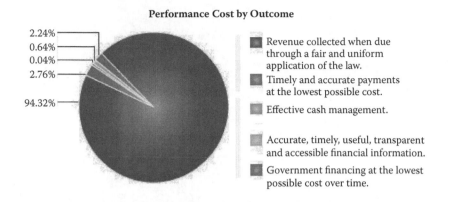

Figure 3.8 Treasury cost pie chart. (Source: U.S. Department of the Treasury, *Performance and Accountability Report, FY 2008,* **2008, 51, www.ustreas.gov/ offices/management/dcfo/accountability-reports/2008-par/Full_Version.pdf.)**

right unit of analysis for performance–cost linkages so that the organization can assess performance results in relation to funding investments.

In order to provide a complete picture, it also is important to take indirect as well as direct costs into account. This includes personnel and administrative costs even if they are funded from a source other than the program or activity being measured. Finally, the cost and performance data on which linkages are based must, of course, be accurate in order for the linkages to be useful. In this regard, we found, not surprisingly, that agencies unable to produce complete and reliable financial data were likewise unable to provide useful cost linkages. We also found instances (fortunately few) in which data used for performance-cost linkages were inconsistent with financial data presented elsewhere in the report.

On the positive side, we identified some 2008 federal agency reports that can serve as models for other organizations. The Department of Labor report linked costs for the current year and several prior years to most of the department's individual performance measures (Labor 2008, 15–16). Likewise, the Transportation Department report had links to its individual performance measures (e.g., Transportation 2008, 101). Several other agencies developed innovative techniques to relate costs to performance. The Treasury Department report presented this information primarily on the basis of performance and cost, as opposed to budgetary resources. Figure 3.8 reproduces a pie chart from the Treasury report as an example.

As the report explained, this approach provided a more accurate picture of the actual costs related to performance since it included "imputed costs, depreciation, losses, and other expenses not requiring budgetary resources" (Treasury 2008, 47). The Treasury report also covered costs for programs funded by sources other than general fund appropriations, such as user fee-financed or nonappropriated fund activities.

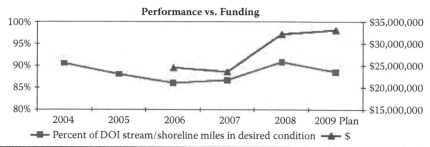

Performance vs. Funding

ID #1614	2004	2005	2006	2007	2008	2009 Plan
Target				88%	89%	89%
Performance	91%	88%	86%	87%	91%	
Miles in desired condition	126,821	131,200	137,173	193,147	247,937	241,982
Miles with known condition	140,096	149,167	159,411	222,830	273,093	273,093
$	Not Available		24,523,638	23,550,163	32,166,294	33,124,376

Figure 3.9 Interior performance-cost chart. (Source: U.S. Department of the Interior, *Performance and Accountability Report, FY 2008*, 2008, 23, www.doi. gov/pfm/par/par2008/par08_final.pdf.)

The Interior Department allocated costs to the 25 representative performance measures featured in its report and, through activity-based costing graphs, showed performance results in relation to funding levels. Figure 3.9, from the Interior report, illustrates this practice.

The report narratives also provided some analysis of the impact of funding levels on performance.

Addressing Major Management Challenges

Up to this point, we have discussed performance reporting in relation to an organization's core program mission(s)—for example, enhancing national security or improving public health and safety—since program performance constitutes the most important aspect of the organization's work, being directly related to achieving mission outcomes. At the same time, virtually all large organizations face major management challenges that, if left unaddressed, can seriously impede or even undermine the organization's ability to accomplish its mission. The impact of management challenges is most critical in the context of outcome achievement. Thus, it is important that performance reports cover those management challenges that are potentially mission critical. Indeed, at the federal level Congress deemed major management challenges to be sufficiently important that the Reports Consolidation Act specifically requires agency performance reports to include a statement by the organization's inspector general that (1) summarizes what the inspector general considers to be the organization's most serious management and performance challenges and (2) briefly assesses the organization's progress in addressing those challenges (31 USC 3516(d)).

Descriptions of major management challenges should include full disclosure of each problem area, the specific steps being taken to resolve or at least mitigate the problem, and an assessment of the organization's progress in this regard. By virtue of the Reports Consolidation Act's requirements, inspectors general play a critical role in federal agency report presentations dealing with major management problems. However, the better reports include a discussion on this subject by agency management as well, which, among other things, responds to the inspector general's presentation. The best federal reports also cover major management challenges identified by other relevant sources, such as the U.S. Government Accountability Office and the Office of Management and Budget. The federal model should apply to most nonfederal organizations as well. The key to effective treatment of major management challenges in a performance report is a strong description and assessment of the challenges by the organization's inspector general, or comparable internal auditor(s), coupled with a response by agency management that outlines specific remedial steps.

Inspector General Assessments

Our reviews of federal reports over the years revealed considerable variation in the quality of inspector general presentations on major management challenges pursuant to the Reports Consolidation Act. In particular, the required assessments of progress, which Congress considered an important barometer (S. Rep. 106-337 2000, 4), often were missing or inadequate. Too many inspector general presentations described the challenges in great detail but offered little, if any, insight into what specific steps were needed to remedy them, whether the agencies were taking those steps, and when they were likely to produce a solution. Frequently, the inspectors general recited much the same list of challenges year after year while providing assessments consisting of nothing more that the tired bromide "progress being made but more remains to be done." This does little to inform the reader or instill confidence that the inspector general is on top of the situation. We have also found that agency management responses tended to be less specific when the inspector general assessment was weak on specifics.

One bright spot over the years was the presentation by the inspector general of the Small Business Administration, an insightful assessment that should serve as a model for other auditors. The Small Business Administration inspector general broke down each challenge into specific elements and offered recommended actions to resolve it. The presentation included tables that used a color-coded system to rate the agency's status with respect to each action and listed remaining actions needed to resolve it. It added a table summarizing the organization's overall progress for each action and challenge. Figure 3.10 is an extract from the inspector general's presentation for 2008.

Challenge 4: SBA's National Guaranty Purchase Center Needs Better Controls over the 7(a) Loan Guaranty Purchase Process

The majority of loans made under the 7(a) loan guaranty program are made with little or no review by SBA prior to loan approval because SBA has delegated most of the credit decisions to lenders originating these loans. SBA's review of lender requests for guaranty purchases on defaulted loans is therefore the agency's primary tool for assessing lender compliance on individual loans and protecting SBA from making erroneous purchase payments. However, OIG audits of early defaulted loans and SBA's guaranty purchase process have shown that reviews made by the National Guaranty Purchase Center (NGPC) have not consistently detected lender failures to administer loans in full compliance with SBA requirements and prudent lending practices, resulting in improper payments.

SBA has taken actions to correct many of the deficiencies identified by the OIG, such as reengineering the 7(a) loan guaranty purchase process to improve the efficiency of the program, increasing the staffing level at the NGPC, and issuing revised standard operating procedures (SOPs) for lender loan processing. SBA has also developed a comprehensive operations manual for the NGPC and trained individuals responsible for making purchase decisions. Further, the agency developed and implemented a statistical sampling methodology to identify improper payments in accordance with OMB requirements. While improvements have been made, additional actions are needed to strengthen guaranty purchase decisions and effectively reduce improper payments, such as ensuring corrective actions are taken when deficiencies in the purchase review process are identified. Also, the agency needs to implement policies and procedures that are required in recommended action 4 below, including: (1) review of the entire lender loan file for early defaulted loans, (2) verification of financial information, (3) identification of collateral at loan inception and after loan default, and (4) verification of borrower equity injections.

Challenge History Fiscal Year (FY) Issued: 2001	Actions Accomplished (Green Status) during Past 4 FYs			
	04-0	05-2	06-0	07-0

Remaining Recommended Actions Needed for FY 2009	Status at End of FY 2008
1. Devote adequate resources to the purchase process.	Green
2. Determine the level of improper payments for the entire loan portfolio in compliance with the improper Payments Information Act of 2002 and OMB guidance.	Green
3. Establish a process to identify and address the risks of improper payments.	Orange
4. Implement effective policies and procedures governing the guaranty purchase process.	Yellow

Note: Green = implemented, yellow = substantial progress, orange = limited progress, red = no progress.

Figure 3.10   SBA inspector general assessment. (Source: U.S. Small Business Administration, Agency Financial Report. FY 2008, 2008, 58, www.sba.gov/ aboutsba/budgetsplans/SERV_ABTSBA_BUDGET_2008AFR.html.)

Agency Management Assessments

In addition to assessments by internal auditors, it is important that an organization's management provide its perspective on major management challenges. Organization management should respond directly to the internal auditor's assessment. While of course the organization need not accept the internal auditor's assessment, it should clearly spell out the areas of agreement and disagreement. Simply ignoring the internal auditor leaves the reader with the impression that the auditor must be right on all points. To the extent that the organization agrees with the internal auditor's problem assessment (or acknowledges additional challenges at its own initiative), organization management should specify the remedial actions it is taking as well as the timing and significance of those actions. The Labor Department's 2008 report provides a model in this regard. As Figure 3.11 illustrates, Labor used a traffic light system to assess its own progress on each challenge listed by its inspector general, presenting its assessments in tables that discuss each challenge, actions taken in fiscal year 2008 to address them, and remaining actions needed along with their expected completion dates.

Similarly, the Transportation Department's report broke down the management challenges identified by its inspector general into their component parts and used a progress meter graphic to self-assess its progress toward resolving each component. Figure 3.12 presents an extract from the Transportation report.

Such specific assessments by internal auditors and organization management provide a solid framework for instilling confidence that the organization is working seriously to address its major management challenges.

Conclusion

The points discussed in this chapter and in Chapter 2 summarize our findings over ten years of evaluating federal performance reports submitted pursuant to the Government Performance and Results Act. They capture what we believe to be the most important attributes of successful reports, as well as the main pitfalls to be avoided. The examples reflect the best practices we have found in federal performance reporting as they evolved over the ten-year span covered by our reviews.

While there is still much room for improvement and progress has been uneven among agencies, most agencies have come a long way since the initial round of reports for fiscal year 1999. Unfortunately, improvements in reporting have not been matched by increased use of performance data by federal managers and decision makers in the executive branch or, most notably, in Congress. Given the magnitude of current concerns over the performance effectiveness and fiscal viability of government at all levels, however, we remain confident that the era of outcome-oriented performance management and accountability is fast approaching.

Top Management Challenge	Issue	Actions Remaining	DOL's Assessment of Its Own Progress
Protect the safety and health of workers	• Implement the Mine Improvement and New Emergency Response (MINER) Act. • Improve oversight of mine emergency response plans (ERPs). • Replace retiring mine inspectors.	• Provide guidance on underground communications. • Review ERPs every six months, evaluate violations, and develop policy clarifications. • Continue implementing localized recruiting.	Yellow
Improving performance accountability of grants	• Ensure that grantees accomplish their grant objectives and enhance monitoring of direct grants. • Ensure adequate documentation of costs for earmark grants.	• Train grant officers on reviewing statements of work and grantees' activities. • Provide technical assistance to grantees. • Conduct federal project officer training for grant monitoring, particularly documentation required of grantees.	Yellow

Figure 3.11 Labor management challenges. (Source: U.S. Department of Labor, Citizens' Report, FY 2008, 2009, 24, www.dol.gov/_sec/media/reports/Citizens2008/CitizensReport.pdf.)

Top Management Challenge	Issue	Actions Remaining	DOL's Assessment of Its Own Progress
Ensure the effectiveness of the Job Corps program	• Promote effective regional monitoring, including ensuring that contractors provide accurate performance data. • Ensure student safety and health. • Assess incoming students for cognitive disabilities.	• Continue data integrity audits of Job Corps centers concurrently with on-site compliance and quality assessments. • Continue implementing the Job Corps Safety and Health Program and enforce the violence and drugs zero tolerance policy. • Train Job Corps academic and career technical managers in instruction for students with learning disabilities.	Green ↑ (Improved from 2007)
Ensure the security of employee benefit plan assets	• Strengthen DOL's oversight authority over plan auditors. • Continue efforts to decrease the number of fraudulent Multiple Employer Welfare Arrangements.	• Continue CPA firm inspection program, focusing on firms that perform a significant amount of pension and health benefit plan audit work. • Post names of individuals and entities against whom DOL obtains health fraud or MEWA injunctions on DOL's public web site.	Green

Figure 3.11 (Continued) Labor management challenges. (Source: U.S. Department of Labor, Citizens' Report, FY 2008, 2009, 24, www.dol.gov/_sec/media/reports/Citizens2008/CitizensReport.pdf.)

1. MANAGEMENT CHALLENGE: CONTINUING TO ENHANCE OVERSIGHT TO ENSURE THE SAFETY OF AN AGING SURFACE TRANSPORTATION INFRASTRUCTURE AND MAXIMIZE THE RETURN ON INVESTMENTS IN HIGHWAY AND TRANSIT INFRASTRUCTURE PROJECTS.

- Targeting oversight actions to ensure the safety of tunnels and bridges

Recent tragic highway incidents underscore the need for FHWA to ensure that its oversight actions target tunnels and bridges that represent high-priority safety risk so that problems are identified, evaluated, and remediated in a timely and thorough manner.

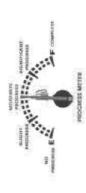

Tunnels

Currently there are no national standards regarding the design, construction, inspection, operations and maintenance of highway tunnels in the Nation. The Federal Highway Administration (FHWA) and the American Association of State Highway Transportation Officials (AASHTO) are working together to provide guidelines and manuals for inspection, maintenance and management of tunnels. As an example, FHWA completed a two-day workshop on tunnel engineering in July that provide an opportunity to gather experts in tunnel ventilation, computer modeling, tunnel operation and response, and to formulate criteria for creation of a pilot program on tunnel fires. Short-term and long-term research, deployment and education programs are needed to assure the safety, reliability and efficiency of our highway tunnels. As such, there are a number of initiatives being considered or under development. In FY 2009, FHWA will develop a pilot program for computer modeling of fires in a tunnel. FHWA will also release a Highway Tunnel Design and Construction Manual that focuses on Construction, Inspection, Operation and Maintenance.

Figure 3.12   Transportation management challenges. (Source: U.S. Department of Transportation, *Performance and Accountability Report, FY 2008*, 2008, 44, www.dot.gov/par/2008/pdf/DOT_PAR_2008.pdf.)

Chapter 4

The State Factor

The Mercatus *Performance Report Scorecard* project evaluated reports produced by U.S. federal agencies. However, there is no reason to presume that the U.S. government has a monopoly on good reporting practices. In this chapter, we examine several state performance reports and use the *Scorecard* methodology to identify best reporting practices in those reports. We evaluated three state reports against our *Scorecard* criteria, awarding scores and noting the principal factors that accounted for those scores. This chapter briefly discusses the scores, then compares the states' reporting practices with each other and with federal practices. Finally, we highlight lessons the federal government could learn from the states, and lessons the states could learn from the federal government.

Both this chapter and Chapter 5 examine reports produced by transportation departments. We chose to compare transportation reports for several reasons. Transportation is a significant function of both national and state governments. Most people experience the results of transportation policies in their daily lives as they commute to work or school, shop, and travel. Compared to many functions of government, transportation performance requires less specialized knowledge to comprehend. The desired outcomes, such as safety and reduced congestion, are relatively intuitive and understandable by a wide variety of readers, both in the United States and internationally.

Table 4.1 illustrates this point by listing strategic goals for the U.S. Department of Transportation, along with the strategic goals enunciated by the three states whose reports we consider in this chapter. Both the federal government and the states have three broad types of outcome goals related to mobility, safety, and the environment. Three of the four departments also have a strategic goal related to internal management.

Mobility is perhaps the most obvious goal for transportation policy. As a colleague once quipped, "Transportation is important. We couldn't get anywhere

Table 4.1 Comparison of Strategic Goals in 2008 Performance Reports

	USDOT	Connecticut	Colorado	Florida
Mobility	Mobility Global connectivity	Quality of life Preservation Efficiency and effectiveness	Mobility System quality	Mobility and economic competitiveness Maintenance and preservation Sustainable investments
Safety and security	Safety and security	Safety and security	Safety	Safety and security
Environment	Environment	Quality of life		Quality of life and environmental stewardship
Management	Organizational excellence	Accountability and transparency	Program delivery	

without it." Under mobility, both the federal and the state reports discuss the speed and reliability with which the transportation system moves people and goods from point A to point B. Reports also sometimes emphasize mobility for particular groups of people, such as the elderly or disabled. The three state reports each have a goal for preservation, maintenance, or system quality that essentially addresses ongoing upkeep of roads and mass transit, which is largely a state responsibility. Departments understandably use different terms at times to refer to the same goals. For example, Connecticut deals with congestion issues as part of its "quality of life" goal, whereas the other reports subsume congestion under a goal explicitly labeled "mobility."

Some mobility-related goals reflect each department's unique circumstances. The U.S. Department of Transportation has a "global connectivity" goal that reflects the national government's role in negotiating agreements and setting policies that affect cross-border transportation. Connecticut's "efficiency and effectiveness" goal reflects a policy decision to get the most service out of existing transportation assets. Florida's "sustainable investments" goal focuses on creative ways to fund new transportation investments whose cost will outstrip available government funding.

All four reports have goals related to safety and security. The principal difference is that the federal report breaks out a separate security goal. Three of the four reports have an environmental quality goal; for Connecticut, environment is part of the "quality of life" goal. Thus, in terms of goals, the federal and state transportation reports have even more in common than we expected when we began the research for this chapter.

Transportation outcomes are arguably more likely to be measurable than the outcomes of some other government agencies, so focusing on transportation reports will likely surface some excellent examples of good reporting practices. The U.S. Department of Transportation was a perennial high achiever on the Mercatus *Scorecard*, finishing in first place four times and never ranking below third. Therefore, when evaluating reports from transportation departments, we are comparing them with one of the best federal reports. If state reports have better reporting practices than the U.S. Department of Transportation, they are likely to be practices not yet widely implemented in the federal government.

This chapter does not claim to present a comprehensive summary of state reporting practices. Such an investigation would be far outside the scope of both the original *Scorecard* project and this book. When we began the research for this chapter, we expected we could simply select some performance reports from states that have a reputation for innovative performance management. However, states utilize a bewildering variety of reporting formats. Based on our online search, about 14 states produce annual reports on a comprehensive set of strategic transportation goals that could be considered analogous to federal GPRA reports. About 20 states either produce no annual report on strategic transportation goals or had no report posted for 2008. The remaining 16 states utilize a variety of alternative reporting formats that are not very comparable to federal performance reports. Some have annual reports that address only some issues, such as highway construction. Several offer "dashboards" or other web interfaces that highlight performance data in place of an annual performance report, and still others have biennial, quarterly, or monthly reports. Faced with this challenging cornucopia, we selected readily accessible annual reports on a comprehensive set of strategic transportation goals from three states in different parts of the country that arguably face very different transportation challenges.

Table 4.2 presents some statistics that illustrate the three states' diversity. Connecticut is a small but relatively densely populated northeastern state. Of the three states, it has the highest percentage of commuters using mass transit—close to the national average—but also a higher than average percentage of people commuting to work alone. The latter probably reflects relatively short driving distances, which makes carpooling less of an economic necessity. Colorado, on the other hand, is a prototypical western state, with a quite large landmass relative to population. Due largely to the longer distances, Colorado has more than four times as much road mileage as Connecticut, more than four times as many airports, and five times as much freight railroad mileage. Colorado also has less transit use, more carpooling, and a higher percentage of people working from their homes.

From a transportation perspective, Florida is in many ways a microcosm of America. Florida has a relatively large land area. The state is also home to 6% of the total U.S. population. Population density is higher than that of Colorado and the national average, but lower than that of Connecticut. The state has large urban centers, such as Miami, Orlando, Tampa–St. Petersburg, and Jacksonville, as well as extensive rural regions. Despite having about half the land area of Colorado,

Table 4.2 Comparative State Data

	United States	Connecticut	Colorado	Florida
Population	304.5 million	3.5 million	4.9 million	18.3 million
Land area (sq. miles)	3.6 million	4,845	103,730	52,997
Population per square mile	85	722	47	345
Transportation expenditures ($2007)	$61.7 billion[a]	$1.7 billion	$3.5 billion	$13.6 billion
Miles of public road	4.04 million	21,363	88,265	121,387
Registered cars and light trucks	238 million	3 million	1.5 million	14.4 million
% Commuting via public transit	5.0	4.4	3.4	2.0
% Commuting alone in vehicle	75.5	78.7	73.7	79.4
% Carpool	10.7	8.8	11.3	10.3
% Working at home	4.1	4.1	6.3	4.5
Airports	13,362	55	254	491
Freight rail track (miles)	170,757	702	3,609	2,982

Source: United States Department of Transportation, Research and Innovative Technology Administration, *State Transportation Statistics*, (2009); U.S. Office of Management and Budget, *Budget of the United States Government, Fiscal Year 2010, Historical Tables* (2009a); www.netstate.com.

[a] Federal government outlays on transportation.

Florida has about 40% more road mileage and almost twice as many airports. These differences reflect Florida's extensive development as well as the need to connect multiple large urban centers, several of which are at opposite ends of the state. The percentage of commuters riding transit is below the national average; the percentage of solo commuters is above the national average.

Despite these differences, the three states' broad strategic goals for transportation are remarkably similar. This allows us to perform something like a controlled experiment, examining how entities with similar goals utilize different reporting strategies.

Scoring Summary

Before turning to our analysis of the state reports, two caveats should be noted. First, as explained in previous chapters, we developed our *Scorecard* criteria to align with the core elements of the Government Performance and Results Act and other statutory provisions that impose specialized requirements for federal performance reports. While federal agencies write their reports with these specific requirements in mind, state reports obviously are not subject to GPRA. So we might not expect to see all of the content in state reports that GPRA and related laws require federal agencies to include in their reports.

Second, the 2008 federal scores reflect the fact that federal agencies had ten years of experience with our criteria. Many regularly took our annual *Scorecard* analyses into consideration in developing future reports. Indeed, each year about half of the agencies requested in-person consultations with members of the Mercatus research team to discuss the strengths and weaknesses of their reports.* In contrast, we are coming at the state reports "cold" in a sense. States had no warning that we would examine their reports, and we have not discussed the *Scorecard* criteria with transportation officials in any of these states. This is another reason we might expect state agencies to have lower scores than federal agencies.

Nevertheless, we believe that the *Scorecard* criteria largely reflect the generic attributes of good performance reporting. GPRA requires agencies to state the outcomes they seek to achieve for the public, measure progress on those outcomes, present credible performance data, note shortcomings, and identify ways to improve. It is hard to argue that a thorough performance report could exclude any of this content. Our experience with the state reports bears this out. Two of the three state reports we reviewed—Colorado and Connecticut—exceeded the 2008 average *Scorecard* score of 36. Colorado received 40 points, and Connecticut received 38. Florida's report scored 34 points, only slightly below average.

Figure 4.1 compares the three state reports' scores with federal scores on our three groups of criteria: transparency, public benefits, and leadership.

---

* Such meetings were free of charge. To avoid conflicts of interest, the Mercatus Center did not do paid consulting for agencies.

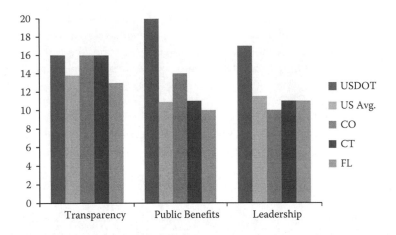

Figure 4.1 State vs. federal scores.

Two of the three states—Colorado and Connecticut—beat the federal average score of 13.8 for transparency and matched the USDOT's score of 16. Florida's report fell short only because it was very difficult to find on the state's web page. Curing that defect would have given Florida a comparable score for transparency.

For public benefits, no state report came close to the USDOT's score of 20. This is the highest score possible. Colorado's score of 14 exceeded the federal average, Connecticut's tied it, and Florida was just 1 point below.

On the leadership criteria, the USDOT bested both the federal average and all three state reports by about 6 points. At first glance, one might think that the federal transportation report outscored the states because most of our leadership criteria stem from specific content required by GPRA. For example, federal agencies must present major management challenges identified by their inspectors general, and they must explain shortfalls in meeting their goals. The three state reports, however, did about as well on the leadership criteria as the average federal report.

On average, therefore, the three state reports did noticeably better than the average federal report on transparency, slightly better on public benefits, and about the same on leadership. But these score totals mask significant differences across reports. Within each category, different reports have different strengths and weaknesses. The following sections summarize our individual evaluations of each report. We conclude by highlighting several positive examples of performance reporting practices from the state reports and a few areas of potential improvement.

Summaries of Individual State Reports

This section presents more detail on our evaluations of the three state reports. The numbers in parentheses indicate their scores for each of our three overarching

Scorecard categories: transparency, public benefits, and leadership. As discussed earlier, the maximum score for each *Scorecard* category is 20 points—thereby adding up to a maximum overall score of 60.

Connecticut

Transparency (16)

The Connecticut Department of Transportation issues annual performance reports and augments them with quarterly reports that update performance results. The department's home page has a prominent, direct link to the current and prior year annual and quarterly reports captioned "Performance Measures" under the heading "Highlights and Initiatives" (www.ct.gov/dot/site/default.asp, last visited September 27, 2010). The department commissioner's introduction to the annual report invites reader feedback and includes report-specific contact information to facilitate feedback. In another feature that enhances accountability and transparency, the quarterly report lists the departmental component that is the "owner" of each performance measure and identifies a contact person within that office. Figure 4.2 provides an example.

The annual report is a manageable 60 pages. It is well organized, clear, very much to the point, and eminently readable. It includes a number of informative tables and graphs. This is a no-nonsense document that provides a wealth of substantive narrative backed up by highly relevant data; there is little rhetoric or

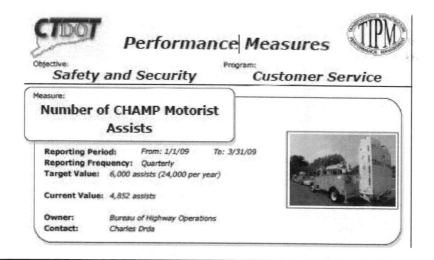

Figure 4.2 Connecticut DOT measurement ownership graphic. (Source: Connecticut Department of Transportation, *CTDOT Performance Measures 2009 Quarterly Update*, 2009a, 6, www.ct.gov/dot/lib/dot/documents/dperformance-measures/pmeasures2009q1.pdf.)

puffery. Acronyms are few and not distracting. A two-page list of performance metrics at the end of the report provides a helpful overview for readers searching for performance information in particular areas. An index at the beginning shows where to find performance material on each goal. Each page has a tab graphic that shows which goal the page covers.

The quarterly report is 32 pages. It consists mainly of one- or two-page presentations that describe results for each measure using a consistent and highly readable format. The narratives are concise and are accompanied by graphs that clearly illustrate performance trends. The quarterly updates on performance results enhance the timeliness of information.

The annual and quarterly reports provide lots of data, but little is sourced. One page does describe how the department actually monitors pavement quality—a useful explanation we have rarely seen in transportation reports. The report is rich in data showing important transportation-related trends over extended time periods. The report narratives frequently elaborate on these trends. Throughout, the report compares Connecticut's performance to that of other states or to regional or national averages. Figure 4.3 shows one such comparison.

This is an excellent technique for conveying context to the reader; the comparisons help show how Connecticut's performance compares to what is reasonably possible.

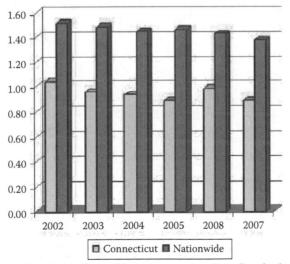

Accident data is obtained from many sources. Compiling the data takes considerable time.The data from the previous year becomes reportable the following December.

Figure 4.3 Connecticut DOT comparison bar graph. (Source: Connecticut Department of Transportation, *CTDOT Performance Measures 2009 Quarterly Update*, 2009a, 3, www.ct.gov/dot/lib/dot/documents/dperformancemeasures/ pmeasures2009q1.pdf.)

Public Benefits (11)

The department's performance metrics have fairly good outcome orientation. The goals and objectives emphasize reducing transportation-related deaths, injuries, and risks; maintaining infrastructure in order to increase vehicle-miles traveled, reduce congestion, and enhance safety; improving on-time transportation performance; and reducing adverse transportation-related impacts on the environment. The nexus between the goals and their implementing performance measures is apparent in most cases.

Slightly over half of the measures clearly capture end or intermediate outcomes. Examples are such basic safety-related transportation measures as the rate of annual highway fatalities and the percent of seat belt usage (Connecticut DOT 2009a, 3, 4). The rest are primarily activity, efficiency, and cost savings measures. The department's performance metrics are solid but not exceptional in outcome orientation. The feature of comparing Connecticut's performance results to those of other jurisdictions is a major positive since the state usually looks good in these comparisons.

One downside is that the report is not very strong in demonstrating how results are attributable specifically to the department's programs and activities. For example, the quarterly report includes a graphic that compares over a 20-year period the number of motorcyclists trained each year—one of its measures—to the number of annual motorcycle crashes (Connecticut DOT 2009a, 5). While this is a useful conceptual approach to attribution, the figures do not demonstrate a strong correlation at least after the initial few years. Since then, the number of riders trained has increased significantly but crashes have remained fairly level. Perhaps additional data could make the correlation more obvious—if, for example, motorcycle ridership has increased dramatically over the years. The report contains some information on the budgetary costs of its programs but does not link costs to the performance metrics at any level. There are some explicit goals that address cost savings.

Leadership (11)

The annual and quarterly reports evidence a commitment to results-oriented performance measurement and accountability. They present a clear picture of safety, infrastructure conditions, and reliability of transportation in Connecticut and how its results compare to those of other jurisdictions.

On the other hand, there are some significant shortcomings in relation to our leadership criteria. While the reports are rich in data and consistently describe trends, there is little additional analysis of performance results or explanations for performance shortfalls. Where shortfalls are explained, they are often blamed on external factors with no discussion of what the department could do proactively to correct the problem. Some shortfalls go wholly unexplained. For example, the quarterly report indicates that the department fell short of its target for highway fatalities per 100,000 in population. There is no direct explanation for this shortfall—only a statement that Connecticut still ranks as the fourth safest state for highway traffic fatalities (Connecticut DOT 2009a, 3). The department states that it uses the performance data to diagnose and solve problems; it just doesn't provide examples in the reports. Also, the reports lack significant analysis of major management challenges and remedial strategies, although they do have a management-related strategic goal tracked by several performance measures. Measures include the percent of construction contracts awarded within 60 days of bid opening and the number of federally funded project closeouts (Connecticut DOT 2009a, 31, 32).

Colorado

Transparency (16)

The department's home page links directly to the 2008 report as well as to performance reports for other years. The web page containing the report provides contact information for the departmental librarian, who could put readers in touch with the officials directly responsible for the report. The report is brief (40 pages), well organized, and clearly written. There is minimal use of acronyms. The report makes effective use of tables and graphics. For example, a one-page table early on in the report presents at a glance the department's measures and 2008 results. Figure 4.4 shows the portion of this table dealing with safety measures.

The report highlights results using traffic light icons. Baseline and trend data, including both targets and actual results, are presented in bar charts. Figure 4.5 provides an example.

Narratives in the detailed description of performance results are concise and informative. The report provides baseline and trend data for its performance measures usually going back four fiscal years. In a useful feature, the baseline and trend data include prior year targets as well as results. The report compares Colorado's performance to that of other states in a few instances, but not nearly to the extent of the Connecticut report. The only major weakness with respect to transparency is the failure to systematically provide data sources for performance measures or to assess data accuracy and validity. Such information would be particularly helpful for the many measures that express targets and results in the form of letter grades. The reader is left to ponder the basis for the assigned grades.

Public Benefits (14)

The report is constructed around three programmatic strategic goal areas that focus primarily on outcomes: safety, system quality, and mobility. The outcome orientation is clearest in the safety and mobility strategic areas. Most performance measures under the safety and mobility strategic goals likewise are outcome-oriented. They include safety measures on accidents, fatalities, and injuries as well as

2008 Performance Summary

	Measure	
	2008 Objective (Based on Available Revenue)	*2008 Actual*
Safety		
Total crashes per 100 million vehicle-miles traveled	283.7	283.7 ●
Fatal crashes per 100 million vehicle-miles traveled	1.00	1.04 ●
Injury crashes per 100 million vehicle-miles traveled	73.0	69.3 ●
Percent of drivers and occupants using seat belts	82.5	81.7 ●
Alcohol-related fatal crashes as percent of all fatal crashes	29.5	39.6 ●
Number of CDOT vehicle accidents	265	373 ●
Number of workers' compensation claims	415	453 ●
Dollar amount of workers' compensation claims (millions)	$5.1	$1.9 ●
Striping, signs, signals, and guardrail maintenance	D+	B– ●

Figure 4.4 Colorado DOT summary performance table extract. (Source: Colorado Department of Transportation, *Fiscal Year 2008 Annual Performance Report*, 2009, 9, www.coloradodot.info/library/AnnualReports/CDOT_2008_lores.pdf/view.)

mobility measures on highway congestion and percent of on-time bus performance (Colorado DOT 2009, 9).

The measures under the system quality goal, which deal primarily with infrastructure condition, are more difficult to interpret. Most of them are expressed as letter grades, the basis for which is not adequately explained in the report. The letter grades are used primarily for a series of maintenance measures, such as roadway surfaces, bridges, and tunnels (Colorado DOT 2009, 9).

Overall, the performance metrics are outcome-oriented. However, they could better demonstrate results if they included strategic objectives in order to add specificity to the strategic goals. Also, they would be more persuasive if more measures were stated as quantified outcomes or, at least, if the basis for letter grade measures was made clear. The report contains a good deal of information on program costs, much of it in conjunction with the overriding theme that the department is seriously underfunded (see below). As illustrated in Figure 4.6, it links budget costs to

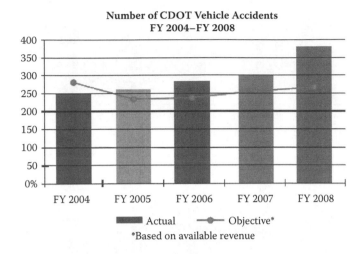

Figure 4.5 Colorado DOT trend data bar chart. (Source: Colorado Department of Transportation, *Fiscal Year 2008 Annual Performance Report*, 2009, 15, www. coloradodot.info/library/AnnualReports/CDOT_2008_lores.pdf/view.)

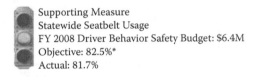

Figure 4.6 Colorado DOT cost by measure. (Source: Colorado Department of Transportation, *Fiscal Year 2008 Annual Performance Report*, 2009, 13, www. coloradodot.info/library/AnnualReports/CDOT_2008_lores.pdf/view.)

the department's performance metrics down to the level of a number of individual performance measures or sets of measures.

Leadership (9)

The report is weakest in this area. Its basic message is reactive rather than forward looking: that the department is doing what it can with inadequate funding. While the narratives describe some accomplishments, they are more focused on a plea for additional resources. For example, the executive summary rather strikingly observes:

> This report does not attempt to address whether CDOT is delivering the transportation system it needs to thrive in the 21st century. The objective is to report on how CDOT is performing based on the resources made available to it.... [The report's performance] objectives

are set within the parameter of the resources provided rather than on an absolute scale. With additional funding the department can set and attain more aggressive objectives. (Colorado DOT 2009, 8)

The report clearly discloses and explains performance results, including shortfalls, but the usual explanation is lack of resources. There is little discussion of remedial strategies other than obtaining more funding. It would be encouraging to find some discussion of innovative strategies the department was at least trying to take in order to enhance its efficiency and effectiveness in the face of its resource challenges. Is the reader really expected to believe that the department is already doing everything as effectively and efficiently as possible, so that the only barrier to improved performance is more resources?

Florida

Transparency (13)

The Florida Department of Transportation home page has no link to any performance report. Using the home page search function, we eventually found a web page captioned "Transportation Performance Reporting in Florida" that contains the department's January 2009 performance report (which covers 2008) along with all other relevant documents. This web page also included a link to the department's performance management office, which provides contact information for staff members responsible for the report. The department's planning and performance web page is the best we have encountered; it collects in one place a wealth of information about the department's performance and accountability and presents it in a user-friendly way. Figure 4.7 reproduces most of the material on this web page.

A major drawback, however, is that the web page was quite hard to find. Providing a direct link to it from the department's home page would greatly enhance transparency.

The performance report is manageable in length (66 pages), well organized, and clearly written. Its use of acronyms is not excessive or distracting. On the downside, it contains a lot of narrative on government processes and activities—who is "collaborating with" whom, what agencies are responsible for what, what new initiatives were launched, etc. We often encounter this kind of exhaustive list of major activities in performance reports. But the material does not say very much about what results are actually being achieved. The report could probably be 25% shorter without this content.

The performance web page includes a link to a separate report from the Florida Transportation Commission, an independent body that oversees the department. The transportation commission report uses lists, graphs, and tables to make the performance information very digestible. It uses minimal acronyms. The department's report would be a lot better if it used this format.

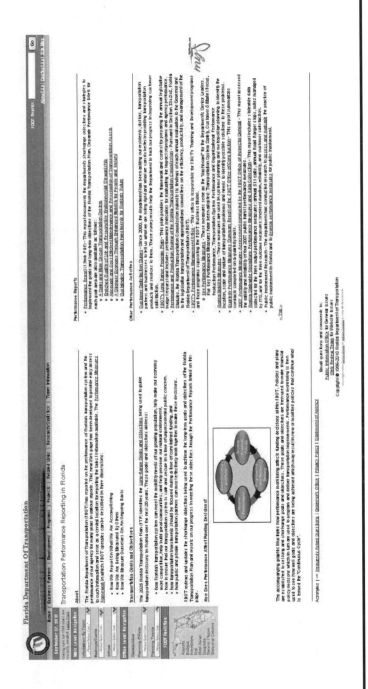

Figure 4.7 Florida DOT performance web page. (Source: www.dot.state.fl.us/planning/performance, last visited September 27, 2010.)

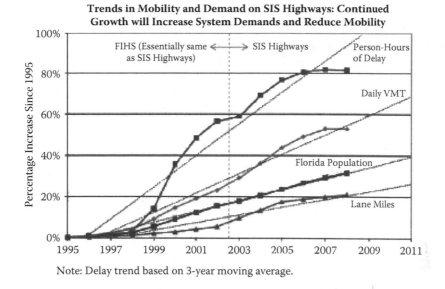

Trends in Mobility and Demand on SIS Highways: Continued Growth will Increase System Demands and Reduce Mobility

Note: Delay trend based on 3-year moving average.

Figure 4.8 Florida DOT mobility trends graphic. (Source: Florida Department of Transportation, *2025 Florida Transportation Plan: Performance Report, December 2009,* 2009, 45, www.dot.state.fl.us/planning/performance/Performance-Report. pdf.)

The department's report consistently sources data presentations and occasionally provides data definitions. The data seem timely and complete. One of the documents on the planning and performance web page is an assessment of selected 2007 performance measures by the department's inspector general. The inspector general's assessment found that the performance measures examined were fundamentally valid and reliable (Florida OIG 2008). The report provides baseline and trend data tables for most objectives going back at least four prior years. The report has a lot of additional data, such as traffic/passenger volumes, data on factors contributing to traffic accidents, vehicle-miles traveled, etc., that help put the main measures in context. Figure 4.8 provides an example.

The tables occasionally compare Florida's performance to national averages, but much less so than Connecticut.

Public Benefits (10)

The department's goals and measures are a mix of outcomes, outputs, and activities. The report is built around five strategic goals from Florida's 2025 strategic transportation plan that have long-range (2025) and shorter-range (2015) strategic objectives. The goals and objectives dealing with safety and security, maintenance, and mobility are fairly outcome-oriented. For example, the short-range objective for the safety goal is a 5% annual reduction in highway fatality and serious injury rates through 2015, and the mobility goal has a short-range objective of increasing transit ridership at twice the average rate of population growth through 2015 (Florida DOT 2009, 6, 56). The quality of life goal has a few long-range objectives that could be regarded as intermediate outcomes, but none of these objectives is quantified. The report supplies some quantification through the additional shorter-range objectives. The full set of performance measures is not readily identifiable, but those that can be found are fairly outcome-oriented.

Neither the department's report nor any of the other source documents linked budget costs to performance metrics at any level. The transportation commission's report lists numerous cost goals for acquisition of rights of way, construction, etc. These do not match the *other* outcomes with costs, but they provide information on cost performance that we rarely see in performance reports.

Leadership (11)

The department's primary focus is on long-term rather than annual accomplishments. Thus, the 2009 report is more of an interim progress report than a report on a particular year's achievements. Although it does use some good outcome metrics and shows some yearly accomplishments, there is little analysis or explanation for annual results. The report contains a good deal of narrative on key programs and strategies to achieve the department's goals over the long haul. There is relatively little discussion of specific changes or remedial strategies to improve performance from one year to the next.

One noteworthy feature is that the department's performance is reviewed by an independent oversight commission, the Florida Transportation Commission. The commission uses its own set of performance measures to evaluate the department. The measures deal primarily with efficiency and cost savings and include:

- More than 80% of construction contracts completed within 20% above the original contract time
- More than 90% of construction contracts completed at a cost within 10% above the original contract amount
- The transportation department's administrative costs are less than 2% of total program costs (Florida Transportation Commission 2008, 12–13)

What the United States Can Learn from State Reports

The three state reports that we reviewed stacked up well against many of our *Scorecard* criteria. Indeed, they reveal potential best practices in each of our three overarching *Scorecard* categories.

Transparency

The state reports were particularly strong in the transparency category. The main features from the reports that contributed to these strong scores are highlighted below.

Accessibility

The Connecticut and Colorado transportation department web sites had all of the accessibility features we look for, including a direct link to the performance report from their web site home pages as well as information enabling members of the public to contact knowledgeable departmental employees with questions or comments. In this regard, the Connecticut quarterly report on performance measures had an excellent feature and potential best practice that we have never encountered in a federal report. The report listed the departmental component that owned each performance measure and named an individual employee contact person within that office. In addition to enhancing transparency, this practice may offer substantive benefits. We often find that federal performance reports are developed by central office staffs, such as the chief financial officer shop, that are separate from those agency components directly responsible for program performance. Identifying performance measure owners who have line responsibility should increase their buy-in with respect to the measures and instill a greater sense of visibility and commitment to achieving results.

The Florida transportation department had the best performance-related web page that we have seen. Captioned "Transportation Performance Reporting in Florida," the web page contained current and prior year departmental performance reports along with a number of other documents relevant to the department's performance. Collecting all of this information in one place and presenting it in a user-friendly way is certainly a best practice example for all organizations. Ironically and inexplicably, the department's home page did not have a direct link to this page—a shortcoming that could be easily fixed.

Length and Readability

All three of the state reports were much shorter than federal performance and accountability reports (average length in 2008: 320 pages) and more comparable in size to the federal citizens' reports described in Chapter 3 (average length in 2008: about 30 pages). Specifically, the state reports were 40 (Colorado), 60 (Connecticut), and 66 (Florida) pages in length. Like federal citizens' reports, the Connecticut and Florida reports linked to other source documents, which were also quite reasonable in length. Among the other positive features of all three state reports, they were clearly written in plain language and did not evidence the heavy reliance on acronyms that we have found in many federal reports.

Data Validation and Verification

One of the source documents on the Florida department's web page was an assessment of selected performance measures by the department's inspector general. According to this document, Florida law requires each agency inspector general to perform validity and reliability assessments of its agency's performance measures and, if needed, recommend improvements. An independent assessment of data validity and reliability provides a real boost to the credibility of organization performance reports. We rarely find such assessments in federal performance reports, and there is no statutory requirement that federal inspectors general conduct such reviews. We regard the Florida law as a best practice that should be emulated at the federal level and elsewhere.

Baseline and Trend Data

Connecticut offers two potential best practices here. First, the transportation department supplements its annual performance report with quarterly reports that update performance results during the applicable year. This unique (in our experience) feature significantly enhances the timeliness of information provided to the public and decision makers. Second, the annual report regularly compares Connecticut's performance results to those of other jurisdictions or to national or regional averages. This is an excellent technique for conveying context to the reader and providing an objective yardstick to assess how well the state stacks up against others. Given the availability of data, other states can and should follow this practice. Indeed, both Colorado and Florida included some comparative data to a limited extent. If the data permit, this might also be a potential best practice for national organizations such as the U.S. Transportation Department.

Public Benefits and Leadership

The state reports did not stand out in these categories as they did in transparency. However, we found several noteworthy features relative to these categories in the state reports.

The Colorado report linked budget costs to many individual performance measures or sets of related measures. This provides a good example for other organizations. Most federal agencies have struggled to identify and link costs to their performance metrics. Interestingly, the Colorado report constructs a major theme around the relationship between budget resources and performance results. The report repeatedly emphasizes that the performance levels it can attain are severely limited by inadequate funding.

Florida offers two potential best practices in the public benefits category. One is the annual independent oversight review and report on the transportation department by the Florida Transportation Commission, an organization whose members, by law, must have private sector management experience. The transportation commission uses its own set of measures to rate the department's performance. The commission's report presents an impressive array of data and findings concerning the department. It includes a response by the department's secretary that describes remedial steps for performance shortfalls with respect to the report's measures. The second potential best practice (closely related to the first) is the commission's use of a set of cost savings goals and measures as part of its performance metrics. These goals provide information on cost performance at a level of detail that we rarely see in performance reports.

Finally, one feature of the Colorado report deserves special mention. While we do not regard it as a best practice, it is an interesting practice that has relevance to performance reporting by virtually all public organizations—federal, state, and local. As noted previously, the Colorado report disavows crafting its performance targets with a view toward "delivering the transportation system [the state] needs to thrive in the 21st century." Rather, the Colorado transportation department expressly sets its performance metrics "based on the resources made available to it." Presumably the department does face serious resource challenges, as do most governmental agencies at all levels throughout the country. However, we have never before encountered a performance report that (at least explicitly) scales back its performance metrics from the outcomes it strategically aspires to achieve to those it says it can afford.

The Colorado report may deserve some credit for highlighting its budget constraints with such candor and directness. Perhaps other organizations should likewise candidly acknowledge the impact of budget constraints; in any event, they should not set performance targets that are patently unachievable based on available funding. At the same time, simply ratcheting down performance levels as the Colorado department does hardly demonstrates public benefits or inspires public confidence. A better alternative might be to accompany its actual performance targets with a description of what performance levels the department believes *will* achieve the transportation system the state needs and how much it would cost to achieve them. This information certainly would afford the public and policymakers a better foundation for making choices. It also would be more credible than the report's mere assertions that the department could accomplish more with additional resources, which lack any specific data or metrics to support them.

What States Can Learn from the Federal Reports

While the state reports generally scored well under our criteria, our reviews disclosed several areas where they could improve.

Data Quality

Of the three state reports, only Florida's consistently provided data sources for its performance metrics. None consistently explained the methods used to develop or apply the data (including potential data limitations). These shortcomings should be easy to overcome in most cases since all three reports seem to be supported by copious data that could be readily sourced. It would be particularly helpful to explain the basis for arriving at performance results for nonquantified measures such as letter grades. Finally, the Connecticut and Colorado reports could benefit from some information on how performance data are verified and validated. The Florida inspector general's presentation provides a good example in this regard.

Performance Metrics

The performance metrics in the three reports were not below average. However, we have found that transportation functions lend themselves particularly well to results-oriented goals and measures given the clearly defined public outcomes involved (e.g., safety and security, reduced congestion, improved transportation reliability, and timeliness) as well as the availability of relevant data. Thus, transportation reports should be expected to score above average for performance metrics. Indeed, the U.S. Department of Transportation 2008 report earned our highest score of 5 on all *Scorecard* criteria directly related to goals and measures. The strategic goals in three state reports were reasonably outcome-oriented; however, the performance goals and measures could be revised to track more outcomes. For example, in the most comparable strategic program area—safety—the U.S. Department of Transportation report lists the following ten clear, quantified, and comprehensive performance measures:

- Passenger vehicle occupant highway fatality rate per 100 million passenger vehicle-miles traveled (VMT)
- Large truck and bus fatality rate per 100 million total VMT
- Motorcyclist fatality rate per 100,000 motorcycle registrations
- Nonoccupant fatality rate per 100 million VMT
- Number of commercial air carrier fatalities per 100 million persons onboard
- Number of fatal general aviation accidents
- Rail-related accidents and incidents per million train-miles
- Transit fatalities per 100 million passenger-miles traveled
- Number of serious incidents for natural gas and hazardous liquid pipelines
- Number of serious hazardous materials transportation incidents (USDOT 2008, 93)

Assessing Performance Shortfalls

None of the three reports systematically explained the reasons for failures to meet performance measures or described remedial strategies to address such shortfalls in the future. Performance shortfalls are inevitable for all complex organizations that set meaningful targets and report candidly. Understanding and learning from them is a key aspect of performance management and an important element of leadership. In fairness, we should note that many federal agencies also are weak in this area. However, the better reports tend to score well here, and Chapter 3 describes several techniques federal agencies use to address shortcomings and improvement plans.

Conclusion

Due to GPRA, many federal agencies had a head start on performance reporting relative to the states. Nevertheless, the state transportation reports we reviewed all compared favorably with the average federal report. None was as good overall as the U.S. Department of Transportation's report. Yet individual states have pioneered some significant best practices that we have rarely, if ever, seen in ten years' worth of federal reports. These include:

- Identify the operating division that owns each performance measure and provide contact information.
- Create a home page that offers one-stop access to all departmental performance information.
- Keep the report brief, using plain language and minimal acronyms.
- Arrange for independent assessment of the quality of performance measures by the agency inspector general or other outside authority.
- Produce quarterly updates to make performance data available when they are actionable.
- Compare the department's performance with the performance of similar departments on the state or national level.
- Link budgetary costs to performance measures.
- Establish an independent oversight body composed of experts with private management experience to review the department's performance.
- Establish goals for costs or cost savings.

Many federal reports, on the other hand, seem to be ahead of the three states we examined in assessing data quality, providing data sources, developing a full suite of outcome-oriented measures, and diagnosing reasons for performance shortfalls.

These examples amply demonstrate that there are significant opportunities to improve the quality of performance reporting simply by sharing best practices across different levels of government. And if we may briefly pat ourselves on the back, the examples also illustrate the value of the Mercatus *Scorecard* methodology as a rough-and-ready technique for quickly identifying best practices.

Chapter 5

The International Context

This chapter continues our comparative approach by evaluating transportation department performance reports from three nations known as leaders in government performance management: Australia, New Zealand, and the United Kingdom.

Like the USDOT and U.S. states, the transportation ministries in these countries all espouse goals related to mobility, safety, security, and environmental concerns (Table 5.1). New Zealand and the United Kingdom both have objectives that are quite analogous to the U.S. strategic goals. The principal difference is that those two countries place more explicit emphasis on transportation for the disabled, elderly, and other disadvantaged populations via their access goals.

Australia, on the other hand, lists three outcomes that do not quite parallel the U.S., NZ, and UK goals: "assisting the government to provide, evaluate, plan, and invest in transportation infrastructure across industry sectors," "fostering an efficient, sustainable, competitive, safe, and secure transport system," and "assisting regions and local governments to develop and manage their futures" (Australia 2008, 23). These statements and the accompanying explanations, however, indicate that the Australian government is concerned with much the same transportation issues as the United States, New Zealand, and the United Kingdom. The first outcome addresses mobility. The second outcome covers all three of the strategic areas covered in the other countries' reports. The third addresses transportation's role in promoting economic development—a goal addressed explicitly in New Zealand and implicitly in the U.S. and UK reports.

Australia, New Zealand, and the United Kingdom are all English-speaking parliamentary democracies. Yet each country has adopted a somewhat different approach to setting performance expectations for agencies and measuring results.

Table 5.1 Comparison of Strategic Goals in U.S. and International Reports

	USDOT	Australia	New Zealand	United Kingdom
Mobility	Mobility Global connectivity	Infrastructure investment Regional development Efficient and competitive transportation system	Economic development Access and mobility	Reliable and efficient transportation networks Access to jobs, services, and social networks
Safety/security	Safety Security	Safe and secure transportation system	Safety and personal security	Safety and security
Environment	Environment	Sustainable transportation system	Environmental sustainability Public health	Environmental performance and climate change
Management	Organizational excellence			

Australia holds agencies accountable for outcomes. Ministers of the elected government specify the outcomes they seek to achieve. Every department must then identify outputs that contribute to these outcomes, as well as performance measures for quantity, quality, price, and effectiveness. Agency plans are submitted as part of the budget, and annual reports communicate the results (Hawke 2007).

New Zealand holds elected leaders responsible for outcomes and government agencies responsible for outputs. In New Zealand, the elected government is responsible for selecting the outcomes it seeks to achieve, identifying the outputs agencies must produce to achieve those outcomes, and purchasing the outputs from the agencies. Legislators hold agencies accountable for producing the outputs they have agreed to produce in exchange for appropriations. To understand what outcomes the government seeks to achieve, one must read the government's multiyear statement of intent (SOI) that accompanies the proposed budget for each department. The SOI lists ultimate and intermediate outcomes, activities, initiatives, and outputs. For each output, it indicates the desired quantity, quality, timeliness, and costs. The agencies report on outputs, not outcomes, in their annual performance reports. The Ministry of Transport typically lists the quantity, quality, timeliness, and cost of each output delivered. We could find no annual document that explicitly reports on outcomes achieved. A report called *New Zealand Transport Statistics* (2009) has some information on longer-term outcome trends, but it is not explicitly tied to the department's annual report.

The United Kingdom's Department for Transport report covers transportation in England and Wales. (Most government transportation responsibilities for Scotland have been devolved to the Scottish Parliament.) The department reports against two overlapping sets of objectives: its own strategic objectives and a set of government-wide public service agreements that are established during comprehensive spending reviews undertaken every two or three years. Public service agreements usually specify outcomes rather than outputs or activities. First established under Prime Minister Tony Blair, the public service agreements commit the government as a whole to achieving delineated outcomes that have noticeable effects on citizens' quality of life. Typical examples have included "reduce congestion on the inter-urban road network in England to 2000 levels by 2010" and "improve punctuality and reliability of rail services to at least 85 percent by 2006" (UK 2008a, 240, 257). A Cabinet subcommittee on public services and expenditure reviews departmental performance (Noman 2008).

Operationally, the transport departments in the three countries achieve their goals through somewhat different organizational structures. Australia has a federal system, relying heavily on state and local governments to deliver most public services using funding provided by the federal government (Hawke 2007, 6). Most investments in road infrastructure, for example, consist of grants to states and territories rather than direct federal provision. The New Zealand Ministry of Transport characterizes itself as "primarily a policy and monitoring agency." It develops policy advice, legislation, and regulation. It also negotiates annual performance agreements with the separate Crown entities (agencies and state-owned companies) that do much of the actual investment in, and management of, the nation's transportation infrastructure: the New Zealand Transport Agency, Maritime New Zealand, Aviation Security Agency, Civil Aviation Authority, Transport Accident Investigation Commission, and several state-owned enterprises (NZ 2008, 5–8). In the UK, the Transportation Department has more direct operating responsibility. It regulates transportation and maintains and operates a network of major roads. Ninety percent of the department's employees work in its seven agencies: the Driving Standards Agency, Driver and Vehicle Licensing Agency, Vehicle Certification Agency, Vehicle and Operator Services Agency, Government Car and Dispatch Agency, Highways Agency, and the Maritime and Coastguard Agency (UK 2008a, 193–96).

Before turning to our analysis of the individual international reports, we reiterate the caveats mentioned in Chapter 4 concerning the application of our *Scorecard* to state transportation department reports. First, our *Scorecard* criteria were developed to align with the Government Performance and Results Act and other statutory requirements that apply to federal performance reports; obviously states and other nations' governments are not subject to these requirements. Second, federal agencies had ten years of experience working with our criteria and reacting to our feedback. By contrast, state and international entities are being exposed to our criteria for the first time here. For these reasons, states and other nations might be expected to face a substantial disadvantage in scoring vis-à-vis U.S. federal agencies. A third caveat should be added in the case of the international agencies. The governmental organizations and structures that other nations use to address transportation functions can be quite different from those of the federal government and U.S. states. These differences can have a major impact on transportation performance reporting.

Despite these differences, it seems clear that many governments are creating systems to make themselves more transparent and accountable to the public. While these systems are different, they all seem to be heading in the direction of more clearly identifying the public benefit arising from government activities.

Scoring Summary

While many differences exist, we found in reviewing the international reports that many generic attributes of good performance reporting extend across international boundaries, just as they do across state lines. All three of the international reports we reviewed had substantial content responsive to our *Scorecard* criteria. All three also had features that could be adopted to improve U.S. federal performance reports.

All three reports posted respectable scores, particularly in light of the caveats noted above. Most impressive was the United Kingdom report's overall score of 39, which placed it well above the federal agency average and would have ranked sixth among the 24 federal agency reports we reviewed for 2008. New Zealand (32) and Australia (31) scored somewhat below the federal average. However, their scores were competitive and matched or exceeded those of a number of federal agencies. Moreover, some of the relatively lower scores they received on individual *Scorecard* criteria may result from our lack of familiarity with their reporting systems and practices. They also lost points under a few criteria due to the absence of specialized content mandated by specific provisions of U.S. law. On the other hand, none of the international reports fared nearly as well as the U.S. Department of Transportation's 2008 report, which earned a score of 53.

Figure 5.1 compares the individual scores of the international reports for each overall category of our *Scorecard* criteria. It also shows the average score by category for the 2008 federal agency reports and for the U.S. Department of Transportation. As a group, the international reports scored very close to the U.S. federal averages. The three reports earned an average score of 12.3 points for transparency, 10.3 points for public benefits, and 11.3 points for leadership. The U.S. federal reports averaged 12.3 points for transparency, 10.3 points for public benefits, and 11.3 points for leadership. The UK report exceeded the U.S. average in all three categories.

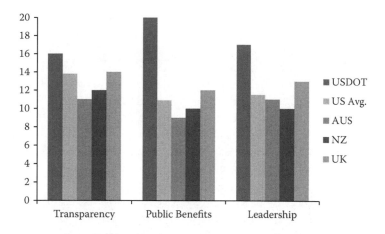

Figure 5.1   International versus U.S. federal scores. Summaries of the individual international reports.

Australia

Transparency (11)

The report was easy to find and manageable to use online. The home page for the Department of Infrastructure, Transport, Regional Development, and Local Government (www.infrastructure.gov.au, last visited October 29, 2010) has no direct link to the 2007–08 report or to any other annual report. However, a search for "annual report" using the home page search feature produced the reports going back to 1996–97. The annual reports also can be found via the department home page link captioned "The Department." The web page containing the report provided contact information and invited suggestions for improving the report; the hard copy report also had report-specific contact information. The report is downloadable in single or multiple HTML and PDF files.

At 446 pages, the report is almost as long as the longest U.S. performance and accountability report we scored for 2008 (467 pages) and well above the 318-page average length for such reports. Mitigating its length somewhat, the main body of the report is 238 pages, with the rest consisting of appendices and financial statements. The appendices cover discrete topics that may be of interest to different audiences. The table of contents lists 13 appendices with more specialized information. They include reports relevant to various policy issues or strategies (the access and equity strategy, the commonwealth disability strategy, and ecologically sustainable development), a list of discretionary grants, airport performance data, a list of new or revised performance indicators since the 2007–08 portfolio budget statement, and a comparison of current and previous outputs and outcomes. Treating specialized topics in this way is a good technique to pinpoint content for readers with different levels of interests.

The report is well organized and easy to navigate. It begins with a brief and pro forma transmittal letter from the department secretary, followed by a one-page guide for readers and the table of contents. The report includes a glossary of terms and a comprehensive index. The body of the report is not heavily laden with acronyms. One novel feature we have not previously encountered is a list of corrections to the prior year report. The substantive portion of the report starts with an introduction and overview that describes many departmental programs and activities but does not discuss performance outcomes. The overview also describes the department's structure and includes charts indicating which departmental units are responsible for which performance outcomes. The detailed performance portion of the report (Chapters 3–5) consists mainly of lengthy text narratives.

The secretary's transmittal letter includes a statement that the department has in place appropriate reporting and data collection procedures and processes that comply with governmental fraud control guidelines. This appears similar to the agency head statement on data completeness and accuracy required by law for U.S. performance reports. The department received an unqualified audit opinion on its financial statements. The report does not provide data sources or methods for performance measures. Such information would be particularly useful since, as discussed hereafter, the report's performance metrics are primarily qualitative and judgmental rather than quantitative. Without more information, it is difficult for the reader to determine the basis for the report's assessment of performance results. The report contains a few tables and narratives that describe transportation trends. However, it does not show baseline and trend data related to the performance metrics. This may be because the metrics are generally not quantitative.

Public Benefits (9)

The Australian government has some transportation-related quantified outcome goals. For example, the report refers to a goal of reducing the road fatality rate by 40% over the decade prior to 2010. However, the performance metrics covered by the 2007–08 report are not outcome-oriented. In fact, most are not quantified. A chart on page 23 sets forth three goals, which it describes as "outcomes." Only one of these goals actually references outcomes, and it is stated at a very high level of generality: "fostering an efficient, sustainable, competitive, safe and secure transport system." Page 23 also sets out a series of "outputs." However, these are descriptions of program and activity areas, such as "infrastructure investment coordination" and "transport safety investigations" rather than performance goals. Chapters 3–5 of the report list performance indicators that correspond to each of the outcome and output areas referenced on page 23. The performance indicators are categorized as "effectiveness" measures (e.g., "stakeholders undertake safety action in response to critical and significant safety issues identified through safety investigations") and "quality" measures (e.g., "Australia's transport safety investigation regime meets international standards"). However, the listed measures are not outcome-oriented. Instead, they focus on activities, outputs, efficiency, and compliance. Very few of the measures have quantified targets; most are qualitative and judgmental. Our overall assessment: given the absence of quantified outcome goals and measures, the report's performance metrics do not effectively demonstrate contributions toward transportation outcomes of public importance.

The report links each group of measures for an output to a "price," which presumably is its budget cost. A table includes both the goal and the actual cost (see, e.g., Australia 2008, 70–72).

Leadership (11)

While the secretary's transmittal letter is perfunctory and nonsubstantive, the overview section begins with an additional presentation by the secretary that does discuss the department's role and some of its accomplishments. The main performance chapters detail a number of accomplishments. Scattered throughout these chapters are vignettes captioned "case studies" and "did you know" that focus on particular achievements. One sidebar, for example, describes the Auslink Black Spot Program, which allows anyone to nominate sections of road that have a proven history of crashes for remedial attention (Australia 2008, 50).

The report uses a clear set of icon categories to rate performance results for each set of measures. Check marks indicate whether the performance indicators are fully, mostly, partially, or not achieved (Australia 2008, 33).

The performance chapters contain narratives discussing activities for each measure. However, there is little content analyzing performance results. Indeed, the report does not systematically describe the basis for evaluating results, nor does it explain shortfalls and improvement strategies. The absence of such explanations is a concern, since a number of measures were rated as falling short of fully achieved.

There is no presentation on major management challenges by audit sources comparable to the inspector general presentations in U.S. performance reports. However, the report devotes a full chapter (Chapter 6) to management and accountability issues. While rather general for the most part, this chapter does provide insight into major management challenges and improvement strategies. The report has significant content throughout on future initiatives and strategies in general and in relation to individual performance measures, although this content is not tied to specific program performance shortfalls. As noted, it also discusses improvement strategies in management areas.

New Zealand

Transparency (12)

The Ministry of Transport's home page (www.transport.govt.nz) (last visited October 29, 2010) has a prominent direct link to the current (2009–10) annual report. The annual reports also can be found by clicking on the home page link "About the Ministry" and from there "Our Publications" and then "Annual Reports," or by searching for "annual reports" using the home page search feature.

The 2007–08 annual report, which we reviewed, is downloadable only as a single PDF file. (The more recently posted reports permit downloading in multiple files.) There is no readily apparent report-specific contact information for the 2007–08 report either online or in the hard copy. The 2007–08 performance report does not convey a comprehensive understanding of the ministry's performance as a stand-alone document. We had to consider two additional sources to gain a fuller perspective: the New Zealand Ministry's *Statement of Intent 2007–2010* (SOI) and its *New Zealand Transport Statistics, July 2009*. Both of these documents were hard to find. The SOI document was not available online, although the ministry staff promptly sent us a PDF copy in response to our email request.

The performance report is 96 pages long and about 3 megabytes. Typical of U.S. performance and accountability reports, it covers both program performance and financial matters. The first 41 pages cover program performance. The performance report is well organized and concise. This report, as well as the other two documents we considered, was exceptionally clear and easy to read. The authors make extensive use of short paragraphs and lists, with very little narrative padding. In a positive departure from most reports, the documents are almost acronym-free. Anyone who thinks acronyms are necessary to write an annual report should read the New Zealand documents! Even when all source documents are considered, however, it is difficult to fully comprehend the ministry's goals and measures. Nowhere on the ministry's web site could we find a summary of New Zealand's performance accountability and reporting systems that would put the information in context.

The 2007–08 annual report generally does not list performance data sources or describe data validation and verification processes. On the other hand, the auditor's letter in the report indicates that the performance information is audited and states that the ministry received a clean opinion on its financial statements. Data are largely complete and timely. However, the tables on performance results reveal several cases in which data systems were not in place to support measures.

The performance measure tables in the annual report show results only for the current and immediately preceding year. Other portions of the report provide additional trend data in a few instances. Specifically, the executive summary and the overview/key findings sections of each chapter tie some of the statistics to broad transportation outcomes. For example, an informative chart, shown in Figure 5.2, relates long-term highway death data to various safety improvement initiatives.

The SOI document has some data on safety, environment, and congestion outcomes, but it is not clear how the reported figures are related to any quantifiable goals. The transport statistics document provides a very comprehensive view of transportation system performance in terms of outcomes. It shows many years of data and has supporting information that helps put the outcome data in context.

Figure 5.2 Impact of safety initiatives. (Source: New Zealand Ministry of Transport, *Annual Report 2007/08: Report of the Ministry of Transport for the Year Ended 30 June 2008*, 2008, 17, www.transport.govt.nz/about/publications/ Documents/Annual%20Report%202008.pdf.)

For example, it lists transportation volume figures as well as congestion and safety outcomes. "Contributing factors" are sometimes listed. However, these statistics are not related back to the performance report's (or any other) specific set of performance metrics. In short, the various documents provide many informative data pieces, but no document ties things together.

Public Benefits (10)

The annual report lists a number of "transportation sector outcomes" and "results sought" (NZ 2008, 23). Most of these are stated in general terms and none are quantified. A few capture outcomes or intermediate outcomes, such as reduced transportation-related deaths and injuries, improved transportation security, and harmful transportation-related emissions reduced. The report also lists selected targets from the New Zealand Transport Strategy 2008. As shown in Figure 5.3, these targets are primarily end or intermediate outcomes.

Those targets expressed as numbers are very long range (2040). However, the annual report also mentions goals (targets) with shorter timeframes—e.g., a 2003 target to reduce highway safety deaths to 300 per year by 2010 (NZ 2008, 17).

Performance measures listed in the annual report are predominantly output, activity, efficiency, and customer service measures (NZ 2008, 23–35). None of the listed measures are outcome-oriented, nor do they relate directly to the goals set forth in the report. The SOI document presents two additional sets of goals and measures (NZ 2007, 23–35, 32–33). Figure 5.4 gives some examples from the first set.

Some of the Targets Included in the NZTS

Ensuring Environmental Sustainability
Halve per capita greenhouse gas emissions from domestic transport by 2040 (relative to 2007 per capita emissions)
Become one of the first countries in the world to widely use electric vehicles
Assisting Economic Development
For identified critical routes: • Improve reliability of journey times • Reduce average journey times
Assisting Safety and Personal Security
Reduce road deaths to no more than 200 per annum by 2040
Improving Access and Mobility
Increase use of public transport to 7% of all trips by 2040 (i.e., from 111 million boardings in 2006–07 to more than 525 million boardings in 2040)
Increase walking, cycling, and other active modes to 30% of total trips in urban areas by 2040

Note: For a full list of targets in the NZTS, please visit www.transport.govt.nz.

Figure 5.3   Selected targets from New Zealand transport strategy 2008. (Source: New Zealand Ministry of Transport, *Annual Report 2007/08: Report of the Ministry of Transport for the Year Ended 30 June 2008,* 2008, 13, www.transport. govt.nz/about/publications/Documents/Annual%20Report%202008.pdf.)

Of this first set, about 40% are outcome-oriented. However, they are not quantified and some are quite general—e.g., "reduced real and perceived security risks for transport users." The second set is described as cost-effectiveness and efficiency measures. They include no outcomes and are not quantified.

Given their general lack of quantifiable outcomes, the New Zealand performance metrics do little to demonstrate contributions toward important public transportation benefits. Those goals that do capture quantified outcomes are too long range to serve this purpose in a compelling way. Moreover, there is little explanation of how the outputs measured actually accomplish the intended outcomes. One exception is the interesting graph captured in Figure 5.2, which juxtaposes road deaths with various policy changes, each of which appears to affect the measured outcome in the following year.

The performance measure tables in the annual report link appropriation costs to each set of output measures. Figure 5.5 provides an example.

Sector Leadership and Support—Work Program

Outcomes (Planned Results)	Intermediate Outcomes (Defining Success)	Interventions
The government transport sector is efficient and effective.	The transport sector is recognized as a benchmark for other government portfolios.	Develop and maintain effective governance, monitoring, and management arrangements and systems.
The transport system is efficient and effective.	Land transport agencies are able to plan and carry out infrastructure development work effectively.	Ensure transport revenue is collected in an efficient manner that meets needs Provide Land Transport NZ with a policy framework to inform the distribution of funding.
Transport participants increasingly understand and meet the costs they create.	Fees and charges reflect the costs of transport enforcement, compliance, and monitoring.	Ensure the process for the review of transport fees and charges is transparent.
Contributes to all the sector outcomes.	Guidance is in place that maximizes the likelihood of achieving the outcomes.	Provide strategic policy direction for the sector.
New Zealand's transport system is increasingly safe and secure.	Reduced real and perceived security rides for transport users. Enhanced coordination and capability of the search and rescue sector. Aircraft operators have a safe aerodrome facility.	Coordinate an emergency response plan for the transport sector. Provide leadership and support to the Search and Rescue Council. Manage the aerodrome according to civil aviation standards.

Figure 5.4   New Zealand statement of intent goals and measures. (Source: New Zealand Ministry of Transport, *Statement of Intent 2007–2010*, 2007, 19.)

Actual 2006–07	Performance Measures	Actual 2007–08	Standards Targets 2007–08
	Quantity		
90%	Key initiatives contained in the annual work program are completed or progressed as agreed, or as subsequently amended by agreement between the minister and the chief executive.	92%	The priority work program is detailed in Part 1 of the Statement of Intent 2007–10.
	Quality		
	Project Management		
80%	All significant project deliverables will be cost-effectively managed by an appropriate business management software tool that will align projects to sector outcomes.	100%	100%
	Feedback		
First biennial stakeholder survey undertaken in October 2006 to establish benchmarks.	Feedback from key stakeholders indicates the ministry is effectively leading policy thinking and research on transport sector issues that are in line with the government's vision for transport. As determined through the biennial stakeholder survey and informal feedback via ministers' and chief executives' meetings.	The next survey is to be completed in October 2008.	≥80% satisfied or better

	Quality Characteristics		
	Policy advice will be delivered in accordance with the agreed policy quality criteria listed in "Policy Advice Quality Characteristics." As determined through delivery recorded against the project plan.	[a]	100%
New	Percentage of policy advice delivered that was subject to quality assurance processes such as peer review.	100%	≥90%
	Timeliness		
90%	Policy and research and evaluation advice will be delivered to minister(s) as appropriate within negotiated deadlines.	100%	100%
	Cost		
$19,528,000	The output is produced within appropriation (GST exclusive).	$19,970,603	$22,889,000[b]

[a] The ministry is developing a system to capture this information; however, this was not in place for 2007–08.

[b] This reduction is due to the completion of funding for specific projects in 2006–07 offset by new funding for coastal shipping and heavy vehicle projects.

Figure 5.5 Output performance measures and cost. (Source: New Zealand Ministry of Transport, *Annual Report 2007/08: Report of the Ministry of Transport for the Year Ended 30 June 2008,* **2008, 24, www.transport.govt.nz/about/publications/ Documents/Annual%20Report%202008.pdf.)**

As the example illustrates, actual cost figures are compared to targets. A note in the financial statements explains how costs are assigned to outputs (NZ 2008, 56). This is a potential best practice.

Leadership (10)

The acting chief executive's introductory message to the annual report lists several significant strategy documents and mentions some major activities; however, it does not describe outcome-oriented performance accomplishments (NZ 2008, 1). Introductions to the SOI document from the minister of transport and the chief executive list several major goals that have a direct effect on the quality of life, such as reducing congestion in Auckland and improving safety (NZ 2007, 3–4). The body of the SOI document provides additional detail on these and other contributions.

The annual report generally discloses enough information for the reader to determine whether measures were met or missed; however, it does not highlight performance results. Highlighting results, as many performance reports do, relieves the reader of the burden of parsing through performance information in order to make this determination. Each set of measures is followed by a "commentary on performance." These narratives consist mainly of lists of activities. They provide little analysis of performance results and no explanation of shortfalls. The report has no systematic discussion of management challenges either by an external auditor or by the ministry itself. One page in the annual report on developing the ministry's capabilities does mention some management challenges related to information technology and staffing issues (NZ 2008, 22).

New Zealand's annual report focuses largely on outputs rather than outcomes. Outcome reporting is more focused on long-range strategies and their implementation than it is on annual performance results. The annual report describes ongoing and future initiatives, particularly the development and issuance of the Transport Strategy 2008, which is a 30-year strategic planning document. The SOI document has considerable content throughout describing future actions that the ministry plans to take to advance each strategic outcome.

United Kingdom

Transparency (14)

The Department for Transport's home page, www.dft.gov.uk (last visited October 11, 2010), did not have a direct link to the 2008 annual report or to any other annual report at the time of our review. A search for "annual report" using the home page search function produced a link to "annual and performance reports" that in turn produced the 2008 report as well as subsequent and prior year versions. The report is downloadable in a single HTML or PDF file or in smaller PDF files for different sections. We found no contact information specific to the report online or in the hard copy.

November 2007

High Speed 1 Complete
2.10 On November 14, 2007, Section 2 of the Channel Tunnel Rail Link, from North Kent to London, was opened to passenger traffic, on time and on budget. This marked the completion of the link and the creation of High Speed 1. As a result, journey times from London to Paris and Brussels have been cut by 40 minutes, to 2 hours 15 minutes and 1 hour 51 minutes, respectively.
St. Pancras Station Restored
2.11 The spectacular St. Pancras International station has been restored to its full 19th-century glory, while at the same time being developed into a major 21st-century gateway to Britain. Highly acclaimed on opening, it presents a dramatic first impression for rail passengers, whether from the Continent or on domestic services from the Midlands.
Fresnel Lenses
2.12 The Vehicle and Operator Services (TOSA) and the Highways Agency joined forces to trial a solution to side-swiping incidents involving left-hand-drive trucks. From November, they began issuing left-hand-drive lorries with window-mounted lenses—known as Fresnel lenses—as they entered the UK at Dover. They gave out 40,000 lenses in the trial, which produced a dramatic 59% reduction in accidents involving left-hand-drive trucks. A further 90,000 lenses will now be distributed, targeting major ports in both England and France.

Figure 5.6   UK report highlights format. (Source: United Kingdom Department for Transport, *2008 Annual Report,* 2008a, 16, http://webarchive.nationalarchives. gov.uk/+/http://www.dft.gov.uk/about/publications/apr/ar2008. Permission to reproduce granted under the UK Open Government Licence, http://www.nation-alarchives.gov.uk/doc/open-government-licence/open-government-licence.htm.)

The report is 322 pages long (7 megabytes), very close to the 2008 U.S. performance and accountability report average length of 318 pages. It begins with a foreword by the department head that highlights many initiatives and a few achievements for the covered year. The body of the report consists mainly of text along with a fair number of graphs and tables. The text is written in plain language and uses a format of succinct numbered paragraphs with many headings and subheadings. All these format features aid readability. Figure 5.6 provides an example of this format, used here to describe specific monthly accomplishments.

Although there is a nine-page glossary of acronyms, they actually are used sparingly in the body of the report. The report is well organized and easy to navigate. It includes a detailed index, a useful feature rarely found in U.S. reports. It also contains many hyperlinks to other source files for more detail on a range of topics.

The department appears to report based on several overlapping sets of objectives and goals: its own strategic objectives and public service agreement (PSA) commitments that support government-wide priorities. This framework is not explained very clearly, so it is somewhat confusing for noninsiders to read and understand what the department is accomplishing in every substantive area. The substantive paragraphs in the main body of the report tend to be lengthy recitations of programs and activities, achievements, current initiatives underway, funding allocations, and future plans. This makes it challenging to pick out specific performance results.

Appendix D describes performance results, although it likewise can be difficult to parse through. It would be helpful to have summary presentations of goals, measures, and results in the main body. Indeed, the report could be one-third the length if it took Appendix D as its outline, added performance measures for all the department's strategic objectives, and then used selected pieces of narrative from the main text as needed to show how the department is or is not accomplishing its goals.

Under the heading "Data Quality," Appendix D presents detailed information on data sources and methods for each measure discussed there. This includes descriptions of data qualifications, issues, and improvement strategies. Some data descriptions give hyperlinks to online sources for additional detail. Figure 5.7 shows one of these presentations, dealing with a measure on reducing travel times.

Overall, the report provides confidence that its data are reliable and that the department devotes serious attention to data credibility. Moreover, the department reports performance on a semiannual basis by issuing autumn performance reports in addition to the annual reports. An example is the *Autumn Performance Report 2008* (UK 2008b). This is a potential best practice not found in U.S. federal performance reporting, which should greatly ameliorate the impact of lagging annual data.

Data Quality

Journey time data for all vehicles other than buses are provided to local authorities by the department. These data are derived from in-vehicle GPS tracking systems. Coverage varies from route to route, and from section to section over individual routes, and some infilling is necessary where sample sizes are low. Journey times for each hour in the target are based on an annual weekday average, excluding school holidays.

Figure 5.7   Assessment of travel time data quality. (Source: United Kingdom Department for Transport, *2008 Annual Report,* 2008a, 253, http://webarchive.nationalarchives.gov.uk/+/http://www.dft.gov.uk/about/publications/apr/ar2008. Permission to reproduce granted under the UK Open Government Licence, http://www.nationalarchives.gov.uk/doc/open-government-licence/open-government-licence.htm.)

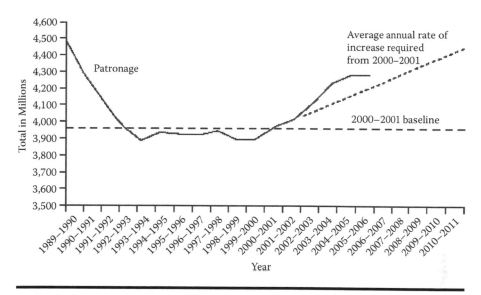

Figure 5.8   Bus and light rail ridership. (Source: United Kingdom Department for Transport, *2008 Annual Report,* **2008a, 265, http://webarchive.nationalarchives. gov.uk/+/http://www.dft.gov.uk/about/publications/apr/ar2008. Permission to reproduce granted under the UK Open Government Licence, http://www.nation-alarchives.gov.uk/doc/open-government-licence/open-government-licence.htm.)**

The narratives in the main body of the report rarely show baselines or goals when they present performance data. A few graphs illustrate trends, but since baselines or targets are not indicated, it is not always clear what the trends mean. The primary source of baseline and trend data is Appendix D. It includes graphs showing such data for each covered measure, and in some cases additional data bearing on performance trends. The data usually go back at least several years and sometimes much longer. Figure 5.8 provides an example.

Some trend data are reported in bimonthly increments. Narratives frequently expand on performance trends. The department's performance reporting is built around long-term goals and performance targets, which are listed in the appendix. This information provides useful context. On the other hand, there is little explanation of the rationale for performance targets. Such explanations would help the reader to assess their reasonableness.

Public Benefits (12)

The department seems to have somewhat overlapping sets of strategic goals and objectives. Reading them together, they capture outcomes or intermediate outcomes for the most part, albeit at a fairly high level of generality. In this regard, an October 2007 framework for transportation planning called "Towards a Sustainable Transport System," referenced in the report, sets out the following five goals:

- Maximizing the overall competitiveness and productivity of the national economy, so as to achieve a sustained high level of GDP growth;
- Reducing transport's emissions of [carbon dioxide] and other greenhouse gases, with the desired outcome of avoiding dangerous climate change;
- Contributing to better health and longer life-expectancy through reducing the risk of death, injury or illness arising from transport, and promoting travel modes that are beneficial to health;
- Improving quality of life for transport users and non-transport users, including through a healthy natural environment, with the desired outcome of improved well-being for all; and
- Promoting greater equality of transport opportunity for all citizens, with the desired outcome of achieving a fairer society. (UK 2008a, 25–26)

Furthermore, Appendix D to the report is built around the PSA targets, which were established through "spending reviews" in 2002 and 2004. The PSA targets generally track the above-mentioned goals and add some specificity to them. For example, one target is to "reduce congestion on the inter-urban road network in England below 2000 levels by 2010" (UK 2008a, 240).

Nowhere in the report can the reader find a comprehensive list of performance measures for each of the department's strategic goals. The report mentions that a full list of performance measures is in a planning document, but it is not clear where the reader could find actual performance data on all measures. Since the report's narratives are organized by function rather than by strategic objective, it is hard to link these measures back to the objectives. Appendix D does list performance indicators to accompany the PSA targets. About three-fifths of these measures are outcomes, such as road casualties, reductions in road travel time, railway on-time performance, and bus punctuality. The rest are intermediate outcomes (air quality), outputs (passenger volumes, pollutant emissions), or activities. Perhaps the PSA targets are supposed to be the department's key goals and measures, but this is not explained. In any event, basing our evaluation on the measures we can identify in Appendix D, they align fairly well with the applicable PSA targets and other goals and generally capture at least intermediate outcomes.

In contrast to U.S. reports, the UK report focuses much more on long-term outcomes than annual results. It uses performance indicators with different timeframes to show progress toward the long-term goals. For some federal agencies, this added flexibility might be a better approach than the GPRA framework that emphasizes annual results for everything.

The report lists many activities that seem related to the department's goals, but does not systematically link specific activities with goal achievement. On the other hand, the line of sight between activities and goals is clarified in many instances. For example, the report (UK 2000a) describes:

■ Reductions in London congestion following the institution of congestion pricing (36–37)
■ How issuance of window-mounted mirrors to visiting left-hand-drive trucks reduced side-swiping incidents (135)
■ The impact of free concessionary fares on increasing bus ridership (263)

The road congestion measures also include stipulations about expected travel volumes, so the reader can understand that achievement or failure to meet a goal may result from travel volume rather than the department's actions. This is an excellent example of presenting performance information in a way that controls for external factors without undue complexity. The department says it will adjust congestion targets if planned changes in traffic volume do not occur. In short, there are some good examples of attempts to control for or establish causality, but these are not typical.

Appendix A to the report has tables breaking down budget costs in various ways and relating them to the department's strategic goals (UK 2008a, 207–215). However, the linkage of budget costs to the report's performance metrics does not go below the strategic goal level. The report has several features that indicate the department uses financial incentives to affect performance in various ways. For example, the department has a "congestion performance fund" that it uses to reward local transportation agencies that meet or exceed their congestion reduction targets (p. 252). Another feature is its cost reduction and "value for money" goals and performance indicators. Cost reduction goals are not supposed to come at the expense of outcomes. The "value for money" concept establishes benefit–cost goals instead of just cost reductions. It is an interesting attempt to compare the aggregate value of the department's activities against aggregate costs.

Finally, Appendix G explicitly addresses the cost of regulation, listing initiatives the department has undertaken under the government's "better regulation" initiative. The appendix mentions a number of regulatory changes that are expected to reduce regulatory costs. This is a worthwhile start toward including comprehensive analysis of the effects of regulation on measured performance and costs.

Leadership (13)

Consistent with the report's overall emphasis on progress toward long-term goals over annual results, the department head's foreword gives more attention to future initiatives than to annual accomplishments. Nevertheless, Chapter 2 lists "key achievements" for each month covered by the report. Some, such as June's announcement of reductions in road deaths, clearly show specific transportation outcomes of interest to citizens. Many others are more prosaic, such as new regulations issued and record sales of the Highway Code.

Appendix D clearly discloses performance results, presenting them in different ways based on the time period covered by the applicable target, e.g., annual performance target "not met" (241); status listed as "ahead" for goal, with only a 2010 target (249). The appendix narratives go into considerable detail (far more than most U.S. reports) in explaining and analyzing performance results and trends. The narratives discuss remedial strategies for some shortfalls but with less specificity and detail than the explanations of results.

Several portions of the report address management challenges and steps to deal with them. Chapter 1 (10–11) briefly describes the results of an external review of the department and a program the department developed to respond to the findings. Chapter 11 discusses a range of financial, administrative, and management matters along with some goals and measures to reduce costs and improve efficiency (184–185). Most notably, Appendix F, captioned "Public Accounts Committee recommendations," seems roughly equivalent to the inspector general presentations found in U.S. reports. It lists findings and recommendations from audits and responds to them with more detail and specificity than most U.S. reports. One missing element is a direct presentation from the auditors on their assessment of the management challenges and the department's remedial steps.

The report is quite forward looking—considerably more so than the vast majority of U.S. reports. From the performance metrics, to the general narratives in the body of the report, to the Appendix D narratives, the report is rich in descriptions of future plans and other initiatives to promote strategic long-term goal achievement. In some cases, the department lists specific measures it intends to take to improve specific aspects of performance. For example, the report observes that the department needs to focus on the most severe accidents because death rates have not declined as fast as injury rates (127–28).

What the United States Can Learn from International Reports

In the area of transparency, we found several positive features in one or more of the international reports that we rarely see in U.S. reports. Both the Australian and UK reports included detailed indexes that greatly facilitate locating relevant information. Further pinpointing relevant content, the Australian report presented specialized topics in an appendix. The New Zealand and UK reports are particularly noteworthy for the clarity of their narratives. The use of concise numbered paragraphs in the UK report provides an excellent text format that could be a model for other reports. Finally, the Australia report's inclusion of corrections from the prior year report is a unique (in our experience) and useful transparency enhancement. Each of these features is discussed in the foregoing individual report analyses.

As described in the individual report analyses, both the New Zealand and UK reports offer good examples in terms of relating costs to performance results. The New Zealand report does a good job of explaining the basis for allocating budget costs to performance measures. The UK report discusses the use of financial incentives to enhance certain performance results.

Apart from the specific features noted above, the most striking lesson that the international reports have to offer, in our view, is their primary focus on long-term over annual performance. As discussed in previous chapters, U.S. reporting under the GPRA centers on annual performance results. This approach is well suited for performance goals addressing economy, efficiency, customer service, outputs, and other activities that readily lend themselves to measurement in annual increments. The approach is less suited to measuring performance results for those government mission outcomes that tend to take longer to materialize, such as improving educational achievement or reducing adverse environmental impacts. The long-term and more strategic approach taken by the international reports may be a better model for outcome measurement. In particular, it affords organizations the option of devising outcome performance goals and measures even if they transcend a single year, rather than force fitting their performance metrics into activities that can produce annual results. While we would not suggest that the core GPRA concept of annual reporting be abandoned, it might be desirable to afford agencies the flexibility to adopt multiyear goals and measures where that approach would lead to more meaningful outcome-oriented performance metrics.

What Other Nations Can Learn from the U.S. Federal Reports

Based on our reviews, the international reports came up short primarily in the area of quantified outcome goals and measures. The Australia and New Zealand reports were particularly weak here. The UK report was significantly better than the other two, but not strong when compared to the better U.S. reports. The more long-term strategic focus of the international reports should, in our view, encourage good outcome-oriented metrics. Thus, it is ironic that the metrics in these reports do not compare favorably with U.S. reports in this regard. It is possible that better performance metrics may exist in other venues that were beyond the scope of our review.

Conclusion

Evaluated against GPRA standards, the annual performance reports from Australia, New Zealand, and the United Kingdom compare reasonably well with U.S. federal

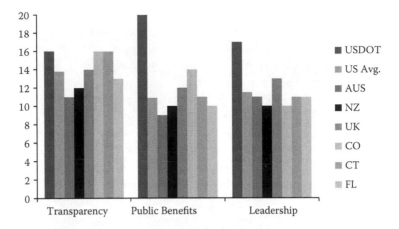

Figure 5.9   Federal, state, and international scores.

and state reports. Figure 5.9 demonstrates this by juxtaposing scores from federal, state, and international reports. In addition to the USDOT, Colorado, Connecticut, and the UK show relatively high transparency scores. For public benefits, the standouts are the USDOT, Colorado, and the UK. Finally, the only clearly better reports on leadership are the USDOT and the UK.

One striking difference between the U.S. and the international reports involves the timeframe for assessing outcomes. The best U.S. reports often attempt to measure incremental changes in outcomes over the course of one or a few years, and they explore ways to improve performance when it falls short. Australia, New Zealand, and the United Kingdom look for outcome trends over much longer timeframes, such as decades. Indeed, New Zealand's reporting structure focuses on annual reporting of agency outputs, with outcomes defined and assessed by elected leaders. Australia's report in particular does a good job of showing progress toward long-term outcomes.

We gleaned numerous good ideas from the Australia, New Zealand, and United Kingdom reports that would improve the U.S. federal reports. These include:

- Corrections from the previous year's report
- An extensive index to help readers navigate the report
- Complete audits of the performance data
- Virtually zero acronyms
- Good linkage of costs with outputs or outcomes
- Inclusion of a mid-year update
- Inclusion of outcome measures with a longer-term focus
- Explanation of how initiatives to improve regulation are linked to agency performance

Interestingly, most of these ideas from the international reports are different from the innovative ideas we saw in the state reports. State reports were especially strong in the transparency category—precisely where the international reports were weakest. In particular, Florida's web site collected a wealth of performance-related information in one place. If we did not understand some aspects of Florida's reporting process, we could find a document that explained it. This would have been extremely helpful for the international reports—even for New Zealand, where one of us had extensive experience in government! More to the point, if we connoisseurs of performance reporting have trouble understanding how a government's performance reporting system works, it is likely even more difficult for a citizen who does not have time to learn all the ins and outs. States also presented many informative uses of baseline and trend data from which the U.S. federal agencies and other nations' agencies could both learn.

The past two chapters have uncovered different strengths and weaknesses in annual performance reports from different states and nations. Clearly, no country or level of government has a monopoly on good reporting practices.

GPRA AND THE QUALITY OF GOVERNMENT

Chapter 6

Regulation—Where Transparency Falls Short

Regulation is one way the federal government directs the use of resources without having the full costs of those resources appear in the budget. Because regulations direct individuals, organizations, and state and local governments to use resources in different ways, most regulatory costs do not appear as federal outlays.

In the United States, regulation arises when Congress delegates some of its lawmaking powers to federal agencies, allowing them to use their specialized knowledge to fill in the details. Laws that enable regulation may be quite broad, such as the legislation that empowers the Federal Trade Commission (FTC) to prevent unfair or deceptive business practices. Or the law may be quite narrow, prescribing precisely what the agency's regulation can and cannot permit. For example, another regulation issued by the Federal Trade Commission requires optometrists to give each patient a copy of his or her contact lens prescription at the conclusion of an eye examination, so that the patient can shop around for contact lenses instead of having to buy them from the eye doctor. Congress passed a law that explicitly directed the FTC to issue this regulation. Regardless of whether Congress grants agencies broad or narrow discretion in writing regulations, the regulations carry the force of law.

Scholars and government analysts can, and sometimes do, disagree over the right ways to measure some of the outcomes and costs of regulation. However, the most heated controversies revolve around what decision makers are supposed to do with information about regulations' benefits and costs once they have it. Some have advocated that a regulation should not be adopted or retained unless the monetized value of the benefits exceeds the monetized value of the costs.* Others recoil at the idea of basing regulatory decisions on consideration of costs at all. Executive Order 12866, which outlines how federal agencies are supposed to conduct regulatory analysis and use the results, takes a middle ground. It states that regulators must determine whether the benefits justify the costs. This clearly directs decision makers to consider information about outcomes and costs without establishing a rigid decision rule. In particular, this would allow decision makers to consider qualitative benefits and costs that cannot be quantified.

Readers may notice that the disagreements over how decision makers should use the results of regulatory analysis mirror disagreements over how decision makers should use the results of program evaluations. If a thorough analysis reveals that a program or regulation is inefficient or ineffective, does that mean it should be abolished, reformed, or furnished with more resources? The principal difference is that the most vicious regulatory debates involve the role of analysis in the decision to *adopt* a new regulation, whereas debates over program evaluation usually involve what to do about an existing program. Resolving either of those kinds of disagreements is outside the scope of this book. In keeping with GPRA's focus on ex post evaluation, we merely consider whether decision makers have access to reliable information about regulatory outcomes after the regulations are in force.

Accountability for regulatory outcomes requires a robust program of retrospective analysis to assess the actual results of regulations after they have taken effect. Executive orders and legislation require regulatory agencies to estimate the benefits and costs of proposed regulations, but little retrospective analysis occurs after regulations are adopted to assess their actual costs and outcomes. Retrospective analysis is necessary because ex ante estimates of regulation's effects are often inaccurate:

- Harrington et al. (2000) compared ex ante government estimates of the benefits and costs of 28 environment, health, and safety regulations with ex post independent estimates. They defined an ex ante estimate as accurate if it was within 25% of the ex post estimate. The ex ante estimate of benefits (pollutant emissions, an output) was accurate for about half of the regulations. Total cost estimates were accurate for only five regulations, and cost-effectiveness estimates (cost per unit of pollution reduced) were accurate for only eight regulations. For both benefits and costs, overestimates were more prevalent than underestimates.
- OMB (2005a) undertook a similar study to determine whether ex ante regulatory analyses systematically over- or underestimated benefits or costs. OMB reported that benefit estimates were inaccurate for 44% of the regulations, and cost estimates were inaccurate for 60% of the regulations. Overestimates of benefits were much more common than overestimates of costs.

* A Senate bill in the 105th Congress (S981) would have required agencies to use benefit–cost analysis to explain their decisions.

■ Harrington (2006) took issue with OMB's claim that benefits are overestimated to a greater extent than costs. Using a larger set of regulations, he found that ex ante regulatory analyses underestimated the benefit–cost ratios about as frequently as they overestimated them. From this, he concluded that government regulatory analyses do not systematically overestimate benefits more frequently than costs. However, Harrington's figures also show that the ex ante analysis was inaccurate for almost three-quarters of the regulations in his sample.*

Though the Harrington and OMB studies disagree on whether ex ante estimates are systematically biased, it is clear from all three studies that many ex ante estimates are inaccurate. We believe that decision makers assessing individual regulations that are already on the books should have accurate information about the actual results of those regulations. Both Harrington's and OMB's studies demonstrate that ex ante estimates are not a good substitute for rigorous retrospective analysis.

Measuring Regulatory Outcomes

A substantial academic literature measures the outcomes and costs of individual regulations, groups of regulations, and laws that authorize regulations. Among scholars and government economists who specialize in regulation, many of the measurement methods are well known and widely used (Viscusi et al. 2005, Zerbe and Bellas 2006). The Office of Management and Budget (OMB 2003a) has a detailed set of guidelines for assessing regulation's effects, titled Circular A-4.

At first glance, retrospective analysis of regulation seems simple: just observe the outcomes of interest before and after adoption of the regulation. Before-and-after comparisons may sometimes be informative, especially if one can make the case that other significant factors did not change in the interim (Winston 1998, Wiseman and Ellig 2007). But such comparisons can often either over- or understate regulation's effects. Statistical analysis is often necessary to compare observed results under regulation with a counterfactual estimate of the results that would have occurred in the absence of the regulation. As Harrington et al. (2000, 301) note:

> For the ex post calculation, the world with the regulation is observed, but the counterfactual is not. To produce an ex post estimate, one must determine the actual outcome empirically and compare it to a hypothetical baseline with the status quo ante.

---

* Harrington provides a full tabulation only of the benefit–cost ratios. When the ex post benefit–cost ratio differs substantially from the ex ante benefit–cost ratio, that means the ex ante analysis inaccurately estimated costs, benefits, or perhaps both.

For instance, gyrating fuel prices may mask the effects of regulation on transportation rates, and so one must control for fuel prices when assessing the effects of regulation on transportation rates. A series of peer-reviewed counterfactual studies found that, after controlling for fuel costs and other factors that affected prices, federal economic regulation of airlines, railroads, and trucking in the 1970s increased transportation prices (Morrison and Winston 1985, 1995, Winston et al. 1990, Winston 1993). In addition, regulation increased travel time and reduced reliability of service. Retrospective analysis revealed that removal of price, entry, and exit restrictions in these three industries generated approximately $50 billion in benefits annually for customers.* The benefits quantified by ex post studies are generally larger than those estimated by economists ex ante (Winston 1993, Ellig 2002).

For economic regulation of transportation, outcomes are relatively straightforward: prices, transit time, and reliability. Some types of social regulation may also have outcomes that are fairly easy to define, measure, and conduct counterfactual analysis upon. Workplace safety regulations seek to reduce workplace injuries and fatalities. Product safety regulations seek to reduce injuries attributable to the design of products people buy. Food safety regulations seek to reduce the incidence of food-borne illnesses that result from chemical, microbial, or physical hazards.

Other forms of regulation have outcomes that may be more difficult to measure. Quantifying the outcomes usually involves complicated chains of causality that require scientific research on the relationship between the regulated activity and human health. Or, the outcomes involve reductions in the likelihood of risks that are not always well understood. Or both.

Environmental regulation presents some classic examples. The ultimate outcomes of clean air regulations are improvements in human health and well-being. Establishing whether a given regulation contributes to those outcomes, and by how much, requires an understanding of the effects of various air pollutants on human health generally, and the health of ecosystems and the health of various vulnerable subpopulations (the elderly, children, people with asthma, etc.) in particular. Security regulation is another example. For instance, post-9/11 federal regulations requiring airlines to reinforce cockpit doors are intended to prevent hijackers from gaining entry to the cockpit and using civilian airplanes as weapons. The likelihood of terrorists trying this again is unknown, and the number of lost lives and amount of property damage could vary greatly depending on the chosen target.

Though establishing causal links between a regulation and outcomes may sometimes be difficult, it beats the alternative: blind faith that a regulation will accomplish the intended results simply because we want it to.

---

* Figure is in 1995 dollars calculated by Crandall and Ellig (1997) from results in Morrison and Winston (1995) and Winston et al. (1990).

Measuring Regulatory Costs

The concept of regulatory costs is somewhat more involved than outcomes, because the true cost of a regulation is its opportunity cost—the value of the next best outcome society had to forego as a result of the regulation. This definition is just an application of the standard definition of *cost* found in most economics textbooks.* But it is profoundly different from the layman's understanding of *cost* as simply an amount of money a regulated entity has to pay to comply with a regulation. The true social cost of a regulation is the total value of everything any member of society had to give up as a result of the regulation. Opportunity costs begin with scarcity. We do not have enough of anything (time, resources) to fulfill all of our wants. This means we have to make choices (such as go to the movies or stay home), and those choices give rise to opportunity costs.

An example is management time associated with regulations. For an accountant, there are no additional managerial costs to dealing with regulations because the managers receive the same salary regardless of how they spend their time. For an economist, the opportunity cost of a manager's time spent dealing with a regulation is choosing not to deal with other management problems, such as improving product quality. Once a choice has been made, the cost is in the past; it is the value of the option not chosen. Individuals ultimately bear all regulatory costs in their roles as consumers, employees, or business owners.

Some regulatory costs may be obvious and easy to measure in monetary terms, such as compliance expenditures. Others may not be so obvious, such as the value of the extra time people have to stand in line at airports due to security screening, or the consequences of behavioral changes as people seek to avoid the increased monetary costs and long lines. One calculation suggests that the post-9/11 airport security measures cost fliers $2.76 billion in extra travel time in 2005 (Ellig et al. 2006, 33–34). Another study found that post-9/11 baggage screening reduced air travel volumes by 6% and generated 129 additional automobile fatalities in the fourth quarter of 2002 as travelers substituted driving for flying on shorter trips (Blalock et al. 2007). Clearly, regulatory costs are not just monetary.

A brief taxonomy of regulatory costs includes:

- ▪ On-budget costs: Government costs of writing and enforcing the regulation.
- ▪ Paperwork costs: Paperwork and other administrative burdens the regulated entities (businesses, individuals, other levels of government, and Indian tribes) bear as a result of the regulation.

---

* Even this definition is a simplification. Cost is the value of the next best alternative the decision maker imagined at the time of the decision (Buchanan 1969). Typically, regulatory cost analysis does not try to get inside the heads of political decision makers, but rather attempts to estimate the total value of what each member of society gives up as a result of the regulation. This is the cost the decision maker ought to be imagining if he or she is concerned about society's overall welfare.

- Direct costs: Expenditures on compliance (i.e., labor and capital), such as the cost of purchasing pollution control equipment for power plants or security screening at airports.
- Time costs: The value of forgone alternatives because people spend their time on activities related to the regulation instead of something else. Examples include a manager's time spent on regulatory compliance and travelers' time waiting in line at airport security.
- Deadweight losses: Reductions in output, quality, safety, or other factors that occur as regulated entities and their customers alter their behavior in response to the regulatory costs and mandates.
- General equilibrium costs: Effects that ripple through the economy if changes in costs or prices of the regulated activity are big enough to affect activity in other markets. If these costs are significant, they may show up as a reduction in gross domestic product.
- Rent-seeking costs: Expenditures by industry and other interest groups to influence the regulatory process so that they can capture or avoid the wealth transfers regulation creates. These costs may stem from an individual regulation or a host of regulations. Therefore, these costs might not change as a result of an individual regulation.

It is hard to know the total cost of regulation, because only a small fraction of the costs of regulation appear in the federal budget. An annual study, "The Regulator's Budget," calculates the on-budget expenditures and employees of federal regulatory agencies using U.S. government data. In 2008, federal agencies spent approximately $43 billion to write and administer regulations (Dudley and Warren 2010, 23).

We know of two principal efforts to measure the overall cost of federal regulation. Neither is perfect, but both suggest the costs are large in an absolute sense.

The first is a series of widely quoted reports commissioned by the U.S. Small Business Administration's (SBA) Office of Advocacy. SBA undertook these reports to determine whether, or to what extent, small businesses bear a disproportionate share of regulatory costs. The most recent study estimates that federal regulation costs approximately $1.75 trillion in 2008 (Crain and Crain 2010). These costs include regulatory compliance costs borne by individuals, organizations, and other levels of government, as well as forgone gross domestic product (GDP). That's equal to 59% of federal outlays in fiscal year 2008.* The report notes that regulations also have benefits, but it does not attempt to measure them.

The SBA report may overstate the costs of regulation. The largest source of regulatory costs in the study is a $1.2 trillion reduction in GDP due to domestic economic regulations (Crain and Crain 2008, 31). This cost is estimated via an international econometric analysis that correlates GDP with the World Bank's

---

* Federal outlays totaled $2.9 trillion in fiscal year 2008 (OMB 2008a, 55).

Regulatory Quality Index plus a number of other control variables that affect GDP. Separately, the study calculates the costs of occupational safety regulations, environmental regulations, homeland security regulations, and tax compliance. To the extent that the World Bank index is correlated with these other forms of regulation or other government policies that reduce GDP, the econometric results might include the effects of some of these other forms of regulation on GDP (Harrington 2006). Therefore, it is possible that the study double-counts some regulatory costs. Nevertheless, the econometric estimate by itself is still $1.2 trillion—a huge sum by any standard.

The other major study of regulatory costs is an annual report on the benefits and costs of federal regulations produced by OMB in response to a congressional mandate, the Regulatory Right-to-Know Act. The legislation requires OMB to produce "an estimate of the total annual benefits and costs (including quantifiable and nonquantifiable effects) of federal rules and paperwork, to the extent feasible ..." (OMB 2010a, 6). Despite the congressional directive to estimate total annual benefits and costs of federal rules, OMB confines its estimate to regulations adopted during the previous ten years. This occurs because OMB relies on prospective estimates produced by federal agencies at the time they adopted the regulations, and "pre-regulation estimates prepared for rules adopted more than ten years ago are of questionable relevance today" (OMB 2010a, 10).

The OMB (2010a) report, which covers fiscal year 2008, estimates that regulations reviewed by OMB and issued by federal agencies during the previous ten years imposed annual costs of between $51 billion and $63 billion, with total benefits ranging between $126 billion and $663 billion. The cost works out to approximately 2% of federal expenditures in fiscal year 2008. Two percent sounds comparatively small, but surely the public is still entitled to transparent disclosure of outcomes for a collection of initiatives costing more than $50 billion annually. And surely at least some of those large claimed benefits are related to agencies' strategic goals under GPRA, and they could be documented and tracked.

The OMB figures likely understate the effects of regulations. The OMB report is not comprehensive, nor is it truly retrospective. OMB readily acknowledges these shortcomings in the report (OMB 2010a, 4). The total figures cover the benefits and costs of major federal regulations enacted during the previous ten years. The report does not have cost or benefit estimates for many of the regulations issued by independent commissions, which are not reviewed by OMB. The totals also exclude regulations for which agencies did not estimate monetary costs or benefits. Even when agencies did calculate monetary values of costs or benefits, they did not necessarily do so for all costs and benefits of the regulation. In most cases, OMB relies on regulatory impact analyses produced by agencies when they proposed the regulations. Thus, the report does not provide an assessment of the actual costs or benefits of the regulations after they were implemented.

Accountability for Regulatory Outcomes

Federal regulations have large effects. However, the agencies that issue them devote little effort to assessing their results after regulations are adopted.

The Clinton administration's fiscal year 1999 budget includes four sentences discussing regulation and GPRA. It notes that regulations "may escape the type of scrutiny that outlay programs receive." OMB also claims that regulations subject to formal benefit–cost analysis receive more scrutiny than tax expenditures and outlays receive (OMB 1998, 106). Every budget since then has repeated this language (see, e.g., OMB 2010b, 241).

It is true that Executive Order 12866, some specific regulatory laws, and the Unfunded Mandates Reform Act require federal agencies to conduct analysis when proposing major regulations (Brito and Ellig 2010). However, these analytical requirements focus on ex ante prediction of the benefits and costs of the proposed regulation and alternatives, not ex post evaluation of actual benefits and costs after regulations are implemented. This is why OMB's annual report on the benefits and costs of federal regulations uses estimates from the regulatory analyses agencies prepared when they enacted the regulations, rather than ex post analyses of the costs and benefits that actually occurred after the regulations were adopted.

Regulatory agencies conduct numerous retrospective reviews of regulations, but these reviews only occasionally provide ex post estimates of costs and benefits of either the regulation or of possible alternatives. A recent GAO report found that nine federal agencies conducted more than 1,300 regulatory reviews between 2001 and 2006, of widely varying scope. The report notes, "Our limited review of agency summaries and reports on completed retrospective reviews revealed that agencies' reviews more often attempted to assess the effectiveness of their implementation of the regulation rather than the effectiveness of the regulation in achieving its goal" (GAO 2007, 16–20).

Agencies rarely make explicit provisions for retrospective analysis at the time they issue individual regulations. Ellig and McLaughlin (2010) examined all 45 proposed regulations in 2008 that were "economically significant"—the same standard that determines whether a regulation gets included in OMB's annual tally of benefits and costs. In only four cases did the agency establish goals or measures for any major outcome the regulation was supposed to produce. In only two cases did the agency enumerate the data it would use to evaluate major outcomes the regulation was supposed to produce. For 16 out of 45 regulations, the agency indicated that it might conduct some type of analysis in the future to assess some of the regulation's effects.

Does this absence of effective retrospective analysis impede accountability for results? We could find no obvious relationship between the extent of an agency's regulatory activities (measured by estimated benefits, costs, or percent of budget devoted to regulation) and the quality of its performance report (measured by Mercatus *Scorecard* scores). The Environmental Protection Agency, which accounts for more than half of the total benefits and costs of regulation in OMB's fiscal year 2008 report (OMB 2010a), received a *Scorecard* score of 36 in fiscal year

2008—essentially equal to both the average and the median. Four agencies with substantial regulatory costs and benefits received higher *Scorecard* scores, and four received lower scores (McTigue et al. 2009). The Nuclear Regulatory Commission devoted 100% of its budget to regulation in fiscal year 2008; it received an above-average score of 40 and tied for 4th place (McTigue et al. 2009). It was the only agency that spent anywhere near 100% of its budget on regulatory activity.

To further investigate the relationship between GPRA and regulation, we performed an econometric analysis to see if the quality of regulatory analysis performed by agencies when they issue regulations is correlated with the quality of agency GPRA initiatives. Ellig and McLaughlin (2010) evaluated the quality and use of regulatory analysis produced by federal agencies in 2008, awarding each regulation 0–5 points on each of 12 criteria derived from the executive order that governs agency regulatory analysis and OMB guidance on regulatory analysis. We explored whether any relationship exists between an agency's GPRA initiatives and its quality or use of regulatory analysis by correlating regulatory analysis scores with the agency's score on the 2008 Mercatus *Scorecard*.

Several of the regulatory analysis scores are of interest:

■ The total score, which measured the overall quality and use of regulatory analysis by the agency for that regulation
■ The score on a question that evaluated whether the agency established goals and measures to monitor the regulation's outcomes in the future
■ The score on a question that asked whether the agency made provisions to gather data to perform retrospective analysis of the regulation's outcomes in the future

In no case were agency regulatory analysis scores correlated with scores on the Mercatus *Scorecard*, once we controlled for other factors that affect the quality of agency regulatory analysis. (Details of the statistical analysis are in Appendix II.) We infer from these results that there is no systematic relationship between the quality of agency GPRA initiatives and the quality of regulatory analysis or retrospective review of regulation. It would be nice if there were, since good regulatory analysis is simply good performance management applied to regulation. But the result is not surprising, since in most agencies completely different offices handle regulatory initiatives and GPRA planning and reporting.

Previous analyses using more granular data from a larger number of agencies find that U.S. regulatory agencies may actually be *less* inclined than other agencies to develop outcome-oriented goals and measures, and this likely impairs their performance. Chun and Rainey (2005a) found statistically significant evidence that regulatory agencies are more likely to suffer from "evaluative goal ambiguity"; that is, regulatory agencies are less likely to use outcome-oriented indicators to gauge their accomplishments and more likely to measure activities and processes. They also found that higher levels of evaluative ambiguity were associated with lower agency scores on managerial effectiveness, customer service orientation, productivity, and work quality in a survey of federal employees administered by the National Partnership for Reinventing Government (Chun and Rainey 2005b). Thus, there is some evidence that regulatory agencies might benefit from tighter integration of their strategic management with their regulatory activities.

International comparisons also suggest that retrospective analysis by U.S. regulatory agencies is weak. The Organization for Economic Cooperation and Development (OECD) periodically produces reports that compare regulatory management practices in member nations. The assessment includes a survey of member nations' ex post regulatory review procedures. Each country receives a score ranging from 0 to 8 based on its responses to a series of questions about retrospective regulatory review. The average score was 4.5; only one nation, Korea, received a perfect score of 8. Other leaders, with scores of 6 or above, were Canada, Spain, Finland, the United Kingdom, Australia, France, and Japan. The United States received a score of 4, ranking 19th out of 31 governments (OECD 2009a, 92).

Integrating Performance Evaluation and Regulatory Analysis

GPRA-style performance evaluation and regulatory analysis should be highly complementary undertakings. The European Commission's guidelines for "impact assessment" of proposed policy initiatives illustrate this point strikingly. The guidelines lay out key questions that must be answered before EU decision makers take action on a policy proposal. Regulations are merely one type of policy proposal that must be analyzed under the guidelines; in a few places, the guidelines point out special considerations to take into account when performing impact assessments of regulatory proposals. Thus, the European Commission document highlights the similarities between regulatory analysis and analysis of the effects of other government policies. As Table 6.1 shows, the EU emphasizes the importance of establishing outcome objectives both because they aid in designing policies and because clear objectives are necessary for ex post assessment.

As the last bullet in the table indicates, the impact assessment must identify specific, measurable, achievable, realistic, and time-dependent objectives for the regulation. Analysts are also expected to establish indicators to help track whether the regulation is achieving its objectives (EU 2009, 28). The guidelines explicitly state that the impact assessment must:

- Name indicators that will show whether the policy is achieving its objective
- Identify monitoring and evaluation methods to assess the policy's effects in the future
- Explain how data used for monitoring will be collected (EU 2009, 49–50)

Table 6.1   What Are Policy Objectives?

All Commission IAs must have clear objectives which are directly related to solving the problems which have been identified.

Only clearly defined objectives will make the level of ambition visible, show that the proposal respects the principles of subsidiarity and proportionality, help ensure coherence of Commission policies, and allow for identification and comparison of options for action and their likely impacts.

Without clear objectives, it is possible to evaluate the extent to which the action has generated its intended effects.

Defining objectives may be an iterative process: the objectives are refined in the course of the IA work. The definition should:

- set out objectives that are clearly linked to the problem and its root causes, respect the subsidiarity and proportionality principles, and correspond to Treaty objectives and Commission priorities and strategies (such as the Lisbon and Sustainable Development Strategies or the EU Chart of Fundamental Rights);

- set out general objectives and translate them into specific and, where appropriate, operational objectives, thus setting a hierarchy of objectives;

- express the objectives in SMART terms (Specific, Measurable, Achievable, Realistic, Time-dependent).

Source: European Commission, *Impact Assessment Guidelines*, 2009, 26, http://ec.europa.eu/governance/impact/commission_guidelines/docs/iag_2009_en.pdf.

Indicators must include "result indicators" that show the effects of the policy on the parties who are directly affected, as well as "impact indicators" that address outcomes. Monitoring should assess compliance, enforcement costs, compliance costs, and outcomes (EU 2009, Annex 13, 76–77).

Despite the kinship between regulatory analysis and performance management, no administration in the United States has yet fully exploited the potential synergies. Executive Order 12866 and OMB Circular A-11 are the primary tools an administration possesses to shape agencies' regulatory analysis and GPRA reporting. At the time we wrote this chapter, the Obama administration had sought public comment on revisions to Executive Order 12866 but had not yet released a revision. The following revisions to these documents would link analysis of individual regulations more tightly with regulatory agencies' strategic planning and GPRA reporting.*

---

* The following section draws heavily on the recommendations in Wray (2009) and Brito and Ellig (2010).

Revisions to Executive Order 12866

1. Incorporate GPRA-Style Performance Measurement into Proposed Regulations

Intuition and evidence both suggest that much of the value of strategic planning and performance measurement stems from what managers learn from going through the process, rather than the value of the plan or report after it is written. As Dwight Eisenhower remarked, "Plans are useless, but planning is indispensable."* Agency efforts have greater focus, direction, and effectiveness when a tangible outcome is defined, measures are identified, and goals are set. There is no reason regulators would not benefit from such an improved strategic focus when writing regulations.

Therefore, Executive Order 12866 should explicitly require agencies to:

- Identify the specific outcomes of value to the public that the regulation is supposed to produce
- Explain how these outcomes are related to the agency's mission and one or more strategic goals in the agency's strategic plan
- Identify what indicators the agency will use to measure progress toward these outcomes
- Estimate ex ante marginal benefits of proposed and final rules that measure, in terms of outcomes, how much of a goal the regulation is expected to achieve
- Determine what kinds of retrospective program evaluations will be necessary to identify how the regulation has affected outcomes
- Track and report the annual progress (through one or multiple regulations) toward achieving a given goal and the social costs expended toward achieving that goal

The proposed outcomes, goals, and measures should be included in any notice of proposed rulemaking so that the public has an opportunity to comment on them. They should also be subject to OMB review, which should focus on ascertaining whether the proposed goals are sufficiently outcome-oriented and whether the proposed measures are valid and verifiable indicators of progress.

There is precedent for regulatory agencies seeking public comment on goals and performance measures for individual regulations. In 2005, the Federal Communications Commission sought public comment on goals and performance measures for telecommunications "universal service" programs (FCC 2005). These programs, created via regulatory proceedings at the FCC, impose charges on interstate telecommunications services in order to subsidize rural telephone companies, telephone service for low-income households, Internet service for schools and libraries, and telecommunications services for rural health care facilities. It is perhaps

---

* http://www.brainyquote.com/quotes/authors/d/dwight_d_eisenhower.html.

unfortunate that the FCC did not seek comment on performance measures until 11 years after GPRA and nine years after passage of the legislation directing the FCC to create the programs, but the FCC's action demonstrates that it is entirely feasible for a regulatory agency to do so.

Our suggested change to Executive Order 12866 is much more specific and detailed than the executive order's current requirements. The executive order does require agencies to assess the anticipated benefits of the significant regulations they propose. But the benefits need not be quantified, and in practice agencies often define them so broadly that outcomes are not well identified (Belcore and Ellig 2008, Ellig and McLaughlin 2010). Nor does the executive order require regulators to link the regulation's outcomes to the agency's strategic goals, identify indicators to measure progress after the regulation is implemented, or set goals for the indicators. In short, there is no real commitment to accountability for results at the time regulations are issued.

A major benefit of our proposal is that it would compel agencies to do the homework necessary to produce truly informative annual performance reports. GPRA Sec. 1116(b)(1) requires annual tracking of outcome indicators in relation to goals. Regulatory agencies, by definition, accomplish at least some of their strategic goals through regulation; an agency that is nothing but a regulatory agency accomplishes all of its strategic goals through regulation. Regulatory agencies should be able to "roll up" outcomes from regulations or groups of regulations into measures of accomplishment of their strategic goals. Alternatively, the principal outcome measures for the regulations that contribute most significantly to achievement of a strategic goal might also be used as outcome measures for the strategic goal.

Table 6.2 illustrates these points. It lists some strategic goals and annual performance goals or measures from actual agency GPRA reports. The performance measures track progress toward a strategic goal, but they could be easily used or adapted to track the effects of individual regulations that contribute toward those goals.

One potential criticism of this proposed change is that it might be taken to imply that the only benefits that count for regulatory analysis are those that can be expressed in monetary terms. We intend no such thing. The best outcome indicators are those that directly measure ultimate outcomes, but such indicators are not always feasible or not always translatable into monetary terms. Sometimes the best indicators available measure only intermediate outcomes. Indicators that measure activity might sometimes be acceptable if rigorous research has documented how changes in the activity actually cause changes in the outcome of interest. Thus, a requirement that regulatory agencies must identify observable indicators for performance evaluation is not the same as a requirement that they must quantify or monetize all benefits or ignore nonquantifiable benefits when deciding whether or how to regulate.

Table 6.2 GPRA Goals and Measures Related to Regulations

Agency/Program	Strategic Outcome Goal	Annual Performance Goals/Measures
Agriculture Department: Food safety and inspection	Reduction in the prevalence of food-borne illnesses from meat, poultry, and egg products	Prevalence of Salmonella on raw meat and poultry products (annual targets expressed as percentage reductions) Percentage of ready–to-eat meat and poultry products testing positive for listeria (annual targets expressed as percentage reductions)
Transportation Department: Railroad safety program	Reduction in transportation-related deaths and injuries	Fewer rail-related accidents and incidents per million train-miles Fewer grade-crossing incidents per million train-miles Fewer train accidents per million train-miles, broken down by cause; human factors, track, and equipment

Source: Wray, Henry, Performance Accountability for Regulations, in Richard Williams (Ed.), *21st Century Regulation: Discovering Better Solutions for Enduring Problems*, Mercatus Center at George Mason University, Arlington, VA, 2009, 30, http://mercatus.org/publication/21st-century-regulation-discovering-better-solutions-enduring-problems.

2. Require Independent Annual Retrospective Cost and Benefit Estimates

Section 5 of Executive Order 12866, Section 610 of the Small Business Regulatory Enforcement Fairness Act, and a variety of agency- or regulation-specific laws require agencies to periodically review existing significant regulations to determine whether they should be modified or eliminated (GAO 2007, 13–16). An expansive interpretation of these requirements would mean agencies should evaluate the costs and benefits of regulations after they have been adopted, regulated entities have complied, and secondary effects have worked their way through the economy. Apparently few agencies have interpreted the language this way, as evidenced by OMB's annual report on the costs and benefits of federal regulations.

To remedy this problem, Section 5 of the executive order should be amended to require agencies to arrange for and publicly release independent annual assessments of the ex post costs and benefits of existing regulations. Such analysis need not be conducted on a regulation-by-regulation basis. It is often possible to group many closely related regulations that aim at the same outcomes and generate the same kinds of costs; indeed, in many cases it may be difficult to identify separate effects of closely related regulations that are already on the books.

An "independent" analysis would be one that satisfies the criteria for independence outlined in OMB guidance:

> To be independent, non-biased parties with no conflict of interest should conduct the evaluation. Evaluations conducted by the program itself should generally not be considered "independent;" however, if the agency or program has contracted out the evaluation to a third party this may qualify as being sufficiently independent. Evaluations conducted by an agency's Inspector General or program-evaluation office would be considered independent. (OMB 2008d)

An annual reporting requirement does not imply that agencies must conduct a *de novo* study of costs and benefits of every regulation every year. If a thorough study occurs in one year and the agency is reasonably confident that underlying conditions have not changed in ways that would significantly alter costs or benefits, then the results of that study should be useful for multiple years. In other cases, certain quantitative relationships used to estimate the effects of the regulations (such as consumer price elasticities of demand) may be relatively stable from year to year, and the agency could update the previous year's study simply by inserting more recent data.

Requiring ex post assessment of costs and benefits of regulations annually would have several benefits. First, the information generated would serve as an input into OMB's annual study of the costs and benefits of regulation, thus permitting OMB to finally produce an annual report consistent with the intent of Congress. Second, periodic retrospective estimates would help agencies assess, and hopefully improve, the accuracy of the prospective estimates they make when considering new regulations. This could occur either because agencies learn specific things that help them better understand how to evaluate similar regulations, or simply because the experience of overseeing ex post evaluations hones the staff's analytical abilities. Third, the requirement would create incentives for regulatory agencies to better integrate regulatory analysis with their strategic planning and performance measurement since they may be able to save a substantial amount of time and effort by devising performance measures for regulations that would track actual cost and benefit outcomes.

Revisions to OMB Circular A-11

Congress required agencies to do strategic planning and performance reporting with the expectation that planning and reporting would lead to better management, different budgeting decisions, and improved performance. Several amendments to Circular A-11 would help ensure that strategic planning and performance reporting live up not only to the letter of GPRA, but to the spirit as well, by incorporating time-tested principles of performance management and regulatory analysis.

1. Require Analysis of Alternatives in Regulatory Strategic Planning and Performance Reporting

GPRA says that agencies must produce strategic plans; it does not explicitly say that agencies must consider alternative ways of achieving desired outcomes. Yet consideration of alternatives is a critical element of sound decision making. "Steer, don't row" was one of the fundamental credos of the reinventing government movement that spawned GPRA (Osborne and Gaebler 1992, 25).

OMB could promote consideration of regulatory alternatives through two changes to Part 6 of Circular A-11. First, the circular should instruct agencies to include in their strategic plans a discussion of the benefits and costs of alternative ways of accomplishing their goals—much like Executive Order 12866 requires agencies to consider a wide range of alternative regulations and alternatives to regulation. Second, the circular should instruct agencies to include in their annual performance reports a discussion of alternative approaches to remedy performance shortfalls (failures to meet goals). Agencies should identify other federal programs that might accomplish the same outcomes more effectively, but they should also be required to consider nonfederal and nongovernmental means of accomplishing the outcomes they failed to achieve.

For regulatory agencies, these changes would effectively clarify the executive order's requirements for consideration of a broad range of alternatives. More importantly, the mandate to evaluate alternatives would be extended to a different level. It would force regulatory agencies to consider alternatives at the broad, strategic level as well as for individual regulations. Because Circular A-11 applies to independent as well as executive agencies, our proposed changes would also encourage independent agencies to consider a wide range of alternatives—something they do not currently have to do unless required by specific legislative mandates.

2. Require Assessment of Costs and Benefits of Regulation in GPRA Performance Reports

Since regulatory agencies accomplish their goals through regulation, they should be expected to understand and report on the results produced by their regulations. A GPRA performance report is the appropriate place for agencies to report on the benefits and costs that resulted from all the regulations that substantially advance their strategic goals. Circular A-11 should require agencies to enumerate in their performance reports the primary regulations or groups of regulations that contribute to the accomplishment of each strategic goal, along with an assessment of outcomes and costs.

If a regulatory agency truly understands how its major regulations or groups of regulations accomplish its goals, this should not be hard to do. As the examples in Table 6.2 imply, if a regulatory agency's strategic goals and measures are outcome-oriented, then these outcomes should be related to (if not identical to) the outcomes its principal regulations are supposed to accomplish. Executive branch agencies should find this requirement easy to comply with if they are also complying with our related proposed change in Executive Order 12866, requiring agencies to report annually on the costs and benefits of their regulations. For independent agencies, this change to Circular A-11 might provide the primary motivation to conduct retrospective analysis.

3. Require Regulatory Agencies to Report on Opportunity Costs

For many types of federal programs, comparing outcomes with the cost to the U.S. Treasury should provide a reasonable means of assessing benefits and costs. But regulation is different. Regulatory agencies accomplish outcomes not by spending federal tax dollars, but by directing citizens to do specific things with their own resources. There is a wide gap between the OMB and SBA estimates of the total cost of regulation, but even the partial OMB estimate amounts to tens of billions of dollars. Therefore, Circular A-11 should explicitly direct agencies to report on the opportunity cost to society of regulations related to their strategic goals, not just their expenditures to promulgate and enforce regulations.

Currently, agencies report performance information in either their annual performance report or in the performance section of their combined performance and accountability reports. They report budgetary cost information in their annual financial report or in the financial section of their combined performance and accountability reports. Identifying the social costs of regulation requires many of the same methods, and is fraught with the same uncertainties, as assessing the outcomes of regulation. Therefore, it is probably more logical to require agencies to report the social cost information with their performance data rather than their financial data.

Encouraging Change

Three tools can encourage compliance with these new requirements. First, OMB could impose budgetary sanctions on agencies that fail to comply. Second, and less draconian, senior executive service contracts can hold managers who are in charge of regulations responsible for the quality of the agency's regulatory analysis. Performance expectations, assessments, and rewards for agency managers who are responsible for developing and implementing outcome-oriented performance metrics for rules should take into account (1) the quality of the goals and measures they produce, (2) the accuracy of performance reporting, and (3) the actions they take in response to reported performance results. Performance expectations and rewards for agency managers of regulatory programs should also be aligned with and structured to achieve the substantive outcome goals and measures to the greatest extent consistent with their individual responsibilities (Wray 2009, 28).

Third, the public comment process for regulations has the potential to create more stakeholder engagement and monitoring than has heretofore occurred with GPRA reports. Stakeholders who participate in regulatory proceedings are already accustomed to furnishing arguments, data, studies, and generally second-guessing every regulatory agency decision. We feel confident that stakeholders would take up the twin challenge of (1) debating desired outcomes and measures when a regulation is proposed and (2) commenting on the regulatory agency's draft GPRA report if the information in the report were more tightly linked to the individual regulations that directly affect stakeholders.

Independent Regulatory Review

The recommendations above could be implemented within the existing framework of OMB regulatory and budget review. Some critics, however, may fear that these changes would give OMB too much power over regulation. Others might reasonably question whether the executive branch would ever take these steps, given that it has not already done so.

An independent regulatory review commission could provide an alternative mechanism to encourage better integration of regulation and performance management. Pennsylvania, for example, has an independent commission that reviews most proposed regulations to determine whether they are consistent with the agency's statutory authority, reflect legislative intent, and are in the public interest. Criteria for determining whether a regulation is in the public interest include the regulation's economic, fiscal, public health, safety, and natural resource impacts. The commission can submit comments and objections when an agency proposes a regulation, and it can return a final regulation to the agency for revisions. It can also review existing regulations to determine whether they are still in the public interest, either on its own initiative or at the recommendation of a state legislator or member of the public (Pennsylvania IRRC 2008). While the Pennsylvania commission focuses on regulatory review functions similar to those performed by OMB, the independent commission model could provide a useful tool for promoting the integration of regulatory analysis and performance management on the federal level.

If Congress believes the executive branch should not—or will not—oversee further integration of regulation and performance management, it could establish a permanent independent commission with responsibility for reviewing proposed regulations and conducting retrospective analysis of existing regulations. Proposed regulations could not move forward until the commission is satisfied that the agency has identified specific outcomes related to the agency's strategic goals that the regulation is likely to accomplish, enumerated indicators that the agency will use to measure the regulation's contribution toward these outcomes, accurately estimated the full cost of the proposed regulation, and made provisions to track and report these outcomes as part of its annual GPRA performance report. The commission could also serve as the independent evaluator that conducts ex post assessments of the benefits and costs of regulations.

Conclusion

Regulation and spending programs are two alternative ways federal agencies seek to accomplish their goals. Comprehensive disclosure and informed decision making require that policymakers and the public have access to information on the outcomes and full costs associated with both of these policy tools.

Currently, agency GPRA reports show the results of spending programs and some regulations, and some of these reports link this information with expenditure data. But the costs that regulation imposes on individuals, organizations, Indian tribes, and other levels of government are not systematically reported or linked to outcomes achieved in agency performance reports. A big reason is that benefits and costs of regulations are predicted when they are adopted but rarely rigorously evaluated ex post.

The executive branch has the ability and the tools to substantially improve disclosure of regulatory outcomes. OMB could facilitate improvement in the analysis of regulatory outcomes by revising Executive Order 12866 and Circular A-11 to mandate more extensive retrospective analysis of regulations and tighter linkage of individual regulations to the agency's overall strategic goals. If Congress does not want OMB to have this much authority, it could establish an independent regulatory review commission to promote integration of regulatory analysis and performance management. Such changes would begin the process of bringing GPRA-style accountability to federal regulatory activity.

Chapter 7

Tax Expenditures— The Silent Partner

GPRA's focus on outcome measurement and performance budgeting seeks to match up federal expenditures with the results they produce for citizens. But sometimes the federal government sacrifices revenue to provide tax breaks for citizens who spend money in ways that accomplish public purposes. The lost revenue is like an expenditure that should be justified based on the outcomes it produces.

Accountability for the outcomes of such tax expenditures, however, is virtually nonexistent on the federal level in the United States. Each year, the congressional Joint Tax Committee and an appendix to the president's budget calculate the revenues forgone from tax expenditures, but tax expenditures are not evaluated like spending programs or compared with spending programs that aim to achieve similar results. Thus, even a good performance budget that matches direct federal expenditures with outcomes will underestimate both the costs of government and the outcomes it achieves. Tax expenditures usually fly under the radar screen, receiving even less scrutiny than spending.

As policymakers seek to cope with the U.S. government's fiscal problems, tax expenditures will likely appear on the table as a source of budgetary savings. But at the current time, the federal government is poorly equipped to make informed decisions about tax expenditures, because it knows little about their actual effectiveness in accomplishing desired outcomes. Until tax expenditures are subjected to the type of analysis envisioned by GPRA, decision makers who want to eliminate or reform tax expenditures will be flying blind.

Defining Tax Expenditures

A *tax expenditure* occurs when a taxpayer receives a deduction, credit, or other tax reduction in exchange for spending money or otherwise using resources in ways the government has decided to encourage. Familiar examples of tax expenditures include deductions for home mortgage interest and charitable contributions, as well as tax credits for purchasing energy-efficient appliances. Sometimes the government employs tax expenditures to increase compensation of its own employees, instead of simply paying them more money. For example, military housing, meals, and some types of combat pay are exempt from income tax; so are certain parking and mass transit expenses federal agencies pay for their employees.

What Counts as a Tax Expenditure?

A fuzzy line separates some tax expenditures from more general tax policy. It seems clear, for example, that the deduction for charitable contributions is a tax expenditure that encourages people to donate money to charities. It also seems clear that a decision to raise or lower income tax rates is a decision about general tax policy, not a tax expenditure. But some ostensible tax expenditures might alternatively be viewed as general tax policy. For example, OMB has categorized the revenue loss from the child tax credit as a tax expenditure under the category of education, training, employment, and social services (OMB 1998, 92; 2007a, 288).

Realistically, though, the child credit might be more accurately viewed simply as a redistributive measure intended to allow parents to shield more income from tax, rather than a tax expenditure that encourages parents to have more children or educate them more extensively.*

Reduced tax rates on capital gains from the sale of securities or other assets provide another timely and controversial example. The budgets from the two most recent administrations reflect differing points of view. The Bush administration argued that differential tax rates for dividends and capital gains on corporate equity do not constitute tax expenditures, because they make the income tax rate on equity capital (33% corporate rate plus individual income tax rate) more nearly equal to the tax rate on other forms of income. Starting in 2005, OMB stopped counting the forgone revenues from these tax rates on corporate equity as tax expenditures (OMB 2007a, 299). The Obama administration's first budget referred to the capital gains and dividend rates as "preferentially low rates" and provided an alternative estimate of the tax expenditure calculated under the pre-2005 method (OMB 2009b, 311, 318).

---

* However, we note that one author's spouse did give birth to a child roughly nine months after both parents attended a seminar with congressional staff in 1997, where it became quite apparent that Congress would enact a substantial child tax credit that year. We leave it to the reader to assess whether correlation implies causation.

These examples highlight a more general point. We cannot know what counts as a tax expenditure without first defining some baseline tax system. One possible baseline is a comprehensive income tax that taxes all income only once. Another is a comprehensive consumption tax. The federal government calculates most tax expenditures using an income tax baseline called the normal tax baseline, which differs somewhat from a pure comprehensive income tax. In some cases, the Treasury Department employs yet another baseline called the reference tax law, an income tax baseline that is closer to the actual U.S. income tax. We take no position on the most appropriate baseline but refer the reader to sources such as OMB (2009b, 296–97), the Joint Committee on Taxation (2008), Burman (2003), Carroll et al. (2008), and Hall (2009) for a more detailed discussion of tax expenditure baselines.

Although reasonable people using different baselines may disagree over whether certain provisions of the tax code belong in the tax expenditure bucket, we should not lose sight of the larger point that the federal government directs substantial private resources toward specific ends via tax policy. Many large and popular tax expenditures count as exceptions under just about any baseline.

Criticism of the Term

Some policy commentators object to the term *tax expenditure* on rhetorical and philosophical grounds. They argue that the term improperly implies that every citizen's income is property of the federal government, and hence any decision to reduce taxes is an "expenditure." A 1999 report issued by the vice chairman of the congressional Joint Economic Committee expressed this view succinctly: "The tax expenditure concept relies heavily on a normative notion that shielding certain taxpayer income from taxation deprives the government of its rightful revenues. This view is inconsistent with the proposition that income belongs to taxpayers and that tax liability is determined through the democratic process, not through arbitrary, bureaucratic assumptions" (Hall 1999). This is not a new argument. In an 1863 British parliamentary debate over tax exemptions for charitable contributions, Sir Strafford Northcote offered this retort to a speaker who sought to account for the exemption as if it were an expenditure: "The Right Hon. Gentleman, if he took £5 out of the pocket of a man with £100, put the case as if he gave the man £95" (quoted in Burman 2003, 620).

Related normative concerns stem from the fact that one's choice of baseline affects what items count as tax expenditures. Different items may receive scrutiny depending on which baseline one chooses. A heavily value-laden judgment about whether the ideal tax system should be based on income or consumption could masquerade as a neutral or technical expert decision about the baseline.

While we sympathize with these concerns, we continue to use the term *tax expenditures* because it highlights our concern about these tax provisions that is most relevant to performance management. Giving a taxpayer a tax reduction in return for using resources in ways the government prefers is a substitute for explicit spending (Gandhi 2010). As Burman (2003, 621) notes, "Even those who believe that lower taxes and smaller government are always a good thing should care about tax expenditures, because the revenues lost to such programs could be used for other purposes—such as lowering tax rates." If the government does not account for the costs and outcomes of these tax breaks, decision makers cannot know whether tax expenditures are more or less effective than spending to accomplish similar objectives. The absence of transparency makes it much more difficult for citizens to hold policymakers accountable for their decisions.

Tax Expenditures Are Big

The total cost of tax expenditures in terms of forgone revenue is enormous and growing. GAO (2005c, 25) reported that the size of inflation-adjusted tax expenditures tripled over the previous three decades, from $240 billion in 1974 to $730 billion in 2004. Figure 7.1 shows the estimated cost of various categories of tax expenditures in fiscal years 1999 and 2008, the time period covered by our *Performance Report Scorecard*. All estimates are from the tax expenditures chapter of the *Analytical*

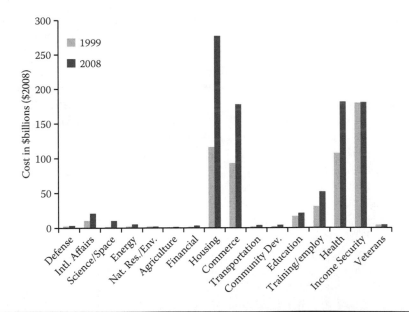

Figure 7.1 Categories of tax expenditures. (Source: Authors' calculations based on data in U.S. Office of Management and Budget, *Budget of the United States Government, Fiscal Year 1999, Analytical Perspectives,* 1998; U.S. Office of Management and Budget, *Budget of the United States Government, Fiscal Year 2008, Analytical Perspectives,* 2007.)

Perspectives volume of the president's budget for these two years. In a few cases, we have combined some categories, recategorized some tax expenditures, or removed those that seem more related to general tax policy.*

Four broad categories account for the vast majority of tax expenditures:

■ Housing ($277 billion in fiscal year 2008): The U.S. tax code heavily subsidizes owner-occupied housing. By far the largest amounts in this category are the deduction for mortgage interest on owner-occupied homes ($89 billion), the deduction for state and local property taxes on owner-occupied homes ($12.6 billion), the capital gains exclusion on owner-occupied home sales ($39 billion), and the exclusion of imputed rental income on owner-occupied homes ($36 billion). These figures are all from 2008, at the height of the U.S. housing boom, but the graph reveals that even in 1999, housing was the second largest category of tax expenditures.

■ Income security ($181 billion in fiscal year 2008): This category combines two categories in the *Analytical Perspectives* volume that both relate to income security. First is a $28 billion revenue loss because some types of social security benefits are excluded from income for tax purposes. By far the largest chunk of the tax expenditure occurs due to the deferral of taxes on pension contributions and retirement savings plans, which cost $111 billion in 2008.

■ Health ($181 billion in fiscal year 2008): Almost all of this figure—$166 billion—reflects the deductibility of medical insurance paid by employers or self-employed individuals.

■ Commerce ($178 billion in fiscal year 2008): Most of this figure reflects favorable tax treatment of capital gains or depreciation rules that depart from the normal tax code for specific industries or situations. We have already discussed the controversy over whether capital gains rates are a tax expenditure or part of broader tax policy. Depreciation likewise is a highly complex topic. The purpose of depreciation rules in a tax system is to accurately define the cost of capital used by businesses, so that a business pays taxes only on revenue that genuinely reflects income, not merely a return of its original investment. Some or all of these provisions may not really be tax expenditures, but rather attempts to more accurately define the true costs associated with capital employed in various business activities. The economic arguments about capital gains and depreciation rules are far outside the scope of this book, so we report these commerce-related numbers but accompany them with a caveat.

---

* To the "income security" category, we added tax expenditures associated with social security and with exclusion of interest paid in life insurance policies, since life insurance is obviously related to income security and many people use life insurance as a tax-deferred savings vehicle. Exclusion of interest paid in life insurance policies was subtracted from tax expenditures related to the financial industry. We excluded the child tax credit from the education category (1999) or the training, employment, and social services category (2008), since this credit is more an issue of general tax policy.

The number of tax expenditures reported by the Treasury Department more than doubled between 1974 and 1984, from 67 to 146 (GAO 2005c, 5–6). That number rose to 161 by 2008 (OMB 2007a, 287). The four categories listed above account for about 36 of the 161 tax expenditures listed by the Treasury Department for 2008. Many of the more obscure ones likely fly completely under the radar, understood only by their congressional sponsors and private sector recipients.

Simply adding up the estimated revenue loss from individual tax expenditures may not create an accurate picture of the total cost. A simple summation ignores economic incentive effects and interactions by which the size of one tax expenditure might affect the size of others (OMB 2007a, 285–86; Joint Committee on Taxation 2008, 14). Poterba and Sinai (2008), for example, calculate that eliminating the tax deductibility of home mortgage interest would generate less revenue than the government estimates, because many homeowners would choose to carry less mortgage debt and keep more equity in their homes. The increase in home equity would come at the expense of taxable investments like stocks and bonds. Similarly, Metcalf (2008) finds that eliminating the deductibility of state and local taxes would generate less federal revenue than Treasury or Joint Tax Committee estimates imply. If individuals' state and local taxes are not deductible, these governments would in part substitute taxes and fees paid by businesses. These would reduce federal business tax revenues by increasing business costs, thus reducing taxable business income. More generally, OMB (2008c, 288) notes that repeal of one itemized deduction might reduce the revenue losses associated with others by inducing some taxpayers to utilize the standard deduction instead of itemizing. For example, if the home mortgage interest deduction were eliminated, many more taxpayers might choose the standard deduction because it would be larger than their remaining itemized deductions.

Though summing the tax expenditure estimates does not accurately measure the revenue loss, it does provide a rough idea of how much resource allocation the federal government accomplishes through tax expenditures (GAO 2005c, 21). Tax expenditures totaled approximately $981 billion in fiscal year 2008. Converted to 2008 dollars to adjust for inflation, fiscal year 1999 tax expenditures totaled approximately $598 billion.

To put these numbers in perspective, federal expenditures totaled $2.9 trillion in fiscal year 2008 and $1.7 trillion in fiscal year 1999 (OMB 2008a, Table 1.1). Therefore, federal tax expenditures equaled about 35% of federal on-budget expenditures. In most years since 1980, outlay-equivalent tax expenditures have exceeded federal discretionary spending.* They have equaled approximately 7.6% of the gross domestic product since the major tax reform of 1986 last pared them back.

---

* Outlay-equivalent tax expenditure is the federal outlay that would be required to provide taxpayers with the same after-tax income they receive as a result of the tax expenditure.

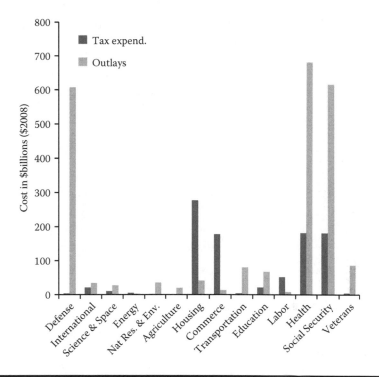

Figure 7.2 Tax expenditures vs. outlays 2008. (Source: Authors' calculations based on data in U.S. Office of Management and Budget, *Budget of the United States Government, Fiscal Year 2008, Analytical Perspectives,* **2007; U.S. Office of Management and Budget,** *Budget of the United States Government, Fiscal Year 2009, Historical Tables,* **2008.)**

Another way to assess the magnitude of tax expenditures is to compare them with on-budget expenditures that appear related to similar outcomes. Figure 7.2 compares tax expenditures in 2008 with outlays on federal functions that seek to accomplish related outcomes. Several results stand out.

In three cases, tax expenditures exceed federal expenditures on similar functions. Tax expenditures related to owner-occupied housing ($277 billion) are more than six times as large as the entire outlays on housing credit and housing assistance ($41.3 billion). Tax expenditures related to commerce ($178 billion) far exceed outlays spent to promote commerce ($13.6 billion), but that's largely because these tax expenditures include those that stem from differential capital gains rates and most accelerated depreciation. Finally, tax expenditures related to job training, employment, and social services ($52 billion) exceed outlays on training, employment, and other labor services ($8.6 billion). This occurs largely because OMB throws most of the tax expenditures related to charitable deductions into the "social services" category; these totaled $45.8 billion in 2008. Thus, housing is the one area in which vast tax expenditures clearly outweigh direct federal expenditures that arguably seek to accomplish related outcomes.

In two other areas—health and income security—direct federal expenditures by the Department of Health and Human Services and the Social Security Administration exceed tax expenditures substantially. However, the sheer size of the tax expenditures in both of these categories still makes them noteworthy. Other federal functions whose tax expenditures are nonnegligible compared to outlays include international affairs, science and space, energy, and education.

A more granular analysis that broke all programs and tax expenditures down by specific outcome would likely identify numerous clusters of areas where tax expenditures are substantial compared to outlays on programs that seek to accomplish similar outcomes. The total size of tax expenditures, as well as their size in relation to agency budgets, provides a strong argument for rigorously assessing their outcomes and comparing them to similar spending programs.

Assessment of Tax Expenditures

In principle, there is no reason one could not identify and measure the outcomes of tax expenditures in the same way the results of spending programs can be analyzed. "Although isolating and quantifying the outcomes associated with tax expenditures is challenging—just as it is for spending programs, research results are useful in demonstrating how particular tax expenditures work or providing insight on ways to refine their design" (GAO 2005c, 56).

Just as with spending programs, meaningful assessment requires accurate definition of genuine outcomes that benefit the public. The analysis must distinguish between inputs (federal revenue forgone and private expenditures that occur as a result of the tax break), outputs (products or services produced), and outcomes (concrete changes that improve citizens' quality of life). For example, some studies sought to assess the effects of the research tax credit by estimating the amount of research spending stimulated per dollar of revenue lost. Research spending, however, is an input, not an outcome. If the tax credit stimulates research spending that creates little or no value for the public, it generates social waste; indeed, the more low-value research it stimulates, the more of society's resources it wastes. The relevant outcomes that should be measured are the social benefits created by the research, such as new products, productivity increases, or cost reductions that would not have occurred in the absence of the tax expenditure (GAO 2005c, 57).

Academic public finance contributes numerous findings that help identify the effects of tax expenditures. In 2008, the National Bureau of Economic Research sponsored a conference that showcased some of the latest research. Desai et al. (2008) consider whether tax credits for investors in low-income housing provide low-income housing more effectively and efficiently than vouchers. Bakija and Heim (2008) estimate how the tax deduction for charitable giving affects the amount of charitable giving, concluding that high-income taxpayers are very responsive to the deduction. Poterba and Sinai (2008) estimate how the tax deduction for mortgage interest and property taxes affects the cost of homeownership. Deductibility of state and local taxes was intended to stimulate state and local spending on projects and services that might have spillover benefits for other jurisdictions, but Metcalf (2008) finds little evidence that this deduction produced such benefits. Eissa and Hoynes (2008) discuss the effects of the earned income tax credit on the number of families in poverty and labor force participation by single mothers.

Decades' worth of references cited in these papers demonstrate that evaluation of tax expenditures has become a robust subspecialty in the economics of public finance. Government analysts could gain a great deal of insight about the outcomes of tax expenditures by updating publicly available research that has already been conducted using already available data. We illustrate this by briefly reviewing some research relevant to the largest set of U.S. tax expenditures: those related to owner-occupied housing.

Owner-Occupied Housing: A Case Study

Owner-occupied housing benefits from four main tax expenditures: deductibility of mortgage interest and property taxes, little or no taxation of capital gains, and no taxation of net imputed rental income. Net imputed rental income is most easily understood by comparing home ownership to renting. A landlord receives a tenant's rent as gross income. To determine taxable income each year, the landlord subtracts mortgage interest, property taxes, maintenance expenses, and depreciation. A landlord who sells a property might also receive a taxable capital gain. To determine the taxable capital gain, the landlord starts with the sales price, subtracts the price he paid for the property, adds any depreciation claimed in prior years, and subtracts the cost of any improvements.

Similarly, a homeowner receives a stream of services from the house, and these services have an implicit rental value. This value is the gross imputed rental income. If the tax code treated landlords and owners the same, the homeowner would have to pay tax each year on the difference between the gross rental value of the house and the mortgage interest, property taxes, maintenance expenses, and depreciation. When selling the house, the homeowner would calculate and pay tax on a capital gain the same way a landlord would. Under current U.S. law, the homeowner does not pay any tax on the net imputed rental income. Most mortgage interest and taxes can be deducted against other income. Most capital gains on owner-occupied housing are not taxed, because the owner can receive $250,000 in capital gains tax-free when selling a home he or she has lived in for two of the past five years. The figure is $500,000 for a married couple.

These tax expenditures reduce the cost of owning compared to renting. The actual value of the tax expenditures depends on the taxpayer's circumstances. The value of the tax expenditure—and hence the subsidy for homeownership—is higher for taxpayers who face higher marginal tax rates. This also means that the overall value of the tax expenditures is higher when the tax system generally imposes higher marginal tax rates. Across-the-board rate reductions, such as those that occurred in 1981 and 1986, reduced the subsidy and increased the cost of owning compared to renting. In addition, increases in the standard deduction eliminate the subsidy associated with the interest and property tax deductions for homeowners whose total itemized deductions are smaller than the standard deduction.

One of the major arguments for the four tax expenditures related to owner-occupied housing is that they increase homeownership, and homeownership generates spillover benefits for society. Glaeser and Shapiro (2003, 64–72) summarize many of the benefits for which researchers have found empirical evidence. Homeowners are much more likely to garden and maintain their homes, which also benefits neighbors. Homeowners are more likely to be knowledgeable about local politics and vote in local elections, and they tend to favor policies that bring long-term benefits to their neighborhoods. There is also some evidence that children of homeowners are less likely to drop out of school. Thus, a simple "logic model" would thus posit that:

1. The tax expenditures reduce the cost of owning relative to renting.
2. Reducing the cost of owning relative to renting produces the intermediate outcome of increased homeownership.
3. Increased homeownership produces various social benefits, which are the ultimate outcomes.

These hypotheses are not difficult to test. The federal government already reports the rate of homeownership. For performance reporting purposes, changes in homeownership attributable to the tax expenditures could be a workable intermediate outcome to track. Economic research has already addressed the effects of the tax expenditures on homeownership and the effects of homeownership on spillover benefits for society.

Table 7.1 summarizes major studies that have quantified the relationship between tax expenditures on owner-occupied housing and the rate of homeownership. Earlier studies tend to show larger effects. This probably occurs because the real value of the subsidy was higher prior to the tax reforms of 1981 and 1986, which slashed marginal rates. Between 1980 and 1990, the user cost of housing for middle-income households increased slightly, but the cost for a household making $250,000 almost tripled due to a reduction in its marginal tax rate from 59% in 1980 to 28% in 1990 (Poterba 1992, 238). Consistent with this observation, Rosen's (1979) simulation for 1970 finds that the tax expenditures increased home-ownership among lower-income homeowners, who face lower marginal tax rates, by only 2.6%, compared to an average of 4.4% for all taxpayers. This is because taxpayers facing lower marginal tax rates receive less of a subsidy. Thus, the effect of the tax expenditures on the relative price of homeownership for middle- and

Table 7.1   Tax Expenditures and Homeownership

Authors	Year	Increase in Homeownership (percentage points)	Notes
Harvey S. Rosen	1979	4.4	Uses cross-sectional data from 1970
Harvey S. Rosen and Kenneth T. Rosen	1980	4.0	Uses time-series data from 1949–1974.
Patric H. Hendershott and James D. Shilling	1982	6–7	Uses time series data from 1995–1979
Harvey S. Rosen, Kenneth T. Rosen, and Douglas Holtz-Eakin	1984	0.4	Estimates effect of mortgage interest and property tax deduction only
Edward Glaeser and Jesse Shapiro	2003	None	

upper-middle-income households today is likely to be similar to the effects on lower-income households in the 1970s.

The most recent study showing a statistically significant result finds that the special tax treatment of owner-occupied housing increases homeownership by about four-tenths of 1% (0.004). Given that there were approximately 75 million homeowners in the United States in 2008 (HUD 2010, Exhibit 25), that implies the tax expenditures for mortgage interest and the property tax deduction may have increased homeownership by about 300,000 units. OMB estimated that the tax expenditures for home mortgage interest and property taxes would cost $111 billion in fiscal year 2008. That works out to a cost of about $370,000 *annually* per additional homeowner created by the tax expenditures. OMB's estimates surely overstate the revenue cost of the mortgage interest deduction to the U.S. Treasury, because if homeowners could not deduct mortgage interest, they would use more equity to purchase homes and forego taxable income from other investments. Poterba and Sinai (2008) estimate that because of these behavioral changes, repeal of the mortgage interest deduction would raise 14% less revenue than one might expect. Even after adjusting for incentive effects, the tax expenditures for owner-occupied housing appear to be an expensive way to promote homeownership.

Is the increase in homeownership worth the cost to the U.S. Treasury? One ingenious study addresses the link between homeownership and spillover benefits by estimating the effect of changes in the homeownership rate on the value of other properties in the same neighborhood (Glaeser and Shapiro 2003). The authors find that a 1% increase in homeownership is associated with a 0.25–0.47% increase in the value of neighboring homes. This finding allows us to estimate the value of the social benefits created by the housing tax expenditures. A 0.4 percentage point increase in homeownership prompted by the tax expenditures would increase home values by between one-tenth and two-tenths of 1%. The Federal Reserve's *Flow of Funds* report lists the total value of owner-occupied real estate in 2008 as $17 trillion. A 0.4 percentage point increase in homeownership thus implies a total increase in housing values of between $17 billion and $34 billion.* The *total* value of the benefits created by the tax expenditures for mortgage interest and property taxes ($17–34 billion) may be less than the *annual* cost ($111 billion).

Policymakers might use this information about outcomes and costs in various ways. Perhaps the figures suggest that the housing tax expenditures really aren't worth the costs and should be scrapped. Or perhaps their cost-effectiveness could be improved by eliminating some aspects that appear to do little to promote homeownership, such as deductibility of mortgage interest on second homes or on home equity loans. Or perhaps the benefits could be targeted more narrowly to lower-income taxpayers, who might be more likely to become homeowners as a result of the tax savings. As with spending programs, the information about outcomes and cost-effectiveness is just an input into the decision; it does not dictate the decision.

Of course, to inform today's policy decisions, the studies on tax expenditures and homeownership should be updated with more recent data to assess the effects of current U.S. policy. A study like Rosen's (1979), which uses one year of cross-sectional data, could be updated regularly using the most recent year's worth of data. Other study designs use multiple years of data; these too could be updated as new data become available. We point to these existing studies merely to demonstrate that scholars already have found ways to gather relevant data and quantify the relationship between tax expenditures, homeownership, and some of the ultimate outcomes believed to flow from homeownership.

Outcomes of Tax Expenditures Not Systematically Measured

GPRA does not explicitly mention tax expenditures. The Senate Governmental Affairs Committee's report on GPRA indicates that the committee expected the Office of Management and Budget to take the lead in assessing outcomes associated with them:

> To increase significantly the oversight and analysis of tax expenditures, the Committee believes that the annual overall Federal Government

---

* One-tenth of 1% (0.001) × $17 trillion = $17 billion. Two-tenths of 1% (0.002) × $17 trillion = $34 billion.

performance plans should include a schedule for periodically assessing the effects of specific tax expenditures in achieving performance goals. (This schedule would be in addition to the primary content of the overall plan—the program performance goals tied to the direct expenditure of funds.) The Committee expects that annual performance reports would subsequently be used to report on these tax expenditure assessments. These assessments should consider the relationship and interactions between spending programs and related tax expenditures. The Committee hopes that such reports will foster a greater sense of responsibility for tax expenditures with a direct bearing on substantial missions and goals. (Senate Committee on Governmental Affairs 1993, 27–28).

The comprehensive analysis of tax expenditures that the Senate Governmental Affairs Committee (now the Senate Committee on Homeland Security and Governmental Affairs) sought never materialized. The tax expenditure section in the *Analytical Perspectives* volume of the president's annual budget does discuss the costs of tax expenditures and acknowledge congressional expectations about outcome reporting.

The first such discussion occurred in President Clinton's proposed fiscal year 1997 budget, issued three years after GPRA and three years before agencies' first performance reports were due. The brief discussion succinctly defines the inputs, outputs, and outcomes attributable to tax expenditures:

In the case of tax expenditures, the principal input is likely to be the tax revenue loss. Outputs are quantitative or qualitative measures of goods or services, or changes in income and investment, directly attributable to these inputs. Outcomes, in turn, represent the changes in the economy, society, or environment that are the ultimate goals of programs. (OMB 1996, 74)

The document states: "OMB and the Department of the Treasury have started to develop a framework for evaluating the performance and economic effects of tax expenditures" (OMB 1996, 73). Four paragraphs suggest outcomes that some prominent tax expenditures seek to achieve. Tax expenditures for retirement savings, for example, could be evaluated to see if they increase retirement savings. The mortgage interest deduction and preferential treatment of capital gains on housing could be evaluated to see how they affect homeownership and the quality of housing (OMB 1996, 73). The Clinton administration's fiscal 1998 budget offers a slightly longer explanation with a few more examples of possible outcomes from tax expenditures, but largely just pledges to work on the issue (OMB 1997, 85–86).

President Clinton's fiscal year 1999 budget is the first to cite the Senate Governmental Affairs Committee's report. It also reports on three pilot studies conducted by the Treasury Department in 1997 to explore evaluation methods. The tax expenditures studied were the tax exemption for worker's compensation benefits, the tax credit for nonconventional fuels, and the tax exclusion for some income of Americans living abroad. Treasury found that the effects of the exemption for worker's compensation benefits are uncertain, in part because states may have considered the tax exemption when setting benefit levels (OMB 1997, 117). For nonconventional fuels, OMB notes that the tax expenditure stimulated production of domestic coal bed methane, but this production probably just displaced other domestic production or imports from stable suppliers like Canada, so it had little effect on energy security (OMB 1997, 110). For Americans living abroad, Treasury identified who benefits but did not report how well the tax expenditure achieved outcomes (OMB 1997, 109). "One finding of the pilot studies is that much of the data needed for thorough analysis is not currently available." For this reason, assessment of data needs and availability would receive high priority (OMB 1998, 105). Although tax expenditures represent billions of dollars of forgone revenues annually, the federal government did not systematically gather the data needed to evaluate their effectiveness. For the first time, the fiscal year 1999 budget offered a two-page list of conceptual evaluation issues broken down by budget function, plus a one-page discussion of the pros and cons of tax expenditures, direct outlays, and regulations as alternative policy tools (OMB 1998, 105–8).

President Clinton's fiscal year 2000 budget pledged to assess the availability of data needed to identify beneficiaries and assess effects of specific tax expenditures, mostly focused on those intended to increase savings. It repeated the two-page list of evaluation issues and the comparison of tax expenditures, outlays, and regulations presented the previous year (OMB 1999, 121–24). The fiscal year 2001 budget largely repeated the prior year's language, adding that the Treasury Department would develop a new panel data set that would follow the same taxpayers over time, which should aid in assessing the effects of tax expenditures intended to increase savings (OMB 2000, 124). Burman (2003, 624) sums up the experience of those years: "Clinton's Treasury Department, of which I was a part from 1998 to 2000, was unenthusiastic about performing these evaluations, reasoning that a comprehensive evaluation of tax expenditures would necessarily raise serious objections to measures enthusiastically advanced by the administration." He notes that the Bush administration brought no change in this treatment of tax expenditures.

President Bush's first full budget, for fiscal year 2002, announced that "the Executive Branch is continuing to focus on the availability of data needed to assess the effects of the tax expenditures designed to increase savings." It provided a brief update on Treasury's panel data sample, noting that it would start with returns filed for 1999. The discussion of conceptual evaluation issues and comparison of tax expenditures, outlays, and regulations were repeated again (OMB 2001c, 77–81). The discussion remained largely unchanged in the fiscal year 2003–2007 budgets, except to note that Treasury had now drawn the panel sample from tax year 1999 returns (OMB 2002a, 113–16; 2003b, 116–19; 2004, 300–3; 2005b, 332–35; 2006, 299–302). Each year, OMB assured the public that "other efforts by OMB, Treasury, and other agencies to improve data available for the analysis of savings tax expenditures will continue over the next several years" (see, e.g., OMB 2006, 299).

In the Bush administration's fiscal 2008 budget, the section on performance measurement and tax expenditures concluded with the now-customary boilerplate statement that "as indicated above, over the next few years the Executive Branch's focus will be on the availability of the data needed to assess the effects of the tax expenditures designed to increase savings" (OMB 2007a, 327). This language originated in the Clinton administration's fiscal year 2001 budget and has been repeated every year since (OMB 2000, 127). However, the fiscal 2008 budget no longer contained the description of the savings data-gathering initiative that was supposedly "indicated above." The Bush administration's final budget, for fiscal year 2009, continued to omit the description of the savings analysis but repeated the final sentence that assures the reader the topic was discussed earlier (OMB 2008c, 328). The Obama administration's fiscal year 2010 and 2011 budgets continued both the repetition and the omission (OMB 2009b, 326–29; 2010b, 240–43).

Based on this record, 1997 appears to be the high-water mark for analysis of tax expenditure outcomes by the executive branch. In that year, the Treasury Department found that one tax expenditure probably failed to achieve the intended outcome, and results of the other two it examined were either uncertain or unknown. In the ensuing 13 years, administrations have pledged to evaluate tax expenditures related to savings, but thus far the only progress appears to be the gathering of panel data. GAO's conclusions still ring true today:

> Since their initial efforts to outline a framework for evaluating tax expenditures and preliminary performance measures, OMB and Treasury have largely ceased to make progress and have retreated from setting a schedule for evaluating tax expenditures. (GAO 2005c, 58)
>
> Over the past decade … the executive branch has made little progress in integrating tax expenditures into the budget presentation, in developing a structure for evaluating the performance of tax expenditures, or in incorporating tax expenditures under review processes that apply to spending programs, as we recommended in 1994. (GAO 2005c, 5)

Annual administration discussions of tax expenditure outcome analysis have largely consisted of boilerplate lists of conceptual issues to be addressed, with little actual progress reported. Indeed, during the past few years, not even the boilerplate appears to have been edited carefully. Thus, accountability for large revenue losses is quite poor.

Evaluating Tax Expenditures: A Proposed Division of Labor

Aside from availability of data, a key obstacle to better outcome analysis of tax expenditures appears to be lack of clear roles and responsibilities.

Within the executive branch, three possible candidates could be responsible for evaluating and reporting the outcomes of tax expenditures: OMB, which has responsibility for overseeing GPRA implementation; Treasury, which oversees tax policy and has access to confidential tax data; or the other executive branch agencies, whose programs sometimes seek to achieve goals similar to those achieved by tax expenditures and who may have personnel with relevant analytical expertise. Obviously, each has important expertise to contribute.

As OMB's response to GAO's 2005 recommendations on tax expenditures illustrates, the problem is not just unclear roles and responsibilities, but conflicting opinions on who should have what roles and responsibilities. GAO recommended that OMB should develop a framework for evaluating tax expenditures, and agencies that administer programs should incorporate related tax expenditures into their GPRA planning, evaluations, and reports. OMB countered that the Treasury Department is in the best position to take the lead in analysis and reporting, because Treasury has responsibility for administering the tax code and access to confidential tax data (GAO 2005c, 82–91).

We suggest the following would be a reasonable division of responsibility that utilizes each entity's expertise appropriately:

1. OMB should take responsibility for articulating an overall framework, plan, and timetable for assessing the outcomes of important tax expenditures. OMB would also facilitate agreement between the Treasury Department and other departments as to the precise role each would play in the analysis of each tax expenditure. Finally, as the entity responsible for the federal government's overall strategic plan and annual report, OMB would coordinate any administration comparisons of tax expenditures with similar spending programs and communicate in the budget any administration recommendations to substitute one for the other.
2. Responsibility for conducting the analysis would be decided for each tax expenditure on a case-by-case basis, depending on the data and expertise needed and available in each agency. In cases where tax data and tax policy expertise are paramount, Treasury might have responsibility for the analysis. In cases where knowledge of specific industries or programs is relatively more important, other departments might take the lead. Of course, various forms of collaboration might also be possible, such as vesting responsibility for analysis of a tax expenditure in Treasury but detailing employees from another department with unique expertise to Treasury to participate in the analysis.

3. As the administrator of the tax code, the Treasury Department would have primary responsibility for reporting the outcomes and costs of all tax expenditures in its GPRA report. Departments that administer related programs and want to include outcome information for related tax expenditures in their GPRA reports would be free to do so.

Conclusion

Our call for performance evaluation of tax expenditures is hardly new. Stanley Surrey, the assistant secretary of the Treasury who introduced the term *tax expenditures* in 1967, hoped that explicit identification of their size would promote "expenditure control" by prompting increased accountability for their results (Joint Committee on Taxation 2008, 3). Thus far, Surrey's hope has not been realized.

There are several reasons. Because tax expenditures are under the jurisdiction of the tax-writing committees and spending is under the jurisdiction of the appropriations committees, Congress does not have an institutional mechanism that forces members to compare the effectiveness of appropriations and tax expenditures that seek to accomplish similar goals. In addition, the lower level of transparency associated with tax expenditures often makes it easier to gain approval of a tax expenditure than an appropriation. Extending GPRA-style analysis to tax expenditures would not solve the jurisdictional problem, but it would surely improve the transparency of disclosure about the results these tax breaks actually do (or don't) achieve.

Chapter 8

GPRA and Performance Management within Agencies

One of GPRA's major purposes was to improve federal managers' ability to manage their programs and activities by providing them with information about results. Has this actually occurred?

Case studies document numerous specific instances in which federal agencies have developed measures of intermediate or final outcomes and used those measures to make decisions. In addition, periodic Government Accountability Office (GAO) surveys have asked federal managers whether they have and use various types of performance indicators. These surveys help identify whether the case studies show typical results that occur widely across the federal government, or isolated exceptions. Survey data suggest that GPRA has indeed improved the availability and use of performance information within federal agencies. Several studies also show that the quality of agencies' GPRA initiatives is correlated with variables that measure perceived performance or the availability and use of performance information. Thus, the available evidence suggests that GPRA has indeed improved the availability and use of the kinds of performance information contemplated by GPRA.

What Should Be Measured, and Why?

GPRA requires federal agencies to develop strategic plans and performance indicators that measure outputs, service levels, and outcomes (GPRA Sec. 4b, 1115). Its statement of purpose includes "promoting a new focus on results, service quality, and customer satisfaction" (GPRA Sec. 2b), which suggests that measures of service quality and customer satisfaction might also be desirable. But the legislation does not simply promulgate measurement for measurement's sake. Its ultimate goal is to "improve federal program effectiveness and public accountability" (GPRA Sec. 2b). In the words of Kamensky, Morales, and Abramson (2005), the objective is not just "useful measures," but "measures used."

This chapter seeks to determine whether GPRA has made a difference by examining case studies and surveys that show whether federal managers have and use the types of performance measures contemplated in GPRA. Periodic Government Accountability Office surveys ask federal managers whether they have and use these kinds of performance measures:

- Outcomes: Direct results achieved through the provision of goods and services by the organization.
- Outputs: Products or services produced, distributed, or provided to service population.
- Efficiency: Cost per unit, productivity measures, ratios of direct to indirect costs, etc. (The 1991 survey refers to these measures as operating ratios.)
- Customer satisfaction: Measures of quality and timeliness from external sources.
- Quality: Measures of quality from internal sources (GAO 1992, 23).

Availability and use of these measures may be a necessary condition for performance improvement, but it is not a sufficient condition. The five categories hardly exhaust the list of measures that could be useful and used. Measures that link outcomes with costs, equity measures, and individual performance measures are also critical for improving government performance.

Measures That Link Outcomes with Costs

GPRA promotes a long-overdue focus on measuring what government accomplishes and how it affects citizens. But in addition to the GPRA measures, managers and policymakers alike need measures that allow them to compare the outcomes achieved by programs, regulations, and tax expenditures with the resources these activities consume. Two key measures are cost-effectiveness and benefit–cost measures.

Cost-Effectiveness Measures

Cost-effectiveness is the ratio of costs to outcomes. It shows the cost of producing one unit of successful outcome (OECD 2009b, 16). Alternatively, dividing outcome by cost shows the amount of outcome produced per dollar spent.

Cost-effectiveness measures are most useful when comparing a set of programs, regulations, or tax expenditures that seek to achieve a similar outcome. Job training programs, for example, frequently measure employment placements—usually defined as the number of program participants who get jobs and remain employed for some specified minimum period of time. Placement and cost data can be used to calculate cost-effectiveness. Table 8.1 shows some cost-effectiveness calculations for job training programs in a pilot study conducted the year after agencies issued their first GPRA reports. Clearly, cost-effectiveness varies widely. The figures suggest that the government could achieve substantially more job placements by reallocating resources from programs that are less cost-effective to programs that are more cost-effective. The appropriate reallocation decision, however, is not obvious from the measures.

Different decision makers might decide differently, depending on the priorities they attach to helping the various target populations the programs serve. The strong emphasis on measuring participants' employment placement and earnings in U.S. job training programs may prompt managers to discriminate against the most disadvantaged applicants and instead seek participants who already have decent placement prospects but would be helped by the extra training. If the goal of the policy is to help the most disadvantaged, this may be a problem (Heinrich 2002, 716). If the goal is to make as many people employable as possible, cost-effectiveness measures probably prompt managers to do what policymakers want them to do (Heckman et al. 1997). Regardless of the goal, cost-effectiveness calculations help inform decision makers about the trade-offs involved.

Cost-effectiveness can also be used to compare programs, regulations, and tax expenditures that seek to achieve similar results. Tengs et al. (1995) performed a now classic meta-study that compared the cost-effectiveness of 500 actual or proposed government programs, regulations, or voluntary measures that could reduce premature deaths. They measured cost-effectiveness in terms of cost per life-year saved. The study revealed stunning differences in cost-effectiveness. Some government expenditures and regulations were very cost-effective, such as media campaigns to increase seat belt use ($310 per life-year saved), chlorination of drinking water ($3,100 per life-year saved), the special supplemental food program for women, infants, and children ($3,400 per life-year saved), and childhood immunizations (zero or negative costs to society on net). Others were quite expensive, such as putting adult monitors on school buses ($4.9 million per life-year saved), arsenic emission control at glass manufacturing plants ($51 million per life-year saved), and setting a chloroform private well emission standard at 48 pulp mills ($99 trillion per life-year saved). Like Tengs and her coauthors, we cannot vouch for the accuracy of all of the estimates in the cited studies. But they clearly indicate wide variations in cost-effectiveness that policymakers should be aware of when choosing which interventions to fund or require via regulation. Indeed, Morrall (1986, 2003) finds that policymakers tend to reject regulatory proposals with very high costs per life saved.

Table 8.1   Cost-Effectiveness Calculations for Job Training Programs

Program Area	Fiscal Year 1999 Appropriation	Placements/ $ Million	Cost/ Placement
School to work (Education)	$149,000,000	1729	$578
Veterans in need (Labor)	$167,000,000	1727	$579
Perkins vocational and technology education (Education)	$1,056,000,000	1515	$660
BIA community development (Interior)	$12,928,000	863	$1159
Adult disadvantaged job training (Labor)	$955,000,000	217	$4608
Indian and Native Americans (Labor)	$53,700,000	149	$6711
Economic independence— refugees (HHS)	$423,000,000	124	$8065
Dislocated workers (Labor)	$1,347,000,000	121	$8264
Migrant and seasonal farm workers (Labor)	$73,000,000	100	$10,000
Youth transition (Labor)	$1,201,000,000	59	$16,949
Welfare to work (Labor)	$1,476,000,000	54	$18,519
Job corps (Labor)	$1,188,000,000	49	$20,408
Tribal postsecondary vocational institutions (Education)	$4,100,000	46	$21,739
Trade-affected workers (Labor)	$131,100,000	34	$29,412

Source: Ellig, Jerry, Maurice McTigue, and Steve Richardson, Putting a Price on Performance: A Demonstration Study of Outcome-Based Scrutiny, Mercatus Center at George Mason University, 2000, 14, http://mercatus.org/sites/default/files/publication/MC_GAP_PriceonPerformance_001201.pdf.

Benefit–Cost Measures

Benefit–cost measures provide another way of comparing different programs, regulations, or tax expenditures. Unlike the private sector, government does not have a financial bottom line that translates the results of diverse activities into monetary values (Key 1940, Wildavsky 1992, von Mises 1946). But to the extent that analysts can roughly estimate the monetary value of outcomes and costs, benefit–cost measures help decision makers compare the value created by diverse programs, regulations, and tax expenditures. Benefit–cost analysis attempts to measure benefits by estimating individuals' willingness to pay for benefits, and it measures costs by estimating individuals' willingness to accept payment for shouldering costs. The most relevant benefit–cost measure for comparing alternatives is *net benefits*—the difference between benefits and costs.

Compared to cost-effectiveness measures, benefit–cost measures allow decision makers to more easily compare projects, programs, or regulations that have multiple outcomes. The monetary value of each type of outcome can be estimated, then summed to calculate total benefits. For the same reason, benefit–cost measures facilitate comparison across policy alternatives that have different outcomes. They thus assist policymakers who must decide how to allocate limited resources among a wide variety of possible objectives.

Benefit–cost measures are not without controversy. We have already alluded to disagreements surrounding benefit–cost analysis of regulation, discussed in Chapter 6. Many objections to benefit–cost measures stem from concern that the quantitative comparison of benefits and costs will become a rigid decision rule that crowds out other legitimate concerns. Such objections lose a great deal of their force if decision makers keep in mind that "benefit–cost analysis is properly regarded as an aid to decision-making and not the decision itself" (Zerbe and Dively 1994, 2). Decision makers can use the results of benefit–cost analysis without subscribing to a "hard" test that requires them to approve only those initiatives whose quantified benefits exceed quantified costs (Graham 2008, 432–37).

Equity Measures

An oft-repeated criticism of performance measurement is that it elevates "efficiency values" above "equity values" (Radin 2006, 91–112). Similar critiques are common in the field of regulatory analysis (Graham 2008). The basic concern here is that performance measurement's focus on efficiency and effectiveness gives short shrift to values of fairness or equity. Indeed, the measures required by GPRA do not explicitly address equity.

To get a handle on how to measure equity, we must first unpack the concept. Equity is a highly subjective concept rooted in one's definition of fairness or justice. To some people, equity means equal distribution of income or results. To others, it means equality of opportunity, equality before the law, or treating similarly situated individuals similarly. To appreciate the full scope of differing definitions of equity, one need only consider the vast difference between the widely different theories of justice developed in classic works by two Harvard University philosophers, John Rawls and Robert Nozick. Rawls' (1971) theory of justice justifies an extensive social welfare state; Nozick's (1974) justifies a minimalist libertarian state.

There is no objective definition of *equity*, nor is there a single, widely accepted subjective definition. As a result, it is not possible to develop a simple, direct measure of equity in the same way one might measure costs or outcomes. A more useful approach that recognizes diverse definitions of *equity* utilizes the economic concept of incidence (Browning and Browning 1979, 273–88). Analysis of incidence identifies which individuals or groups ultimately bear the costs and receive the benefits of programs, regulations, or tax expenditures. Outcomes (or costs) can be measured separately by race, gender, geographic location, or income level (Berman 1998, 61).

Incidence analysis does not directly tell us whether the resulting distribution of benefits and costs is equitable. Different observers with different values or different definitions of justice may reach different conclusions. But measuring how outcomes or costs differ for different subgroups provides crucial information that informs various observers' assessments of equity.

Individual Performance Measures

Yet another argument for additional performance measures comes from principal–agent theory, a branch of economic reasoning that has heavily influenced new public management reforms (see, e.g., Scott et al. 1997). Principal–agent problems arise when one party cannot perfectly monitor and direct another party's actions on his or her behalf. The first party (the principal) faces the challenge of crafting a contract or other compensation system that rewards the second party (the agent) for taking actions that create value for the principal. Any homeowner who has ever sold a house and wondered whether the real estate agent was always acting in the homeowner's interest knows what it's like to be a principal trying to control an agent. Relationships between government managers and employees, political appointees and the permanent civil service, the president and agency heads, and voters and their elected representatives are all examples of principal-agent problems.

Performance measures at the individual level can help solve principal–agent problems by creating a basis for rewarding individuals based on their contributions to the agency's strategic goals. This is the reasoning behind the U.S. reforms that seek to link senior executive service pay more closely to accomplishment of the agency's goals (OPM 2007). Such links between individual and organizational performance are especially important when employees are expected to use their imagination and creativity to solve problems, rather than simply follow bureaucratic rules. If employees have fewer rules to follow (because we believe this frees them to create more value), then they need some guide to value creation other than rules.

GAO (2003) case studies have found that high-performing public organizations follow a number of management practices that help mitigate principal–agent problems by linking individual goals and performance measures with organizational goals. These practices include aligning individual performance expectations with organizational goals, tracking performance gaps and requiring follow-up corrective action, and linking pay to individual and organizational

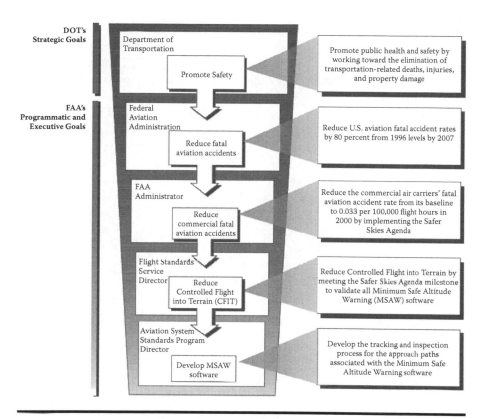

DOT's Strategic Goals

Department of Transportation

Promote Safety

Promote public health and safety by working toward the elimination of transportation-related deaths, injuries, and property damage

FAA's Programmatic and Executive Goals

Federal Aviation Administration

Reduce fatal aviation accidents

Reduce U.S. aviation fatal accident rates by 80 percent from 1996 levels by 2007

FAA Administrator

Reduce commercial fatal aviation accidents

Reduce the commercial air carriers' fatal aviation accident rate from its baseline to 0.033 per 100,000 flight hours in 2000 by implementing the Safer Skies Agenda

Flight Standards Service Director

Reduce Controlled Flight into Terrain (CFIT)

Reduce Controlled Flight into Terrain by meeting the Safer Skies Agenda milestone to validate all Minimum Safe Altitude Warning (MSAW) software

Aviation System Standards Program Director

Develop MSAW software

Develop the tracking and inspection process for the approach paths associated with the Minimum Safe Altitude Warning software

Figure 8.1 Linking individual goals with strategic goals. (Source: U.S. Government Accountability Office, Results-Oriented Cultures: Creating a Clear Linkage between Individual Performance and Organizational Success, Report GAO-03-488, 2003, 7.)

performance. Figure 8.1 presents one example, showing how the Federal Aviation Administration derived a manager's individual goal (development of Minimum Safe Altitude Warning software) from the Department of Transportation's strategic safety goal.

In reality, linking individual performance and organizational performance is much more complex than our description above suggests. Heinrich and Marschke (2010) analyze an extensive list of potential problems. For example, not all individual performance measures will motivate the performance that citizens ultimately want from their government. Rather, the indicators chosen as individual performance measures must be correlated with the *value* the employee creates for the agency and, ultimately, taxpayers. Value may be multifaceted, or some aspects may be difficult to measure (Heinrich and Marschke 2010, 189–90).

Individuals also have more complex motivations than simple economic models assume. A great deal of research addresses whether government employees possess intrinsic motivation to promote the public good that is more important to them than financial incentives. If so, then pay for performance may have little effect or may even be counterproductive (Heinrich and Marschke 2010, 191–92).

But even if government service attracts individuals less motivated by financial gain, individual performance measures linked to organizational goals still serve the crucial function of informing government employees how they can best direct their efforts to promote the public good. It is thus no surprise that GAO (2008, 11–13) consistently urges federal agencies to create a line of sight between individual performance and organizational results.

Clearly, GPRA does not exhaust the list of measures necessary to manage performance effectively. Nevertheless, it is hard to see how one could measure cost-effectiveness, benefit–cost, equity, or individual contributions to organizational performance without first developing the types of organizational performance measures GPRA requires or implies. This chapter investigates whether GPRA has pushed federal agencies to take those crucial first steps.

The Baseline: Pre-GPRA Planning and Measurement

Strategic planning and performance measurement did not begin with GPRA. Any attempt to assess the effect of GPRA on the availability and use of performance information in agencies must take into account the pre-GPRA state of affairs. When Congress held hearings on GPRA in 1991, the Senate Governmental Affairs Committee (now the Committee on Homeland Security and Governmental Affairs) asked GAO to survey major federal agencies to identify the current status of strategic planning, performance goals, standards, and measures. GAO surveyed 103 agencies with more than 1,000 employees or $500 million in annual outlays. These agencies accounted for 92% of outlays and 87% of employees in fiscal year 1991 (GAO 1992, 21).

GAO surveyed agencies, not individual managers, so the responses likely came from the individuals most familiar with each agency's goals and measures. The survey asked whether agencies used specific types of performance measures in "all or part" of their operations. Thus, an affirmative response need not mean a particular type of measure was widespread in the agency. The results are not strictly comparable with later surveys, which come closer to gauging the prevalence of various practices in each agency because GAO sent them to a sample of managers in each agency. Nevertheless, the results demonstrate that a certain degree of strategic planning and measurement occurred before GPRA's enactment.

The 1991 survey asked about the five types of performance measures related to GPRA that also appear consistently in subsequent GAO surveys. A majority of agencies reported that they used these measures somewhere in the organization. As the first column of numbers in Table 8.2 shows, virtually all agencies claimed to measure outputs. Seventy percent said they measured outcomes. The performance

Table 8.2   Use of Performance Measures, 1991 GAO Survey

	Used Somewhere in Agency	Used by Office of Agency Head	Used by HQ Staff	Used By HQ Line	Used by Regional/ District Office	Used by Field Operations Unit
Outcome	70	64	64	63	46	48
Output	98	97	96	94	69	77
Efficiency	72	61	69	63	45	48
Customer	62	58	60	55	40	44
Quality	81	66	76	76	58	61

Source: U.S. Government Accountability Office, Program Performance Measures: Federal Agency Collection and Use of Performance Data, Report GAO/GGD-92-65, 1992, 23, 25.

measure with the lowest positive response, customer satisfaction, was still measured in about two-thirds of agencies.

A separate set of questions asked agencies to indicate who uses the various measures that currently exist. Table 8.2 reports these results in columns 3–7. In all cases, use of performance measures is much more prevalent at headquarters than in regional or district offices or in the field. Yet even the lowest positive response—use of customer satisfaction measures at regional or district offices—occurred in 39% of agencies that had customer satisfaction measures.

Another set of questions sheds some light on pre-GPRA use of performance measures. GAO asked agencies how satisfied or dissatisfied they were with their performance measures for four uses: to make budget decisions, manage programs, ensure accountability, and measure results or outcomes. In each case, more than two-thirds of agencies said they were very satisfied or somewhat satisfied with their performance measures for these purposes (GAO 1992, 29).

Strategic planning was also widespread. Two-thirds of agencies had a single, long-term plan that sets goals or objectives for the entire organization. Half said that all or most of their goals are measurable. Two-thirds said that they translate long-term goals or objectives into annual or semiannual operating plans (GAO 1992, 27–28).

Despite these encouraging signs, GAO cautioned that planning was not tightly linked to performance reporting. Few agencies could use their performance measures to assess progress toward long-term goals articulated in their strategic plans. Only nine of the 103 agencies had a unified strategic plan with measurable goals, an office that collects performance measures, and regular consolidated reports—three characteristics necessary to link planning with performance reporting (GAO 1992, 9–10). In follow-up interviews to validate the survey responses, GAO "found that measures were typically generated and used by program-level units within an agency and focused on measuring work activity levels and outputs or compliance with statutes" (GAO 2004a, 31). Moreover, only one-third of agencies said that program performance measures are reflected in senior executive or senior management performance contracts (GAO 1992, 28).

There is another reason the 1991 survey responses might be overly rosy. The survey indicates that strategic planning, performance measurement, and use of performance information occurred to some extent in most agencies. It does not indicate how widespread these practices were within agencies.

In 1997, GAO began surveying individual managers rather than agencies. The 1997 survey asked managers to recall whether they had and used performance measures three years previously, in 1994. Responses to these questions, shown in Table 8.3, indicate that availability and use of performance information was not widespread. The most prevalent performance measure was outputs. Only about a quarter of managers said they had output measures for their programs in 1994. About one in five managers said they had outcome or quality measures, and even lower percentages had customer satisfaction or efficiency measures. Similarly, low percentages of managers said their performance measures were used to develop the agency budget, make funding decisions for the program, or make changes to the program.

Table 8.3 Percentage of Federal Managers Reporting They Had or Used Performance Measures for These Purposes to a Great or Very Great Extent in 1994

Availability of Performance Measures	
Outcome	18.6
Output	26.6
Efficiency	16.9
Customer satisfaction	10.6
Quality	18.9
Uses of Performance Information from Their Programs	
Develop agency budget	16.2
Make funding decisions for the program	14.1
Make changes to the program by managers above my level	8.7

Source: U.S. Government Accountability Office, The Government Performance and Results Act: 1997 Implementation Will be Uneven, Report GAO/GGD-97-019, 1997, 103–106.

Three conclusions emerge from the early GAO surveys. First, some type of strategic planning and performance measurement occurred in most agencies before GPRA. Second, links between planning and reporting were often tenuous. Third, performance measurement and management were not necessarily widespread within agencies. Thus, GPRA had the potential both to increase the availability and use of performance information, and to link organization-wide goals and measures more closely to goals and measures for individual programs.

Case Studies of Performance Management

Case studies help put meat on the dry bones of performance management. Federal agencies use performance information for a variety of internal management purposes: to identify where corrective action is needed, motivate and develop improvement plans, identify and share best practices, communicate results to employees, allocate resources, set priorities, and develop agency budgets. Hatry et al. (2005) reviewed 16 case studies showing how federal agencies have used performance information. Examples include:

- In 2000, the Education Department's Division of Adult Education and Literacy required states that receive grants to report on the number and percentage of clients who improved their literacy levels; proceeded to further education and training; obtained a high school diploma or equivalent; or obtained, kept, or advanced on the job. The division used these data to identify states for site visits and additional technical assistance, to determine which states should receive monetary incentives, and to prepare its own budget requests.
- Another agency in the Education Department, the Rehabilitation Services Administration in the Office of Special Education and Rehabilitative Services, requires state agencies receiving grants to report on six indicators related to employment outcomes for people with disabilities. Indicators include the percentage of program participants who get and retain a job for 90 days and the percentage who receive a job at or above the minimum wage. State agencies with poor performance must develop plans to improve or face the prospect of reduced funding. A similar grant program for nonprofits and other providers of vocational training has used a similar set of indicators to identify grantees with unsatisfactory performance, and several grantees are de-funded each year. The agency also uses performance indicator information to identify entities that need technical assistance, develop assistance plans, and identify best practices.
- In 1998, HUD established the Real Estate Assessment Center to monitor the condition of public housing through on-site visits. Two key outcome measures are the physical condition of housing and resident satisfaction.

Each public housing authority receives a score based on those two outcomes plus an assessment of its finances and management. HUD uses the scores to decide which housing authorities must develop improvement plans, determine which authorities should receive technical assistance or sanctions for poor performance, prioritize use of resources, and reward high performers with bonus capital funds and public recognition. Numerous public housing authorities significantly improved their performance as a result of this rating system (Hatry et al. 2005, 236–46).

Although many of the case studies cited by Hatry and his coauthors occurred after GPRA, few of them appear to have resulted directly from GPRA. One exception is GAO's 1996 case study of the Coast Guard, which it labels "one of the first examples, if not the first example, of the use of outcome data derived from GPRA" (Hatry et al. 2005, 262). The Coast Guard's Office of Marine Safety, Security, and Environmental Protection seeks to prevent marine accidents. Prior to 1994, the office focused on inspecting vessels, and it measured its success by counting inspections and inspection results. In 1994, the Coast Guard's marine safety program became a GPRA pilot program. In its January 1994 business plan, the Coast Guard shifted from focusing on activities and outputs (like inspections) to outcomes (like reducing the number of fatalities and injuries).

In the marine towing industry, equipment and material failures accounted for only 20% of casualties; human error accounted for a whopping two-thirds of casualties. Working with the towing industry, the Coast Guard developed guidelines and training programs to reduce human error. As a result, the industry fatality rate fell by 70%, from 91 per 100,000 employees in 1990 to 27 per 100,000 in 1995. The Coast Guard accomplished this improvement in outcomes with fewer personnel and a smaller budget. "According to the Coast Guard, the program achieved its results by giving field commanders greater authority and by investing in activities and processes that went most directly to the goal of reducing risks on the water" (GAO 1996, 37). This example demonstrates how a clear focus on outcomes, combined with outcome measurement and analysis of their causes, can drive changes in program strategies, priorities, and resource allocation that lead to better results.

Other studies identify how agency managers have used performance information since GPRA, although they do not always document how the decisions led to changed outcomes. GAO (2005e) identified four ways agencies can use performance information and provided a number of examples, outlined in the sections below.

Develop Strategy and Allocate Resources

The National Highway Traffic Safety Administration (NHTSA) used its Fatality Analysis Reporting System database to identify the 13 states that accounted for 46% of alcohol-related driving fatalities. NHTSA offered additional funding for stepped-up law enforcement and a media campaign. The Small Business Administration used financial and human capital data in its decision to terminate support for a program started in the 1990s that made computers and Internet access available to entrepreneurs. SBA-created business information centers were supposed to require minimal federal support, because they used hardware, software, and library resources donated by information technology companies. Agency data, including an annual survey of employee time allocation for various programs, revealed that SBA still devoted $11 million worth of resources annually to the program. This cost information, along with the realization that computers and Internet access had become much more widely available to small business owners, led SBA to discontinue its role in this effort.

Identify Problems and Take Corrective Action

The Employee Benefits Security Administration (EBSA) employed a contractor to survey individuals whose inquiries or complaints were referred to the enforcement staff. The survey provided an index number that allowed EBSA to compare its customer satisfaction with that of other organizations, but the standardized questions gave EBSA little useful information on specific aspects of its performance. In 2003, a new contractor designed a specialized survey that found many customers received no communication from EBSA while their complaints were being resolved—a process that could take up to two years. As a result, in 2005 EBSA changed its standard operating procedures so that customers were contacted within 30 days of their complaint and received quarterly updates on progress.

A Veterans Health Administration network covering several Mid-Atlantic states found in the first quarter of 2004 that it might not meet its goals on cardiovascular performance measures if one facility failed to improve on a measure that assessed whether heart patients received six kinds of instructions upon discharge. The network added data fields to patients' electronic medical records that would prompt facilities to ensure that patients received the instructions. By the end of the year, the lagging facility received a "fully satisfactory" score.

Recognize and Reward Performance

By the end of fiscal year 2004, the Federal Aviation Administration's performance-based pay system covered 78% of employees. Employees can receive pay increases for meeting individual goals and for outstanding performance. In addition, funds previously used for increases within pay grades were reallocated to an organization-wide increase that is awarded based on whether the agency as a whole meets goals for 31 key performance measures. At the Veterans' Health Administration, half of a network director's annual performance evaluation depends on how well the network scores on its performance measures, "which include clinical waiting times, the percentage of patients receiving cancer screenings, and patient satisfaction."

Identify and Share Effective Approaches

Two of the National Weather Service's performance goals are to improve its flash flood warning accuracy and lead time. In 1995, the Pittsburgh Weather Forecast Office implemented a new monitoring system. When performance data revealed that the new system improved accuracy, the Weather Service began implementing the system nationwide in 2002.

A more extensive set of case studies focused explicitly on GPRA implementation was published in 2006. Frederickson and Frederickson (2006) studied five agencies within the Department of Health and Human Services (HHS): the Health Resources and Services Administration (HRSA), Centers for Medicare and Medicaid Services (CMS), National Institutes of Health (NIH), Indian Health Service (IHS), and the Food and Drug Administration (FDA). HHS faced numerous challenges in implementing GPRA from the very beginning. The department is a diverse "holding company" composed of many autonomous programs that have traditionally been treated as such by decision makers (Radin 2006, 132–49). Effective delivery of HHS programs often requires the cooperation of third parties, such as states, health care providers, and Indian tribes. These entities may have their own ideas of what constitutes success, and they may or may not be enthusiastic about supplying performance data (Frederickson and Frederickson 2006, 20–27). Given these difficulties, perhaps it's no surprise that HHS's early strategic plans and annual performance plans received criticism from congressional leadership and GAO (Radin 2006, 146). On the Mercatus Center's *Scorecard*, the department's annual performance report ranked 20th, or worse, for the first eight years.

Nevertheless, individual HHS agencies have often developed or improved performance information since GPRA. And in fiscal year 2007, the HHS report climbed to fifth place with a score of 37, several points above the average. In fiscal year 2008, HHS's score remained essentially the same (36 points), though it dropped in the rankings because many other agencies improved their reports from the previous year.

HRSA provides some of the best examples of explicit health outcome measures, offering specific goals for reductions in infant death rates per 1,000 live births, maternal death rates per 100,000 live births, neonatal death rates per 1,000 live births, and death rates due to HIV infection. Similarly, the Indian Health Service measures some health outcomes: decreased obesity rates in Native American children, decreased injury mortality rates, and increased blood sugar control among diabetics. One of the FDA's health outcome measures is reduced medication errors in hospitals (Frederickson and Frederickson 2006, 56, 199, 136).

More common in most of the five HHS agencies are intermediate program outcome measures that have been proven to cause health outcomes or might plausibly be linked to health outcomes. Thus, IHS has performance measures for childhood immunizations and pneumococcal and flu vaccinations for adults. Medicare measures the percent of surgical patients receiving antibiotics to reduce infection and the percent of beneficiaries who have access to care (Frederickson and Frederickson 2006, 82, 112). NIH initiated its GPRA efforts with a qualitative performance reporting method that outlined specific discoveries and broader clusters of advances in medical science that had been supported by NIH research grants. After NIH underwent OMB's Program Assessment Rating Tool (PART) analysis in 2004, it developed much more specific, quantitative performance measures, such as: "By 2011, assess the efficacy of at least three new treatment strategies to reduce cardio-vascular morbidity/mortality in patients with Type 2 diabetes and/or chronic kidney disease"* (Frederickson and Frederickson 2006, 104). In both cases, however, NIH measured program outcomes, not health outcomes. Similarly, many of FDA's measures are program outcomes that might be precursors of health outcomes, like improvements in Americans' awareness of various health facts or reductions in the amount of time it takes to approve new drugs or devices.

Finally, the agencies also measure a lot of processes, activities, and outputs. GPRA does call for measurement of outputs as well as outcomes. The output measures include the number of health centers or members of the target population served (HRSA, Medicaid); percent of beneficiaries receiving various preventive procedures (Medicare, IHS); progress in research administration, training, and facilities (NIH); or the number of inspections (FDA) (Frederickson and Frederickson 2006, 56, 82, 101, 119, 136). Agencies usually wanted to avoid responsibility for health outcomes because so many factors other than government programs affect health outcomes (Frederickson and Frederickson 2006, 175).

Not all of the performance measurement initiatives described above can be attributed exclusively to GPRA. NIH's qualitative accounts of research discoveries are more extensive versions of the types of accounts the agency had previously used to justify its budget requests. The FDA's commitment to measure and reduce approval times for drugs stems from a pre-GPRA law, the Prescription Drug User Fee Act of 1992 (Frederickson and Frederickson 2006, 100–1, 134–35).

Frederickson and Frederickson (2006, 45, 185) argue that GPRA's most important contribution may be to improve management of federal programs by improving communication and coordination between federal agencies and the third parties they often rely upon to deliver services, such as states, contractors, research grant recipients, health care providers, and Indian tribes. HRSA's Maternal and Child Health Bureau, for example, initiated a 16-month discussion process that culminated in state officials' agreement on 18 process, output, and outcome measures for the bureau's state block grant program. However, since the HHS case studies focus on implementation of performance measurement, it is not clear how much impact most of the performance measures have actually had.

In general, the case studies demonstrate that at least some federal agencies are capable of measuring outcomes and using that information to make decisions. GPRA has prompted some agencies to develop more outcome-oriented performance

---

* PART is discussed in greater detail in Chapter 9.

measures, though sometimes these are "program outcomes" that might more accurately be classified as outputs. These results, however, vary from agency to agency. (Another key agency use of performance information—performance budgeting—will be covered in Chapter 9.)

Progress over Time

The case studies concretely demonstrate how agencies have used performance information, but they do not show whether the results are typical or exceptions. GAO surveys of federal managers reveal how widespread the availability and use of performance information has become since GPRA. Since 1997, GAO has periodically surveyed managers in the federal agencies covered by the Chief Financial Officers Act. These agencies account for the vast majority of federal spending, and they are the same agencies covered by the Mercatus Center's *Performance Report Scorecard*.

The surveys tell a decidedly mixed story about improvement in the availability and use of performance information over time. Sometimes the results also depend on whether one looks at averaged responses for all federal managers, or averaged responses for agencies. Averaged responses for federal managers indicate that availability of performance information has increased, but use has not. Averaged responses for agencies, however, suggest that both availability and use of performance measures have increased. These findings are not contradictory; they simply mean that smaller and medium-sized agencies were more likely to have increased both the availability and use of performance information by large amounts.

Figure 8.2 shows the percentage of federal managers who said they had various types of performance measures in 1994, 1997, 2000, 2003, and 2007. The latter years show marked improvements from 1994 and 1997. For example, only 18.6% of managers said they had outcome measures for their programs in 1994; the figure rose to 31.8% in 1997. By 2003, 55% of managers said they had outcome measures for their programs. The number receded to 48.9% in 2007—still well above its level in either 1994 or 1997. For each type of performance measure, differences between 1997 and 2007 are statistically significant (GAO 2008, 4).

Figure 8.3 shows less sanguine results for uses of performance information. The average percentage of managers who said they use performance information to a great or very great extent for various purposes increased slightly, but not by much. Use of performance information to allocate resources, for instance, increased by just 5 percentage points between 1997 and 2007, from 44.8% to 49.8%. The largest increase occurred in the use of performance information to reward employees who report to the manager, which rose from 38% in 1997 to 51.1% in 2007. This is the only improvement in the use of performance information that was statistically significant (GAO 2008, 6).

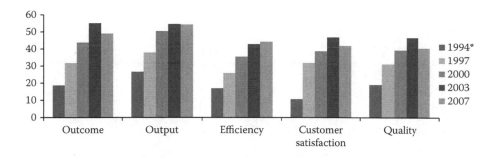

Figure 8.2   Percentage of federal managers who reported having specific types of performance measures to a great or very great extent.* 1994 values are managers' recollections when asked in 1997. (Source: Authors' calculations from data in U.S. Government Accountability Office, The Government Performance and Results Act: 1997 Implementation Will be Uneven, Report GAO/GGD-97-019, 1997; U.S. Government Accountability Office, Managing for Results: Federal Managers' Views on Key Management Issues Vary Widely Across Agencies, Report GAO-01-592, 2001; U.S. Government Accountability Office, Results-Oriented Government: GPRA Has Established a Solid Foundation for Achieving Greater Results, Report GAO-04-38, 2004; U.S. Government Accountability Office, Government Performance: Lessons Learned for the Next Administration on Using Performance Information to Improve Results, statement of Bernice Steinhardt, Report GAO-08-1026T, 2008.)

In a May 2001 report, GAO (2001) noted that survey results for individual agencies vary widely. The same holds for improvements between 2000 and 2007. Results on availability and use of performance information change if we calculate an average response for managers in each agency and then average the agency responses. By counting each agency's average equally, this method implicitly gives more weight to responses from smaller agencies with fewer managers. But it helps us identify whether an appreciable number of agencies have experienced improvements.

For two years—2000 and 2007—GAO surveyed a large enough sample of managers to calculate valid average responses for each individual agency. Table 8.4 shows averaged agency responses for 24 agencies covered by the CFO Act in 2000 and 2007.* Availability and use of performance information improved for every type of performance measure and every type of use.

The changes in Table 8.4 are larger than the changes shown in Figures 8.2 and 8.3 for every survey question except one. For use of performance information to allocate resources, the government-wide average change of 6.8 percentage points in

---

* The GAO survey covers all 24 CFO Act agencies, plus separate breakouts for the Centers for Medicare and Medicaid Services (HHS), Federal Emergency Management Agency (DHS), Federal Aviation Administration (DOT), Forest Service (USDA), and Internal Revenue Service (Treasury). We included the responses from managers in those five subcomponents in the averages for their parent departments.

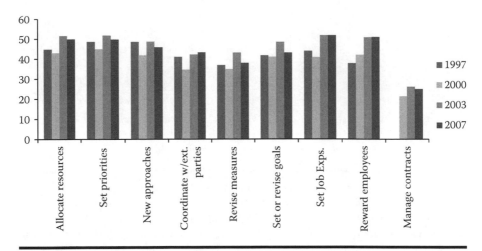

Figure 8.3 Percentage of federal managers who reported using performance information for specific purposes to a great or very great extent. (Source: Authors' calculations from data in U.S. Government Accountability Office, The Government Performance and Results Act: 1997 Implementation Will be Uneven, Report GAO/GGD-97-019, 1997; U.S. Government Accountability Office, Managing for Results: Federal Managers' Views on Key Management Issues Vary Widely Across Agencies, Report GAO-01-592, 2001; U.S. Government Accountability Office, Results-Oriented Government: GPRA Has Established a Solid Foundation for Achieving Greater Results, Report GAO-04-38, 2004; U.S. Government Accountability Office, Government Performance: Lessons Learned for the Next Administration on Using Performance Information to Improve Results, statement of Bernice Steinhardt, Report GAO-08-1026T, 2008.)

Figure 8.3 exceeds the agency average change of 4.9 percentage points in Table 8.4. Improvements in the availability of outcome and efficiency measures are highly statistically significant; improvements in the other uses are marginally significant. Improvements in almost all of the uses of performance information are statistically significant.

These results suggest that, when measuring changes in the availability and use of performance information, there is a great deal of variability across agencies, and many agencies have seen substantial improvement. Table 8.5 shows that this is in fact what happened. For every question, at least one agency experienced a very large increase—almost always by 20 percentage points or more. A handful of agencies experienced declines between 2000 and 2007. The largest decline was always much smaller than the largest gain. A noticeable number of agencies—usually more than one-quarter—had improvements exceeding ten percentage points. At least half the agencies usually saw improvements exceeding five percentage points. Clearly, numerous agencies substantially improved managers' availability and use of performance information between 2000 and 2007.

Table 8.4   Agency Average Percentage of Managers Reporting That They Had or Used Performance Measures for These Purposes to a Great or Very Great Extent

	2000	2007	Difference	T-Statistic
Availability of Performance Measures				
Outcome	45.5	53.9	8.4	2.80***
Output	53.4	59.4	6.0	1.92*
Efficiency	36.2	45.2	9.0	3.34***
Customer satisfaction	36.6	43.2	6.6	1.97*
Quality	36.9	43.1	6.2	1.98*
Uses of Performance Information in Their Programs				
Allocate resources	45.6	50.5	4.9	1.99*
Set priorities	46.4	53.2	6.7	2.48***
Adopting new approaches/work processes	42.5	51.3	8.8	3.18***
Coordinate with external parties	35.7	45.4	9.7	4.17***
Refine program performance measures	38.2	44.5	6.3	2.37***
Set or revising performance goals	43.3	50.2	6.9	2.67***
Set job expectations for employees/ manage	42.8	55.0	12.3	4.80***
Reward employees/manage or supervise	43.6	52.7	9.1	3.19***
Manage contracts	24.2	28.8	4.5	1.51

Source: Authors' calculations based on 2000 and 2007 survey data furnished by GAO.

Statistical significance: *, 90%; **, 95%; ***, 99%.

Econometric Studies

In at least half of major federal agencies, availability and use of performance information has improved since GPRA was enacted in 1993. But what role did GPRA play in this improvement? Would availability and use of performance information have improved anyway, without GPRA? One way to answer these questions is to see if

Table 8.5 Percentage Point Change in Agency Average Availability or Use of Performance Measures, 2000–2007

	Average Change	Biggest Increase	Biggest Decrease	Number with Increase Exceeding 10%	Number with Increase Exceeding 5%
Availability					
Outcome	8.4	39 (NRC)	−6.3 (USAID)	7	13
Output	6.0	16.8 (NRC)	−8.3 (Interior)	6	11
Efficiency	9.0	20.5 (Treasury)	−0.8 (USDA)	11	15
Customer	6.6	33.2 (NRC)	−7.1 (Interior)	6	12
Quality	6.2	20.1 (NSF, Treasury)	−5.1 (Defense)	6	12
Use					
Allocate resources	4.9	35.8 (NRC)	−12.8 (USAID)	4	11
Set priorities	6.7	24.7 (NSF)	−12.8 (OPM)	6	14
New approaches	8.8	35.9 (NSF)	−17.1 (OPM)	7	12
Coordinate	9.7	18.8 (DOT)	−5.4 (HUD)	10	14
Refine measures	6.3	27.1 (NRC)	−20.5 (SBA)	7	12
Set goals	6.9	25.1 (NRC)	−14.1 (SBA)	9	11
Set job expectations	12.3	33.9 (NSF)	−9.3 (Commerce)	14	18
Reward employees	9.1	31.1 (NRC)	−19.8 (SBA)	8	13
Manage contracts	4.5	28.8 (NSF)	−10.4 (HUD)	3	9

Source: Authors' calculations based on 2000 and 2007 survey data furnished by GAO.

there is a correlation between the quality of an agency's GPRA efforts and the quality of management or availability or use of performance information in the agency.

Several econometric studies have established that such correlations do in fact exist. One such study deals with ambiguity in GPRA documents and the quality of management, as perceived by federal employees. Another finds links between the quality of agencies' GPRA reports and their scores on the Bush administration's Program Assessment Rating Tool. A third finds that agencies' Mercatus *Scorecard* scores are highly correlated with the GAO survey results on the availability and use of performance information.

GPRA and Perceived Quality of Performance

In a pair of articles published in the *Journal of Public Administration Research and Theory*, Chun and Rainey (2005a, 2005b) developed several measures of "organizational goal ambiguity" and used these measures to evaluate 115 federal agencies. They measured evaluative ambiguity by calculating the percentage of GPRA performance indicators that were either subjective or workload-oriented, as opposed to objective and results-oriented. A higher percentage of subjective and non-results-oriented indicators meant more evaluative ambiguity. They measured priority ambiguity with an index based on the number of strategic goals and annual performance targets the agency had. More goals and targets meant more priority ambiguity (Chun and Rainey 2005a, 13–14).

Higher levels of evaluative ambiguity were associated with lower agency scores on managerial effectiveness, customer service orientation, productivity, and work quality in a 2000 survey of federal employees administered by the National Partnership for Reinventing Government. Higher levels of priority ambiguity were correlated with lower scores on managerial effectiveness, but not the other factors (Chun and Rainey 2005b, 545–48). In other words, federal employees perceive that their agencies are better managed, more customer-focused, more productive, and produce higher-quality work when GPRA performance metrics are more outcome-oriented. They perceive that the organization is better managed when it has less ambiguous priorities, as evidenced by fewer strategic goals and performance targets. Thus, two practices often seen in high-quality GPRA plans and reports are at least correlated with employee perceptions of their agencies' effectiveness.

GPRA and PART Scores

Another study examined the relationship between the quality of agencies' GPRA reports and the scores their programs received on the Bush administration's Program Assessment Rating Tool (PART). PART sought to apply GPRA principles at the program level. PART was a framework "used to evaluate a program's purpose, design, planning, management, results, and accountability to determine its overall effectiveness." It was also intended to help OMB and Congress make performance budgeting decisions. PART questionnaires contained questions divided into four categories: program purpose and design, strategic planning, management, and results. Each section received a score between 0 and 25 points. The program's total score was a weighted average of the four scores: purpose and design (20%), strategic planning (10%), management (20%), and results (50%). If information on results was available, a program could be rated effective (85 points and above), moderately effective (70–84 points), adequate (50–69 points), or ineffective (0–49 points). Regardless of the numerical score, a program could also be rated "results not demonstrated" if it had not established goals and measures and collected data to evaluate performance.

Manchester and Norcross (2008) sought to determine factors that affected PART scores. One of the factors they included was the quality of an agency's GPRA efforts, as measured by the score its GPRA report received on the Mercatus *Scorecard* for the year the PART evaluation occurred. Programs' total PART scores and scores for each of PART's components (program purpose and design, strategic planning, program management, and program results) were regressed on the agency's Mercatus *Scorecard* score and a number of other variables. These variables included program age, size (measured by budget), agency mission complexity, agency ideology, program type (such as direct federal service provision, regulatory, etc.), and whether the program is mandatory or discretionary. Regression analysis revealed that an agency's *Scorecard* score has a positive effect on the PART scores its programs receive. A 1-point increase in an agency's *Scorecard* score is correlated with a 0.35 point increase in its overall PART score. *Scorecard* scores had the biggest effect on the program results component of PART. A 1-point increase in *Scorecard* score was associated with a ½-point increase in the program results PART score.

The maximum possible PART score is 100. The highest PART score any agency received was 96.7. The maximum possible PART results score is also 100. The highest PART results score any agency received was 100. The average Mercatus *Scorecard* score between 2004 and 2007, the years covered by their study, was 34. Manchester and Norcross's results imply that an agency producing a GPRA report with an average score would have received PART scores 12 points higher than an agency that produced no GPRA report. An agency with an average GPRA report would have received PART results scores 17 points higher than an agency that produced no GPRA report. Manchester and Norcross (2008, 16) conclude:

> Agencies better at meeting GPRA's reporting requirements may have an advantage in completing individual PART assessments. These agencies likely possess the resources and experience to answer PART's questions in a way that satisfies budget examiners, because they are well-versed in GPRA compliance (Gilmour and Lewis 2005). Or as Breul (2004) suggests, through GPRA, agencies are developing the outcome and output information that PART attempts to extract in its questionnaire.

GPRA and GAO Survey Results

One of the authors of this book undertook an econometric study that directly investigated links between GPRA and the availability and use of performance information. Ellig (2010) correlates the quality of agency GPRA reports (measured by the agency's Mercatus *Scorecard* score) and the availability and use of performance information (measured by the GAO survey responses). The study includes a number of variables controlling for institutional factors that might affect the availability and use of performance information, including agency leadership's perceived commitment to performance management, agency size, mix of program types in the agency, complexity of the agency's missions, agency ideology, and elected officials' interest in performance management as perceived by agency managers. An agency's Mercatus *Scorecard* score is positively correlated with the percent of managers who say they have all five types of performance measures in the GAO surveys. Scorecard scores are also positively correlated with many of the uses of performance information.

The second column of numbers in Table 8.6 lists the regression coefficients from Ellig (2010). The coefficients indicate that a 1-point increase in an agency's *Scorecard* score is associated with a 0.3–0.65 percentage point increase in managers reporting that they have or use performance information for various purposes. Successive columns in the table help determine whether this is a large or small effect. We multiplied the regression coefficients by the average *Scorecard* score for the years covered by the study (33.8 points), the standard deviation of the *Scorecard* scores (8.3 points), the highest *Scorecard* score (55 points), and the lowest *Scorecard* score (17 points).

The table is easiest to understand by means of an example. The General Services Administration's (GSA) report earned a score of 34 in 2007, about equal to the average score in the sample. The "Average Scorecard Score" column shows that GSA's *Scorecard* score is associated with a 14 percentage point increase in managers reporting that they have outcome or output measures, a 10 percentage point increase in managers saying they have efficiency measures, a 16 percentage point increase in managers saying they have customer satisfaction measures, and a 13 percentage point increase in managers saying they have quality measures. Compared to average affirmative responses of 40–57%, these are quite large increases that might be attributed to the quality of GAO's GPRA report.

Similarly, GSA's average score is associated with a 22 percentage point increase in the number of managers who say they use performance information to allocate resources. Increases for other uses of performance information are as follows: set priorities (12 percentage points), develop new program approaches (19 percentage points), coordinate with external parties (12 percentage points), revise measures (11 percentage points), and set or revise goals (12 percentage points). The average affirmative response rate ranged between 41 and 50%; GPRA again seems to account for a large portion of the affirmative responses.

Table 8.6 Size of GPRA Quality Effect on Availability and Use of Performance Information

	% Average Affirmative Response	Regression Coefficient	× Average Scorecard Score	× Standard Deviation Scorecard Score	× Highest Scorecard Score	× Lowest Scorecard Score
Availability						
Outcome	50	0.40	14	3	22	7
Output	57	0.40	14	3	22	7
Efficiency	41	0.30	10	2	17	5
Customer satisfaction	40	0.48	16	4	26	8
Quality	40	0.39	13	3	21	7
Uses						
Allocate resources	49	0.65	22	5	36	11
Set priorities	50	0.35	12	3	19	6
New approaches	48	0.56	19	4	31	10
Coordinate with external parties	41	0.34	12	3	19	6
Revise measures	42	0.31	11	2	17	5
Set or revise goals	47	0.34	12	3	19	6

The GSA example shows that an agency with a GPRA report earning the average score would have 10–16 percentage points more managers responding that they have the indicated performance measures, compared to an agency that produces no GPRA report. An agency with an average report would have 10–22 percentage points more managers saying that they use performance information for the listed purposes. As the first column of numbers in the table indicates, between 40 and 57% of managers said they had the types of performance measures listed in Table 8.6 or used performance information for purposes listed in the table. Therefore, merely producing an average GPRA report appears to make a big contribution to the availability and use of performance information.

The Department of Transportation achieved the highest GPRA report score in the sample, 55 points in 2007. The "Highest Scorecard Score" column shows that this score is associated with much larger increases in the number of managers saying that they have or use performance information—between 17 and 36 percentage points, depending on the question. A GPRA report that is one standard deviation better or worse than average is associated with a 2–5 percentage point change in affirmative responses. But even a report with the worst score is much better than no report at all! The Defense Department's 2007 report, which earned the worst score, is nevertheless associated with a 5–11 percentage point increase in affirmative responses. GPRA apparently has a statistically significant and large correlation with the availability and, in many cases, the use of performance information.

Of course, correlation does not imply causation. Perhaps some third factor explains why agencies that produce better GPRA reports are also more likely to have and use performance information in their programs. But none of the institutional factors used in the regressions are correlated with *Scorecard* scores. In the absence of some other explanation, it seems plausible that higher-quality GPRA initiatives leave agencies better equipped to develop performance measures for individual programs.

Conclusion

One of GPRA's most important contributions could be improvement in the use of performance information by federal managers (Frederickson and Frederickson 2006, 185, Hatry et al. 2005, 200, Joyce 2007). Indeed, this was one of the principal rationales listed in the legislation.

GPRA has achieved this goal, though perhaps not to as great an extent or as uniformly as proponents had hoped. To be sure, agencies collected performance information before GPRA, but however one interprets the case studies and the GAO survey results, performance measurement has become more common since GPRA. As one agency official noted, "Without GPRA, we would still be counting widgets" (Metzenbaum 2009, 28).

Agencies do not always satisfy GPRA's directive to measure outcomes. However, they often attempt to measure program outputs that can be linked to outcomes.

Availability of five types of performance measures tracked by GAO surveys, including outputs and outcomes, has increased. Use of performance information has increased noticeably in more than half of the CFO Act agencies. Finally, the quality of agency GPRA efforts is correlated with federal employees' perceptions of agency management and work quality, program PART scores, and the availability and use of performance information for programs and projects. When it comes to internal management of agencies, GPRA has likely made a difference.

Chapter 9

Toward Performance Budgeting?

One of GPRA's major purposes was to improve congressional budgeting decisions by providing better information about program results. The legislation mentions three possible means of increasing the availability of this information to Congress. First, the measures in annual performance reports should show agency progress in achieving their strategic goals. Second, GPRA requires agencies to list program evaluations in their annual performance reports, which should help point legislators toward detailed evaluations of individual programs. Third, the legislation authorized pilot programs on performance budgeting. Performance budgeting matches proposed expenditures with outcomes and shows how the amount of outcome is expected to vary with changes in the level of spending.

Budget decisions in government actually involve multiple steps. Agencies must first formulate their budget requests and negotiate with the Office of Management and Budget (OMB); this step creates the president's proposed budget, released the first week of February. Next, Congress enacts and the president signs a budget that may or may not conform to the president's original requests. Then, agencies engage in another round of decision making as they implement the budget with whatever discretion Congress permits. GPRA could therefore affect budget decisions in four ways: by altering agency budget requests, by altering agencies' management of resources after they receive their budgets, by altering the president's budget recommendations to Congress, or by altering actual budget decisions made by Congress (Joyce 2007, 96).

Chapter 8 already dealt with issues related to budget execution—that is, allocation and management of financial resources where the agency has discretion.

Many of the case studies cited in that chapter show how agencies used performance information to inform discretionary resource allocation. The agency averages in Table 8.4 (Chapter 8) show that between 2000 and 2007, about 5% more managers said they use performance information to allocate resources in their programs, and about 7% more said that they use performance information to set priorities. These are not huge changes, but they indicate some progress. Table 8.5 indicates that 11 agencies saw a greater than 5% improvement in managers saying that they use performance information to allocate resources, and 14 agencies saw a greater than 5% improvement in managers saying that they use performance information to set priorities. As with many of the other changes in the availability and use of performance information, noticeable improvement seems to be concentrated in about half the agencies.

In this chapter, we focus on the use of performance information to shape presidential budget requests and congressional appropriations decisions. Over time, one would expect that effective use of outcome information would lead to reallocation of expenditures from programs that do not produce results to programs that do. As Blanchard (2006, 6) notes, "The notion that budget allocations should favor higher-performing programs is the defining principle of performance budgeting." However, this is not a rigid, automatic process. Some programs may fail to produce results because they are poorly structured, have vague goals, or receive insufficient funding (Moynihan 2008, 127–29, Joyce 2007, 93–94, Blanchard 2006, 8). Fixing those problems could transform some ineffective programs into effective ones. Nevertheless, one would expect that better outcome information would lead decision makers to terminate or shrink at least some programs in order to reallocate resources to more effective ones that seek to achieve similar goals. Certainly some OMB staff hoped this would happen (Moynihan 2008, 128). Altered patterns of funding thus provide one highly observable indicator that helps gauge whether performance information has had any effect on budget decisions.

Agency Performance Budgets

In the late 1990s, OMB began to discuss the need to restructure budget accounts to better align resources with results. Some agencies began experimenting with performance budgets. EPA submitted its first performance budget for fiscal year 1999. In July 2003, OMB directed agencies to develop performance budgets that integrated their GPRA-mandated annual performance plans into their congressional budget justifications beginning with fiscal year 2005 (GAO 2005a, 38).

A major goal of this change was to better link costs with information about goals and outcomes. Federal appropriations accounts and programs do not necessarily match up with agency strategic goals, measures, or outcomes. Some performance goals cut across multiple accounts or programs, and appropriations for an individual program may not measure the full cost of achieving that program's goals (GAO 2005a, 24). The Department of Veterans Affairs' burial program, for example, was funded by six different appropriations accounts (GAO 2005a, 70). OMB also sought to restructure appropriations accounts so that managers responsible for particular outcomes would have greater ability to reallocate resources to achieve those outcomes, since managers normally lack authority to reallocate funds between appropriations accounts (GAO 2005a, 43, 72–73).

A general, statistical indicator of agencies' progress in using performance information for budgeting would be changes in agency evaluations on "budget and performance integration," one of five management priorities in the President's Management Agenda articulated by the G. W. Bush administration in 2001. The goal of budget and performance integration was succinctly stated: "Over time, agencies will be expected to identify high quality outcome measures, accurately monitor the performance of programs, and begin integrating this presentation with associated cost. Using this information, high performing programs will be reinforced and non-performing activities reformed or terminated" (OMB 2001a, 29). The President's Management Council, in consultation with experts in government and academia, developed a set of standards for evaluating agencies' success in budget and performance integration. OMB issued a quarterly scorecard indicating each agency's achievement and progress, using color codes of red (unsatisfactory), yellow (mixed results), and green (success). A 2001 baseline evaluation of 26 federal agencies that account for virtually all federal spending awarded just three agencies with yellow for mixed results; none achieved green (OMB 2001b). By the end of 2008, 19 agencies had "gotten to green" on budget and performance integration (now renamed "performance improvement"); the remainder were rated yellow (OMB 2008b).

Case studies suggest that performance budgeting has become more widespread in federal agencies and affects managers' decisions. Two of the earliest innovators were the National Aeronautics and Space Administration (NASA) and the Small Business Administration (SBA).

NASA was the first federal agency to achieve a green rating on budget and performance integration (Blanchard 2006, 9). Prior to performance budgeting, NASA budgets for programs and projects included only direct costs, such as contracts and project support. Civil service employees were paid out of a separate part of the budget over which project managers had no control and no responsibility. General and administrative (G&A) costs, such as agency-wide management, facilities, and safety, were not assigned to specific programs either. G&A costs amounted to about 5.4% of NASA's budget. Costs of individual centers that host multiple programs, such as the Kennedy Space Center in Florida, account for another 9.1% of the budget; prior to performance budgeting, these were not charged to programs either (Blanchard 2006, 25–26).

These practices created a knowledge problem and an incentive problem. Neither top NASA management nor managers of individual programs knew what the programs actually cost, because personnel and overhead costs were not included as program costs. Not knowing the full cost, they could not compare costs with outcomes or estimate what it might cost to achieve an incremental improvement in outcomes. Program managers, meanwhile, had strong incentives to claim as many civil service employees as they could, because these individuals were essentially a free resource. The employees worked on projects, but project managers were not responsible for the budgets that paid their salaries or travel expenses (GAO 2005a, 72).

NASA's performance budget sought to allocate all costs to individual programs and projects. The costs of civil service employees were allocated to the program in which each employee worked; managers now had an incentive to seek additional employees only if they thought the improved results would justify the additional cost. NASA allocated general and administrative costs to projects and programs in proportion to each program's share of the total budget. Costs of centers were charged to each program based on the total workforce (civil service plus contract employees) each program had at each center. Costs of other internal services, such as facilities, computing, and telecommunications, were charged to each project based on usage.

These kinds of cost allocations create a more transparent picture of each program's actual costs. In addition, they create incentives for program managers to economize on the use of resources they can directly control (such as personnel and internal services), carefully consider costs they can indirectly influence (such as allocations from centers based on workforce numbers), and at least question costs that are allocated to them like a tax (central G&A). NASA sought and achieved changes in its appropriations structure to reflect this new cost accounting system. For example, the general appropriations account for "mission support" was eliminated, and these resources instead are included in program budgets. Out of nine agencies whose performance budget initiatives were studied by the Government Accountability Office (GAO), NASA was the only agency that convinced Congress to change its appropriations accounts to fully reflect its performance-based budget initiative (GAO 2005a, 59, 78).

Ironically, NASA's effort to better identify costs of programs did not appear to have much of an effect on its GPRA reporting. Its budgetary changes occurred between fiscal years 2003 and 2005. After fiscal year 2003, NASA never scored higher than a 2 on the Mercatus *Scorecard*'s criterion 8, linkage of results to costs.

The Small Business Administration began using an "activity-based costing" model to calculate the full costs of programs in fiscal year 1999. Since 81% of the SBA's operating costs were personnel costs, in fiscal year 2002 the agency introduced a web-based survey that allowed employees to track their time spent on specific activities. The costs of activities occurring within specific programs were, of course, charged to those programs. Costs of activities that occur at the agency or field operations level were allocated to programs based on factors believed to drive these costs. Employee benefits, for example, were allocated based on the number of full-time employees, and rent was allocated based on square footage used. This activity-based costing system revealed that in fiscal year 2004, the SBA devoted $9.5 million in personnel time to the Business Information Centers discussed in

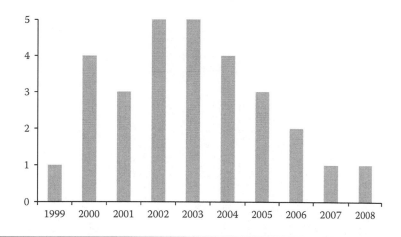

Figure 9.1 SBA's Mercatus *Scorecard* score on linking results with costs.

Chapter 8. The centers had an explicit appropriation of only $396,000 (Blanchard 2006, 30–31). Now aware of the true resource costs, SBA management opted to discontinue the program.

In contrast to NASA, SBA emerged as an early innovator in linking results to costs in its GPRA report. Figure 9.1 shows that on criterion 8, linkage of results to costs, the agency earned a 4 in fiscal year 2000 and a 3 in fiscal year 2001, followed by back-to-back 5's in fiscal years 2002 and 2003.

In 2000, SBA broke down costs at the performance indicator level, though not at higher levels like strategic goals (McTigue et al. 2001, 10). In 2002, it added cost per user and cost per output measures for some activities (McTigue et al. 2003, 13). The SBA improved its presentation further in fiscal year 2003 to become the recognized leader at that time (McTigue et al. 2004, 25). SBA (2004, 61), in turn, touted its high Mercatus *Scorecard* score for linkage of results to costs in its fiscal year 2004 performance and accountability report. Tables in the "Management's Discussion and Analysis" section broke costs down by strategic goals and long-term objectives under those goals. SBA presented this cost information going back to fiscal year 2000. Some tables also included calculations of costs per outcome or output.

Figure 9.2 shows an example from the fiscal year 2003 report. This particular objective involves the SBA's advocacy program, which intervenes with other federal agencies to find ways of reducing or mitigating regulatory costs on small businesses. The table shows several outcome measures, an output measure, and total costs associated with this long-term objective. It provides several years' worth of past data, annual goals, and a long-term goal. SBA's score slipped in subsequent years only because other agencies made major strides in taking cost information down to level of annual performance goals and individual performance measures. (See Chapter 3 for a description of best practices involving linkage of results with costs as of fiscal year 2008.)

Long-Term Objective 1.1: Minimize the Regulatory Burden on Small Business through Effective Advocacy

Key Results and Cost-Related Performance

SBA Outcome Measures	Results and Resources							
	FY 2000 Actual	*FY 2001 Actual*	*FY 2002 Actual*	*FY 2003 Goal*	*FY 2003 Actual*	*FY 2004 Goal*	*FY 2005 Goal*	*FY 2003– 2007 Goal*
SBA Annual Outcome Measures								
1.1.1 Achieve a yearly regulatory cost savings that increases at a rate of 10% annually over a base amount of $3.8 billion set in 2002, due to advocacy intervention, by FY 2008.								
	$3.6B	$4.4B	$21.1B[a]	$4.0B	$6.3B	$4.6B[b]	$5.1B	$24.5B
1.1.2 Ensure 66 federal agencies have in-house expertise on how to comply with the Regulatory Flexibility Act (RFA) as amended by the Small Business Regulatory Enforcement Fairness Act of 1996, by FY 2008.[c]								
	N/A[d]	N/A	N/A	N/A	N/A	25	25	66
1.1.3 Achieve a total of 50 states that have formally considered legislative or executive action to increase regulatory flexibility for small business, by FY 2008.								
	N/A	N/A	N/A	N/A	N/A	10	10	50
1.1.4 Insert advocacy data and reports into the curricula at 80 of the top 100 universities with major entrepreneurship programs, by FY 2008.								
	N/A	N/A	N/A	N/A	N/A	16	16	80

SBA Annual Output Measures

SBA Output Measures	FY 2000 Actual	FY 2001 Actual	FY 2002 Actual	FY 2003 Goal	FY 2003 Actual	FY 2004 Goal	FY 2005 Goal	FY 2003–2007 Goal
Research publications	25	17	18	20	30	20	20	100

SBA Annual Cost

SBA Outcomes Cost	FY 2000 Actual	FY 2001 Actual	FY 2002 Actual	FY 2003 Goal	FY 2003 Actual	FY 2004 Goal	FY 2005 Goal	FY 2003–2007 Goal
Total regulatory burden assistance cost ($000)	7,126	7,175	7,780	9,709	8,680	11,239	TBD	TBD

Figure 9.2 SBA linkage of results with costs, fiscal year 2003. (Source: U.S. Small Business Administration, Performance and Accountability Report, Fiscal Year 2003, 2003, 46, http://www.sba.gov/idc/groups/public/documents/sba_homepage/sba_010475.pdf.)

In 2005, GAO released a series of performance budgeting case studies at nine agencies that made the most significant changes to integrate performance information into their budgets: VA, NASA, the Department of Justice (DOJ), the Environmental Protection Agency (EPA), SBA, Commerce, Housing and Urban Development (HUD), Labor, and the Department of Transportation (DOT). Some proposed changes in their appropriations account structures; others sought to make changes within appropriations accounts. All restructured their congressional budget justifications to better match budget resources with strategic goals, objectives, or performance goals. VA, for example, sought to eliminate appropriations accounts for construction, grants, and program administration, and instead receive these resources as part of appropriations accounts for individual programs (GAO 2005a, 60). EPA had five appropriations accounts in fiscal year 2005: environmental programs and management, science and technology, state and tribal assistance grants, buildings and facilities, and office of the inspector general. Instead of organizing its budget justification around these accounts, EPA used its five strategic goals: (1) clean air and global climate change, (2) clean and safe water, (3) land preservation and restoration, (4) healthy communities and ecosystems, and (5) compliance and environmental stewardship. Since appropriations accounts supported multiple strategic goals, the agency included crosswalk tables that showed the relationships between the two ways of categorizing costs (GAO 2005a, 50–51).

The performance budgeting initiatives had positive effects for agency management. NASA's new appropriations structure gave managers more flexibility to use budget resources for procurement, facilities, or general administration. EPA received more flexibility to reprogram funds within strategic objectives (GAO 2005a, 62–63). Several agencies told GAO that budget restructuring prompted managers to focus more on the agencies' strategic and performance goals. Officials at OMB, NASA, EPA, and VA all said that consolidating budget requests based on strategic goals and performance measures had improved coordination among different parts of agencies that had to work together to accomplish the strategic goal. "OMB staff explained that there is more coordination among EPA's program offices because programs that support common goals and objectives have to 'sell' themselves together under the new planning and budget structure." Seven of the nine agencies said budget restructuring revealed how resources matched up with goals and objectives (GAO 2205a, 68–69). Commerce and EPA told GAO that they used performance budgets for internal management even though Congress continued to appropriate funds to individual programs rather than strategic goals or outcomes (GAO 2005a, 87–88).

Presidential Budget Recommendations

In addition to requiring agencies to produce performance budgets, the G. W. Bush administration undertook another systematic initiative intended to link performance information with budget recommendations. In February 2003, the administration released its system for reviewing the performance of most federal programs, called the Program Assessment Rating Tool (PART). PART sought to link measurement of program results with GPRA's requirements for measurement of the agency's overall results. OMB Circular A-11 instructed agencies to use the same performance measures for GPRA and PART when plans and reports include programs that have been "PARTed" (Brito and Ellig 2009, 39).

As our description of PART in Chapter 8 makes clear, a PART score was a noisy signal of actual performance. Half of the PART score depended on factors other than results. While it may be critically important for agencies and OMB to analyze a program's purpose, design, strategic planning, and management, these are not outcomes. At best they might be inputs or leading indicators of performance. Even within the results category, which accounts for the other half of the PART score, not every question identified the quantity, quality, or value of results the agency produced. The five questions applicable to all agencies were:

1. Has the program demonstrated adequate progress in achieving its long-term performance goals?
2. Does the program (including program partners) achieve its annual performance goals?
3. Does the program demonstrate achieving improved efficiencies or cost-effectiveness in achieving goals each year?
4. Does the performance of this program compare favorably to that of other programs, including government, private, etc., with a similar purpose and goals?
5. Do independent evaluations of sufficient scope and quality indicate that the program is effective and achieving results? (OMB 2008d, iv)

A program needed to achieve results and document them to receive a high PART score. But a middling score could mean that a program scored either high on results but low on the other three factors, high on the other three factors but low on results, or moderately on all factors including results. To understand what outcomes an agency produced, one would need to consult the underlying documents, data, and studies used to justify the PART score. The PART score, therefore, might summarize a lot of information, but to make an informed budget decision, one would want to dig much deeper (Accenture et al. 2009, 13).

Nevertheless, several studies have found some degree of correlation between PART scores and presidential budget requests. A GAO analysis of the first year of PART data found that PART scores were positively correlated with the recommended funding changes in the president's fiscal 2004 budget, but only for small "discretionary" programs—the programs that require a congressional appropriation decision each year. A 1-point increase in a small discretionary program's PART score was associated with a 1.07% recommended funding increase in the president's budget. However, PART scores explained only about 15% of the variation in the president's budget requests; other factors likely had a larger impact (GAO 2004b, 42–46).

Gilmour and Lewis (2006a) found that the effect of PART scores on administration budget proposals for fiscal 2004 depended on the political orientation of the program's department. The G. W. Bush administration proposed larger budget increases for programs with higher PART scores in "Democratic" departments, but PART scores had either no effect or a negative effect on recommended funding in "Republican" departments. For fiscal 2005, however, Gilmour and Lewis (2006b) found that PART scores had a positive, statistically significant effect on budget recommendations, and political factors had little effect. A 1-point increase in the PART score was correlated with a 0.40–0.47% increase in recommended funding. Consistent with GAO (2004b), the authors found that the effect was concentrated in small programs, where a 1-point increase in the PART score was associated with a 1.28% increase in recommended budget.

Norcross (2005) and Norcross and McKenzie (2006) examined the relationship between PART ratings and presidential budget requests for fiscal years 2006 and 2007. Table 9.1, drawn from these studies, shows the percent of programs with various ratings that the president's budget recommended for funding increases, decreases, or no change. The president's budget usually recommended funding

Table 9.1 PART Ratings and Funding Changes Recommended in the President's Budget

	Ineffective	Adequate	Moderately Effective	Effective	Results Not Demonstrated
Fiscal 2006					
Increase	5%	43%	51%	61%	30%
No change	9%	22%	11%	4%	28%
Decrease	86%	36%	38%	35%	41%
Fiscal 2007					
Increase	11%	37%	56%	61%	26%
No change	14%	21%	13%	10%	31%
Decrease	75%	42%	31%	28%	42%

Source: Norcross, Eileen, An Analysis of the Office of Management and Budget's Program Assessment Rating Tool, working paper, Mercatus Center at George Mason University, 2005, 19, http://mercatus.org/publication/analysis-office-management-and-budgets-program-assessment-rating-tool-fy06; Norcross, Eileen, and Kyle McKenzie, An Analysis of the Office of Management and Budget's Program Assessment Rating Tool for Fiscal Year 2007, working paper, Mercatus Center at George Mason University, 2006, 22, http://mercatus.org/publication/analysis-office-management-and-budgets-program-assessment-rating-tool-fy-2007).

reductions for programs rated ineffective. Effective programs were most likely to get funding increase recommendations, followed by moderately effective and then adequate programs. However, the table also reveals that the relationship between PART ratings and funding recommendations was far from automatic or mechanical. Funding increases were recommended for more than one-third of effective, moderately effective, and adequate programs. Funding reductions were recommended for about one-third of effective and moderately effective programs. Since the "results not demonstrated" programs were programs for which insufficient information about results was available, clearly something other than PART ratings drove the budget recommendations for those programs.

Proposed program terminations provide another way to search for links between PART ratings and presidential budget recommendations. Thirty-two of the 99 programs proposed for termination in the fiscal 2006 budget had undergone PART reviews. Ten of these programs were rated ineffective, six were rated adequate, and 16 were results not demonstrated (Norcross 2005, 19–20). In the fiscal 2007 budget, seven programs proposed for termination were ineffective, eight were adequate, two were moderately effective, and 15 were results not demonstrated (Norcross and McKenzie 2006, 24). For fiscal 2008, 37 programs recommended for termination had been PARTed. Five were ineffective, six were adequate, four were moderately effective, and 22 were results not demonstrated (Norcross and Adamson 2007, 29). Thus, most programs recommended for termination were either ineffective or results not demonstrated. The administration did not recommend terminating any effective programs.

For all three years, the budget's *Major Savings and Reforms* document claims that PART ratings were one factor affecting many of the termination recommendations, but not the only factor. Clearly, factors other than PART reviews must have been responsible for the terminations or cuts in programs that had not yet been PARTed. Two-thirds of the 154 programs proposed for elimination or termination in fiscal year 2006 had not been PARTed (Hughes and Shull 2005, 4). Thus, the available studies suggest that PART ratings affected the G. W. Bush administration's budget recommendations to some extent, though not to a great degree.

Congressional Budget Decisions

In general, Congress has displayed less interest in performance-based budgeting than the president. In the early years of GPRA, House Majority Leader Dick Armey took an active role in assessing agencies' strategic plans and performance plans. Apparently few appropriators or committee chairs shared his enthusiasm. In her study of GPRA implementation by the Department of Transportation, for example, Curristine (2002, 42) notes, "Indications from interviews with appropriators show that they will not use performance measures in making funding decisions on highways."

The congressional response to the administration's attempt to reformat agency budget justifications submitted to Congress for fiscal years 2004 and 2005 is instructive. Congress rejected most of the performance budgeting formats. GAO (2005a, 91) noted, "While some agencies have demonstrated that sustained commitment by agency leadership is important to move budget restructuring forward, this commitment has not yet been shared by congressional appropriators and other decision makers." Moynihan (2008, 124) quotes one OMB budget examiner on the congressional response:

> The good government types and the government oversight committees are supportive, but they have very little clout. The appropriations committees have been much less enthusiastic. My committee was outright hostile. They think that the performance information in the budget produced a lot of paper but nothing they found useful.

Extensive GAO case studies revealed that committees usually preferred to use information organized by program and categories of expenditures rather than strategic goals:

> Congressional appropriations subcommittee staff for the most part continued to state a preference for and rely on previously established budget structures. Appropriations subcommittees and staff said that the changes in budget accounts and presentations shifted the focus away from programs and items of expenditures of interest to congressional appropriators and instead highlighted strategic and performance goals. While these staff expressed general support for budget and performance integration, they objected to changes that replaced information, such as workload and output measures, traditionally used for congressional appropriations and oversight with the new performance perspective. (GAO 2005a, 7)

The Environmental Protection Agency (EPA) had structured its budget requests around strategic goals since fiscal 1999. Nevertheless, Congress required the EPA to continue to break budget requests down by program as well, and this is the information Congress used to make appropriations. Appropriations subcommittee staff generally did not use the performance-based budget to conduct their work, but rather the program-based information they requested from EPA. In 2004, the House and Senate appropriations subcommittees required that the EPA reformat its budget justification using appropriations accounts and programs rather than strategic goals. Information on strategic goals and objectives became a supplement (GAO 2005a, 14–17, 78, 164).

Similarly, appropriations committee staff did not use the performance-based information from the Labor Department, but consulted budget justifications from earlier years and requested supplementary information (GAO 2005a, 95). In 2004, the House Appropriations Committee directed Veterans Affairs "to refrain from incorporating 'performance-based' budget documents in the 2005 budget justification submitted to the Committee, but keep the Performance Plan as a separate volume." When the department submitted a restructured performance-based budget for 2005, the committee responded, "If the Department wishes to continue the wasteful practice of submitting a budget structure that will not serve the needs of the Congress, the Congress has little choice but to reject that structure and continue providing appropriations that serve its purposes" (GAO 2005a, 79). The committee directed HUD "not to submit or otherwise incorporate the strategic planning document or its structure into its fiscal year 2005 Budget Justification submission to the Committee." HUD did not submit a performance budget for fiscal year 2005, and the committee reiterated its directive that strategic planning documents or formats were not to be included in future budget submissions (GAO 2005a, 80). After telling the Departments of Transportation, Treasury, and independent agencies to revert to the traditional budget justification format, the committee warned, "If the Office of Management and Budget or individual agencies do not heed the Committee's direction, the Committee will assume that individual budget offices have excess resources that can be applied to other, more critical missions" (Moynihan 2008, 123). Similarly, the Senate Appropriations Committee told the Labor Department that it should use performance information for management purposes but should submit its budget requests in the traditional appropriations format rather than a performance budget format (GAO 2005a, 81). Congress accepted only NASA's proposed revisions to its appropriations accounts (GAO 2005a, 78).

Different committee staff cited different reasons for rejecting the administration's performance-based budget formats. Committees often preferred to appropriate funds by functional area or program, sometimes disagreed with the agency's strategic goals, expressed concern that strategic goals would change when the agency's strategic plan changed, and questioned whether some agencies could track expenditures by strategic goal. Some staff noted that the new format omitted some useful information, such as unit cost, workload, and output measures; historical spending trends; and funding levels broken down by program or state. Some said there was too much performance information, too much narrative, or that the information was poorly organized and formatted (GAO 2005a, 81–85).

Some of these reasons suggest that the committees simply did not want to appropriate funds based on outcomes. Others imply that committees saw the prospective value of performance budgeting but did not think the agencies' performance budgets provided the right information in the right way.

A content analysis of appropriations documents for the fiscal year 2004 budget suggests Congress had little interest in using performance information at this time. Moynihan (2008) examined appropriations bills, accompanying conference reports, and oversight and appropriations hearings in search of performance discussions. In

3,257 single-spaced pages of text, he found that "performance" was mentioned just 57 times in reference to expected or projected program performance, 21 times when committees urged agencies to use performance information, 109 times when legislators asked agencies for more data, and 47 times in reference to actual program achievement. Only nine of these latter instances involved citation of quantitative performance indicators. "The documents examined show no discussions of legislators using the [performance] information themselves" (Moynihan 2008, 131–33).

Another possible indicator of congressional receptivity to performance budgeting would be congressional reaction to PART. PART attempted to match up performance information with individual programs. This could potentially overcome one objection to the performance budgeting initiatives described above – that they provided performance information at the level of strategic goals and objectives instead of at the programmatic level. A 2005 GAO study cited several examples of committee hearings or legislation that related to PART. Nevertheless, GAO (2005b, 49) concluded, "Despite its efforts, OMB has had limited success in engaging Congress in the PART process."

Even if Congress did not use PART, it may have acquiesced in presidential recommendations that were informed by PART. Table 9.2 shows that congressional budget decisions on PARTed programs were often consistent with the president's proposals, with two exceptions. First, Congress was much less likely than the president to cut funding for ineffective programs and much more likely to increase funding for these programs. Second, for fiscal 2007, Congress increased funding for a much smaller percentage of the effective programs that the president recommended, and decreased funding for a much larger percentage.

There is, however, little evidence that Congress considered PART ratings when it made these decisions. An analysis of committee reports in the 109th Congress, which approved the fiscal year 2006 and 2007 budgets, revealed that only about 6% of them had PART-related content, which leads the authors to conclude that Congress used PART "on a limited basis." One subcommittee even banned departments under its jurisdiction from including PART information in its fiscal 2008 budget submission (Frisco and Stalebrink 2008).

Little appears to have changed during the last two years of the Bush administration. Metzenbaum (2009) interviewed congressional staff in 2008 to ascertain their impressions of GPRA and PART. Congressional staff told her they were interested in seeing performance information, and several cited examples of agencies that did a good job of integrating such information into their budget requests. However, staff still had trouble finding the information they wanted for making budget decisions. Echoing GAO's (2005a) findings, one staffer noted,

> We kept saying, "What the hell is this? They are acting as if we appropriate by goals, not programs. We do not appropriate by goals. We appropriate by program. We want them to tell us information by specific program area." (Metzenbaum 2009, 26)

Table 9.2   PART Ratings and Funding Changes Approved by Congress

	Ineffective	Adequate	Moderately Effective	Effective	Results Not Demonstrated
Fiscal 2006					
Increase	18%	47%	53%	59%	34%
No change	4%	13%	12%	5%	25%
Decrease	79%	39%	35%	36%	42%
Fiscal 2007					
Increase	30%	33%	43%	48%	24%
No change	41%	29%	23%	14%	42%
Decrease	30%	38%	34%	38%	33%

Source: Norcross, Eileen, and Joseph Adamson, An Analysis of the Office of Management and Budget's Program Assessment Rating Tool for Fiscal Year 2008, working paper, Mercatus Center at George Mason University, 2007, 28, http://mercatus.org/publication/analysis-office-management-and-budgets-program-assessment-rating-tool-fy-2008; Norcross, Eileen, and Kyle McKenzie, An Analysis of the Office of Management and Budget's Program Assessment Rating Tool for Fiscal Year 2007, working paper, Mercatus Center at George Mason University, 2006, 23, http://mercatus.org/publication/analysis-office-management-and-budgets-program-assessment-rating-tool-fy-2007).

Why the Divergence?

The available studies suggest that performance information has had some influence on agency management and presidential budget recommendations, but very little influence on congressional budgeting decisions. Two different types of explanations could account for this divergence. Perhaps the quality of the performance information and the format in which it is presented are simply not yet good enough for Congress to rely upon to make decisions. Alternatively—or perhaps additionally— the relative lack of congressional interest can be explained by the different political incentives congressional appropriations committees and the president face to monitor agency outputs, efficiency, and outcomes.

Quality and Format

As noted above, congressional staffers, and sometimes even agency managers, told GAO (2005a) about a number of inadequacies in the performance budgets agencies submitted for fiscal years 2004 and 2005. Perhaps if agencies improved their ability to track spending versus outcomes as the spending occurs, added historical trends and other information Congress found helpful, and also showed spending and results by program, appropriations committees would find performance budgets more useful. Greater dialog with the committees might also help. OMB directed agencies to consult with congressional committees when they redesigned their budgets, but apparently such consultation did not occur in many cases (GAO 2005a, 93). It's no surprise that many committees rejected performance budgets if they had not agreed to the format up front and had little or no role in shaping it to meet their needs.

Inadequacies in agency performance budgets, however, do not explain why congressional committees directed agencies to revert to older, non-performance-based formats. If committees actually wanted to use performance budgets, they could have instructed agencies to fix the problems in their performance budgets, rather than telling them to go back to the old way. There was a clear opportunity here to begin a dialog, albeit belatedly. There is little evidence that committees took advantage of that opportunity.

Congressional indifference to PART also suggests that Congress was less interested in performance than the executive branch. One of the big objections to performance budgets was that they organized information by agency strategic goals rather than by program. Congress appropriates money to programs. PART, however, organized performance and cost information by program rather than by strategic goal. PART performance measures often showed which strategic goal or goals an individual program supported. Even though PART presented information on programs, it apparently had little influence on congressional budget decisions.

Divergent Political Incentives

Under the American constitutional system of checks and balances, conflict between the president and Congress over performance budgeting is inevitable. This conflict occurs even when the same political party controls Congress and the presidency. Republican congressional leaders heavily criticized the Clinton administration's GPRA implementation, but it was also a Republican Congress that rejected the G. W. Bush administration's performance budgeting and PART initiatives.

This conflict does not arise simply because the legislative and executive branches are two separate entities who both want power. Both branches, after all, are ultimately accountable to American voters. Especially when the same political party controls both branches, one might imagine that the president and congressional leaders would have a similar interest in performance management because both must respond to the same electorate. On the contrary, the deep-rooted conflicts between the president and Congress arise precisely because they are elected by different constituencies.

Members of the U.S. Congress represent particular geographical constituencies. The appropriations committees and subcommittees make most budget decisions. Committee members tend to be "high demanders" of the services provided by the agencies over which the committee has jurisdiction (Niskanen 1994c, 250–51). High-demand members may have many constituents who benefit from the agencies' program outcomes (such as, for example, a large number of blue-collar factory workers who need vocational retraining). Alternatively, a high-demand member may have constituents who benefit greatly from the expenditures even if they are not direct consumers of the services (such as employees of a large military base in the member's district).

In both cases, the member's district or state receives concentrated benefits from the expenditures or outcomes, while the entire nation pays the costs of those particular programs. "Each legislator will want to procure a project that is larger than optimal because he or she no longer internalizes the full marginal cost of the project" (Primo 2007, 44). Legislators and voters as a whole, however, would be better off if the government funded only those programs that produced benefits to the entire nation that exceed the costs to the entire nation, and if those programs operated at maximum efficiency and effectiveness.

To the extent that their constituents benefit from program outcomes, committee members have some reason to monitor agencies' performance. But they also face two countervailing incentives that discourage them from monitoring. First, some of their constituents may profit personally from agencies' inefficient or less effective expenditures. Appropriations for weapons systems the Defense Department says it doesn't need are an extreme example of this type of expenditure. Improved accountability for outcomes would likely reduce or eliminate those kinds of expenditures, thus reducing benefits that flow to some individual districts. Second, individual members of Congress must decide how to divide their time and staff resources between activities that benefit their own constituencies almost exclusively (such as answering mail, speaking at community events, and helping constituents get federal money) and activities whose benefits are spread across the entire nation. Monitoring the efficiency and effectiveness of federal programs is often a good example of the latter activity (Niskanen 1994c, 251–54). Thus, committee members will likely devote less time and effort to monitoring the efficiency and effectiveness of government programs than the typical or "median" voter would like.

The president, on the other hand, is elected by the entire nation. To win in a two-party system, the president usually has to appeal to the median voters. Therefore, the president has a stronger incentive than the members of appropriations committees to reflect the preferences of the median voter (Niskanen 1994b, 227). Given these differing political incentives, it is no surprise that the U.S. executive branch shows more interest than congressional appropriations committees in using performance information to make budget decisions.

Getting Performance Budgeting Back on Track

At the outset of GPRA, many hoped that transparent disclosure of performance information would itself increase the political benefits and reduce the costs of monitoring agencies' performance. Annual performance reports would make voters more aware of government performance and reduce congressional monitoring costs. With some segment of voters better informed and more vigilant, members of Congress would find that improved efficiency and effectiveness of programs attracts votes. Thus far, this has not happened to any great extent.

Another possible way to increase congressional focus on efficiency and effectiveness would be process reforms that promote budget decisions based on benefits and costs to the nation as a whole rather than just benefits and costs to individual members' constituencies. Several options include:

Budget amendment rules. Primo (2007) finds that enforceable spending limits prompt "agenda setters" to propose funding for programs that are more efficient, or at least less inefficient, in the sense that they better balance cost to the nation with benefits to the nation. A budget rule that allows spending bills complying with a preset spending ceiling to proceed to a floor vote without amendments would likely induce committees to make more efficient spending recommendations (Primo 2007, 74–81).

One significant challenge, however, is crafting an enforcement mechanism for the budget rule. Either house of Congress can adopt a rule establishing spending caps, but Congress can override those rules when it passes the final budget. Scholars have suggested that supermajority requirements to pass appropriations bills could, at least in some cases, make it harder for legislators to enact budgets that contain many inefficient programs, since they need to get buy-in from a larger number of representatives whose constituents pay the costs (Primo 2007, 53–54; Niskanen 1994b, 227–28). The most effective enforcement, however, would come from external entities, such as the judiciary. Judicial enforcement would occur if the budget rule were written into the Constitution. This approach, of course, has pros and cons:

> If members are able to agree on a rule that requires them to take tough actions, they need to give the rule bite. Unlike a statute, which a determined Congress can easily change, a constitutional budget rule would require years to change. Members who wish to evade a constitutional rule do not have the luxury of altering it on the fly.
>
> This relative inflexibility is both a blessing and a curse. If well designed, the rule will have an important positive impact. If poorly designed, however, it may negatively influence the budget process for many years.... For this reason, it is better to have no constitutional amendment than an easily evaded or poorly constructed one. (Primo 2010, 27)

Spending and performance commission. Another option would be a commission to examine and terminate ineffective discretionary spending programs modeled on the Base Realignment and Closure Commission. In 1988, Congress created this commission of independent experts to identify military bases for closure based on military need. The commission's recommendations were implemented unless Congress voted to disapprove the entire list of base closures. Brito (2010) suggests that the commission succeeded for five reasons:

- It was an independent, blue-ribbon panel that contained no current officeholders with constituent interests to protect.
- It had a clear mission and clear set of performance-based criteria for assessing military bases.
- Congress had to vote on the commission's recommendations as an "all or nothing" package. The majority of members, who did not have bases slated for closure in their districts, would naturally vote for this package.
- The recommendations took effect unless Congress affirmatively voted otherwise and the president signed the joint resolution. Thus, the commission's recommendations were difficult to overturn, and Congress could acquiesce in them by doing nothing.
- The use of a commission gave members of Congress who lost military bases political cover; they could blame the commission and other members of Congress for base closures.

A spending and performance commission, composed of independent experts examining programs according to performance-based criteria specified by Congress, would issue recommendations that became operative unless Congress passed, and the president signed, a joint resolution of disapproval. This process would allow legislators to vote in favor of performance-based budgeting without having to explicitly vote against individual programs that may be politically popular even if they are ineffective.

Give budget committees the final say. Both the House and the Senate have budget committees that draft annual budget resolutions establishing overall levels for revenues, outlays, budget authority, deficits, and the public debt. Outlays and budget authority are broken down into broad functional categories, such as defense and transportation. Spending gets subdivided among the appropriations subcommittees, which appropriate money to programs. If the totals that result from decisions of the appropriations and tax-writing committees deviate from those in the budget resolution, a "reconciliation" bill makes adjustments.

The congressional budget process lacks a mechanism that forces Congress to weigh the costs and outcomes of individual programs and then make decisions based on the national interest. Members of the budget committees consider aggregate totals, but not program outcomes. Members of appropriations subcommittees make decisions only in the areas within their subcommittee's jurisdiction. These members tend to be the high demanders of spending on their subcommittee's programs, because their constituents either receive the spending or benefit from the program's outcomes.

One way to prompt a comparison of costs with outcomes from a national perspective would be to give the budget committees the final say on all appropriations and revenue measures. This would allow the budget committees to reconsider individual appropriations or tax provisions in light of the aggregate spending and revenue targets. It would also allow the budget committees to make spending decisions among competing priorities based on outcome information, instead of just allocating money to budget functions. Many parliamentary systems have precisely this type of mechanism, in the form of a finance and expenditure committee that must approve budgets.

A skeptical reader might interpret these kinds of recommendations as mere statements of ideological preference for smaller government. That interpretation misses the point entirely. Like diners who order too many bottles of wine because they're splitting the check equally, legislators are led by current institutional incentives (as if by an invisible hand!) to approve more programs that are less efficient than either they or their constituents would prefer in more sober moments under different rules. Changing the "rules of the game" to focus legislators more on efficiency and effectiveness and less on bringing home rewards to their individual constituencies could make legislators and the public better off by prompting legislators to choose a mix of programs and spending that gives the public greater value for its money.

Conclusion

GPRA was intended to improve agency management and congressional budget decisions by improving the quality of government performance information. The Mercatus *Scorecard* project clearly indicates that the quality of performance information has improved. GAO surveys, in conjunction with *Scorecard* data, show that GPRA has also improved the availability and use of performance information by federal managers. The G. W. Bush administration undertook a major effort to integrate performance with budget information and use the former to inform the latter. But Congress rarely used GPRA-oriented performance information in budgeting.

Individual members of Congress win reelection by bringing federal expenditures to constituencies in their districts or states, while the costs are shared among all taxpayers in the nation. They face weaker incentives to monitor programs for efficiency or effectiveness, since these benefits are often not concentrated on constituents in specific states or districts but rather are shared with program beneficiaries and taxpayers nationwide. Given this reality, it is perhaps not surprising that appropriations debates focus more on distribution of expenditures than on effectiveness or the benefit–cost analysis of expenditures.

GPRA authorized experiments in performance budgeting. But nothing in GPRA required Congress to use performance information in budgeting. The paucity of performance budgeting is a predictable result of the incentives most legislators face. No one has yet developed a magic pill that turns politicians into statesmen. To give performance budgeting a fighting chance, policymakers need to restructure the budget game in ways that constrain the tyranny of concentrated benefits and dispersed costs.

Chapter 10

Conclusions

Federal performance reporting improved significantly from the time the first GPRA reports were issued for fiscal 1999 through fiscal year 2008—the most recent year covered by our *Scorecard* reviews. Also, there is some evidence that GPRA has improved the availability and use of performance information within federal agencies. On the other hand, there is scant evidence that performance information has thus far had a significant impact on budgetary allocations or other policy decisions, particularly within Congress. Furthermore, the application of GPRA principles to regulatory activity has been incomplete, and their application to tax expenditures is virtually nonexistent. Given all of this, what does the future hold for GPRA and outcome-oriented performance accountability in the federal government?

Performance reports certainly can be further improved, as can the statutory framework for reporting. Indeed, significant changes to GPRA were enacted during the last days of the 111th Congress. In the final analysis, however, it is important to recognize that GPRA and performance reporting are fundamentally means to an end—not ends in themselves. They serve only as tools for the public, agency managers, and policymakers in the executive branch and Congress to use to accomplish the real end: performance-based, outcome-oriented policymaking. They will achieve their full potential and impact only when the public demands outcome-oriented performance accountability and policymakers have the political incentives to provide it. Given the state of the nation's economy, our dire fiscal situation, as well as widespread public dissatisfaction with the performance of the federal government and Washington gridlock, the day may be fast approaching when performance accountability and outcome-oriented policymaking will (must) become a reality.

Improving Performance Information

There are three main avenues for improving performance data. One, of course, is to continue to build upon best practices and enhance federal agency performance reports under GPRA. Previous chapters offer a number of suggestions to do this based on our ten years of experience from the *Scorecard* project, as well as our analysis of state and international performance reports. Second, recent administrations have undertaken initiatives to augment GPRA reports. The Bush administration developed the Program Assessment Rating Tool to scrutinize federal program performance. The Obama administration launched an initiative to develop federal agency high-priority performance goals. Third, Congress in 2010 enacted legislation to enhance GPRA itself and otherwise to make performance data more relevant and useful.

Program Assessment Rating Tool

The Bush administration Program Assessment Rating Tool (PART) focused on individual federal programs—more than 1,000 of them in all. The PART process used a standard set of diagnostic questions to assess each program. These questions included the following:

- Is the program purpose clear?
- Does the program have a limited number of specific long-term performance measures that focus on outcomes and meaningfully reflect the purpose of the program?
- Does the program have a limited number of annual performance goals that demonstrate progress toward achieving the long-term goals?
- Does the program have ambitious targets and timeframes for its long-term measures?
- Does the program achieve its annual performance goals?
- Has the program demonstrated adequate progress in achieving its long-term performance goals?

Programs assessed under PART were rated as "effective," "moderately effective," "adequate," or "ineffective." An additional rating category of "results not demonstrated" was used for programs that lacked adequate performance metrics or data to permit a determination of their level of performance. (See GAO 2004b and 2005b for general descriptions of the PART process.)

PART developed a wealth of data on program performance and outcomes. In this regard, one of its most striking features was the decline in the number of programs that received the "results not demonstrated" rating, from 50% of all assessed programs for fiscal year 2004 to only 21% for fiscal year 2008 (Norcross and Adamson 2007, 6–7). Also, while PART came under some criticism for not being well integrated with GPRA (GAO 2004b, 6–8; Metzenbaum 2009, 31–32), its focus on individual programs actually fit better with the federal budget process than GPRA's agency-wide perspective. Since Congress typically legislates and appropriates on the basis of individual programs, the PART assessments arguably should have more immediate and practical relevance to decision making by congressional authorizers and appropriators than GPRA performance reports. Another positive aspect of PART assessments is that they provided a consistent basis to compare the relative effectives of the host of federal programs, both within and across agencies, that have overlapping goals and objectives—such as the literally hundreds of federal programs targeted at employment, economic development, housing, poverty reduction, and many other important public outcomes.

Unfortunately, as Chapter 9 and GAO analyses show, Congress rarely used PART performance data in its deliberations (GAO 2009b, 18). This lack of interest probably stemmed primarily from the same congressional indifference to performance data that has stymied use of GPRA data.

High-Priority Performance Goals

Thus far, the Obama administration's principal effort to advance outcome-oriented performance management and accountability is the High-Priority Performance Goal Initiative. As described in the fiscal year 2011 budget, the premise underlying this initiative is that "the ultimate test of an effective performance management system is whether it is used" (OMB 2010b, 73). The budget description observes that while both GPRA and PART produced better performance information, they have not led to increased use of that data. OMB (2010b, 73–74) also states that the GPRA and PART time-frames did not provide agency managers with sufficiently timely feedback to assess and diagnose performance. The budget provides the following overview of the initiative:

> To encourage senior leaders to deliver results against the most important priorities, the Administration launched the High-Priority Performance Goal initiative in June 2009, asking agency heads to identify and commit to a limited number of priority goals, generally three to eight, with high value to the public. The goals must have ambitious, but realistic, targets to achieve within 18 to 24 months without need for new resources or legislation, and well-defined, outcomes-based measures of progress. (OMB 2010b, 74)

The budget goes on to list the high-priority goals for cabinet departments and a number of independent agencies (OMB 2010b, 75–90). The agency-by-agency listing captures some important public end or intermediate outcomes. For example:

■ Agriculture Department: By the end of 2011, increase agricultural exports by $2 billion (p. 76).
■ Department of Education: Improve high school graduation rates and college completion rates (p. 78).

- Department of Health and Human Services: By the end of 2011, decrease by 10% from the 2005–2007 baseline the rate of Salmonella illnesses, outbreaks and individual cases (p. 80).
- Department of Homeland Security: Reduce wait times for airline passengers to less than 20 minutes by 2012 (p. 80).
- Departments of Housing and Urban Development and Veterans Affairs: Reduce the number of homeless veterans to 59,000 by June 2012 (p. 82).
- Department of Labor: Reduce fatalities resulting from common causes by 2% per year in Occupational Safety and Health Administration-covered workplaces and by 5% in mining sites (p. 83).
- Department of Transportation: Reduce the risk of accidents during aircraft departures and landings by reducing the number of runway incursions by 5% from the 2008 baseline by 2011 (p. 84).

Overall, however, the list does not focus heavily on outcomes. Rather, most listed items appear to be output, activity, or efficiency goals and measures. One challenge in interpreting the goals and measures is that many are stated in somewhat "inside the beltway" language with frequent caveats and qualifications. This makes it difficult to readily grasp their importance in relation to public outcomes. Another challenge is that many are expressed as raw numbers that obscure their impact on the problem being addressed. For example, the Justice Department goals and measures include increasing the percentage of terrorism investigations targeting top-priority threats by 5% and increasing the caseload of certain white-collar crimes by 5% (OMB 2010b, 82–83). It is not clear whether or how achieving these numbers will actually translate into making the nation more secure from terrorism or reducing white-collar crime. Similarly, it is hard to assess the significance of the Social Security Administration's goal to reduce disability hearing decisions to an average of 270 days in relation to the agency's severe backlog in this area (OMB 2010b, 89). As described in previous chapters, we have found a wide range of clearly stated and important outcome goals and measures in agency GPRA reports. Thus, it would not be difficult to find additional outcomes to highlight for inclusion in the initiative.

It would be premature to assess the effectiveness of the High-Priority Goal Initiative given its recent vintage. More to the point, the initiative has now been subsumed and expanded considerably by the GPRA Modernization Act of 2010. Thus, the likely focus for the next several years will be on implementation of the new law and evaluation of its effectiveness.

GPRA Modernization Act of 2010

During the 111th Congress, both the House of Representatives and the Senate considered legislation to amend GPRA and otherwise enhance the development and use of performance data. This effort ultimately resulted in enactment of the GPRA Modernization Act of 2010, Public Law 111-352. It is reproduced in Appendix III.

The original version of the new law was introduced on April 28, 2009, as H.R. 2142, the proposed "Government Efficiency, Effectiveness, and Performance Improvement Act of 2009." The main purpose of the original bill was to require agencies to conduct assessments of each of their programs at least once every five years. The required program assessments were quite similar to those of the Bush era PART process. The original bill also revised the statutory timeframe for submission of GPRA strategic plans to coincide with the presidential election cycle, instead of every five years. Currently, strategic plans are not in sync with the electoral cycle. This leads to the potential anomaly (which occurred in 2008) of agencies submitting a new round of strategic plans shortly before a presidential transition. In addition, the bill codified provisions of a Bush administration executive order requiring the establishment of agency performance improvement officers as well as a performance improvement council, composed of such officers and others, to be chaired by the OMB deputy director for management.

The House Committee on Oversight and Government Reform reported an amended version of H.R. 2142, which passed the House on June 16, 2010. The amended version of the House bill dropped the PART-like individual program assessments in favor of a mandate for high-priority performance goals along the lines of the Obama administration initiative. On the Senate side, S. 3853, captioned the "GPRA Modernization Act of 2010," was introduced on September 28, 2010. The Senate bill included an agency high-priority performance goal mandate similar to the House-passed bill and the Obama administration initiative. However, the Senate bill added a number of new features, including a mandate for a set of outcome-oriented, crosscutting performance goals. Eventually, the Senate passed H.R. 2142 after amending the text to incorporate its language and, on December 21, 2010, the House concurred in the Senate amendment.

As enacted, the GPRA Modernization Act of 2010 retains a number of provisions that date back to the original House bill: the change in agency strategic plan submissions to a four-year cycle that coincides with presidential transitions, the mandate for agency performance improvement officers and the performance improvement council,* and various provisions to enhance the transparency and availability of performance information as well as to encourage greater congressional and public input into the development of performance goals and measures. Other major features of the act include:

■ Agency high-priority performance goals. These goals are to cover two years and reflect the agency's highest priorities. They must have ambitious targets that can be achieved within two years, as well as clearly defined quarterly measures. The agency must identify an official, known as a goal leader, who is responsible for achievement of each priority goal.

---

* In a related provision, the act designates the deputy head of each agency to serve as its "chief operating officer" and exercise overall responsibility for improving the agency's management and performance.

■ Federal government priority goals. These goals are to be identified in the federal government performance plan and generally cover four years. They will consist of outcome-oriented goals covering a limited number of crosscutting policy areas as well as crosscutting management goals. The federal government performance plan must identify the agencies, programs, regulations, tax expenditures, policies, and other activities contributing to each federal government performance goal; specify the contribution of each agency, program, regulation, and tax expenditure toward achieving the goal; and establish common performance measures with quarterly targets for each goal. A designated government official will have lead responsibility for coordinating achievement of each goal.

■ Progress toward achieving the agency high-priority goals and federal government goals is to be assessed quarterly and reported on a web site maintained by OMB.

■ Agency performance plans and reports are to analyze the accuracy and reliability of performance data as well as data limitations and how they will be addressed.

The GPRA Modernization Act implements numerous ideas advanced by public management experts during the presidential transition (see, e.g., Metzenbaum 2009, Accenture et al. 2009). We believe the provisions of the new law are quite positive on the whole. Enhancing the transparency of performance information and its availability to the public is an important objective. Coordinating strategic plan submission cycles with presidential administrations is a commonsense correction to an obvious glitch in the current law. Likewise, encouraging greater congressional involvement in the full range of performance planning and reporting is certainly a good thing. More congressional participation in the development of performance metrics at the front end should stimulate more congressional buy-in and use of the resulting data in its decision making.

Other worthy features are the mandates for both agency-specific and government-wide priority goals in order to focus maximum attention on the most important public outcomes that the federal government pursues. The requirement that agencies identify all programs, tax expenditures, and regulations that contribute toward these goals is especially welcome, given the paucity of attention the latter two topics have received in performance reporting and the regulatory review process. Indeed, we recommend that the same holistic approach of considering the impact of all relevant spending programs, regulations, and tax expenditures be applied to all agency GPRA goals. Identifying government officials with specific responsibility for goal achievement is another good feature that could be extended to all GPRA goals. In this regard, all such designated officials should have direct line responsibility within their agencies for goal achievement; this role should not be passed off to staff organizations.

We also are encouraged by the provisions bolstering attention to performance data quality and government-wide major management challenges. With regard to management challenges, however, we believe it is important to retain the current emphasis on agency-specific major management challenges as well, particularly those identified by agency inspectors general.

On the down side, it is unfortunate that the final legislation did not retain the mandate for individual program assessments from the original House bill. After all, program-specific data are the most immediately and directly relevant type of performance information for much executive branch and congressional policymaking under current legislative and budgetary practice. As Chapter 9 shows, congressional staff have repeatedly expressed a preference for performance information organized by program. Program-specific assessments also add an important element to performance accountability that ties everything together. The administration could, of course, reinstate these assessments, making any modifications from the Bush era process that it deemed appropriate. If this does not occur, Congress might reconsider a statutory mandate along these lines. In either case, the ideal system would require evaluation of the outcomes of each major program, tax expenditure, and regulation that is supposed to contribute toward a particular goal. Only then will decision makers be able to identify what the public receives for its money and find the most effective ways to accomplish public purposes.

Finally, we have some concern over the more frequent reporting timeframes required by the new law. In particular, agency high-priority goals are to be achievable within two years, and progress is to be reported for both agency high-priority and federal government goals four times each year. Moreover, the enacted bill includes additional reporting requirements in the case of performance shortfalls occurring over multiple years. These requirements obviously promote the worthy objective of enhancing performance accountability on a real-time basis. However, they may have the unintended consequence of encouraging agencies to ratchet down their goals and measures to those that can show positive results over the allotted time periods. It can be difficult to achieve—or, in many cases, demonstrate—meaningful progress toward important public outcomes in such short increments of time. Agencies will face a very real temptation to pull back from measuring outcomes and instead measure activities and outputs, in order to have measures that can indicate some type of progress over shorter time periods. OMB and Congress will need to oversee the process from this perspective in order to ensure that the shortened timeframes do not compromise the quality of goals and measures.

Performance and the Debt Crisis

No amount of improvement in the availability, timeliness, and substantive content of performance data will matter if decision makers are not interested in using it. Up to now, most federal decision makers, particularly those in Congress, have been satisfied to pursue business as usual—emphasizing the front-end delivery of federal largesse (including tax breaks) to favored programs, activities, and constituencies over scrutinizing the performance results (or lack thereof) they actually achieve in terms of public benefits. Simply put, the current political incentive structure in Washington does not reward efforts to enhance performance accountability. Unless and until this political calculus changes, even the best performance information will fall on deaf ears.

There are growing signs that business as usual in Washington may indeed be on the verge of change amid mounting evidence, and increasing public acknowledgment, that our current fiscal situation is unsustainable. While not necessarily agreeing on the specifics, a wide range of experts advocate fundamental reform of current federal programs and activities on both the spending and revenue sides.*

The current deficit crisis, coupled with waning public confidence in the effectiveness of the federal government, makes a compelling case for comprehensive fact-based, outcome-oriented scrutiny of federal program performance. Accountability for outcomes isn't just a good idea; it's now a fiscal imperative. In 2005, Comptroller General David Walker offered a prescient warning:

> Our nation is on an unsustainable fiscal path. Long-term budget simulations by GAO, the Congressional Budget Office (CBO), and others show that, over the longer term we face a large and growing structural deficit due primarily to known demographic trends and rising health care costs. Continuing on this unsustainable path will gradually erode, if not suddenly damage, our economy, our standard of living, and ultimately our national security. All reasonable simulations indicate that the problem is too big to be solved by economic growth alone or by making modest changes to existing spending and tax policies. Rather, a fundamental reexamination of major spending and tax policies and priorities will be important to recapture our fiscal flexibility and ensure that our programs and priorities respond to emerging social, economic, and security changes and challenges.
>
> Ultimately, this reexamination will entail a national discussion about what Americans want from their government and how much they are willing to pay for those things. (Walker 2005, 2)

---

* Among them are three bipartisan plans issued in late 2010: the National Commission on Fiscal Responsibility and Reform (popularly known as Bowles-Simpson), the Bipartisan Policy Center Debt Reduction Task Force (popularly known as Domenici-Rivlin), and a plan authored by Bill Galston of the Brookings Institution and Maya MacGuineas of the New America Foundation. For example, Bowles-Simpson proposed the elimination of all tax expenditures (National Commission on Fiscal Responsibility and Reform 2010, 30). Domenici-Rivlin recommended eliminating most tax expenditures, specifying in an appendix those to be retained (Bipartisan Policy Center Debt Reduction Task Force 2010, 40, 132). The Galston-MacGuineas plan (2010, 6) proposed reducing tax expenditures by 10%. The Committee for a Responsible Federal Budget (2010) issued a summary table comparing the main features of these plans as well as other proposals along the same lines.

GAO projected that federal spending would rise from about 20% of the GDP in 2004 to between 30 and 45% of the GDP by 2040. By 2040, interest on the federal debt would consume virtually all federal revenues (Walker 2005, 7–8).

Due to the 2008 financial crisis and recession, the fiscal situation has only gotten worse since the GAO made its projections. In 2010, the Congressional Budget Office (CBO 2010) released a pair of equally unattractive budget scenarios in its long-term budget outlook. The baseline projection assumed most aspects of current law continue. The alternative projection assumed that widely anticipated and predictable changes in law will occur, such as increases in Medicare reimbursements for health care providers and measures that hold tax revenues at about 19% of gross domestic product (GDP). Under either scenario, noninterest federal spending would rise to between 24 and 26% of the GDP by 2035, well above the 40-year historical average of 18.5%. Under the baseline scenario, federal debt held by the public would rise from 62% of GDP in 2010 to 79% in 2035. This projection assumes that federal revenues would take 23% of the GDP by 2035, well above the historical norm. Under CBO's more realistic alternative projection, federal debt would balloon to 100% of the GDP by 2023 and 200% by 2037.

Echoing Walker's warning about "known demographic trends," CBO (2010, i) noted: "The sharp rise in debt stems partly from lower tax revenues and higher federal spending related to the recent severe recession and turmoil in financial markets. However, the growing debt also reflects an imbalance between spending and revenues that predated those economic developments."

Neither of CBO's budget scenarios is likely to be sustainable in practice. Figure 10.1 shows federal debt held by the public as a percent of the GDP. Figures before 2010 are actual; figures after 2010 are projected. The chart shows that federal debt swelled from

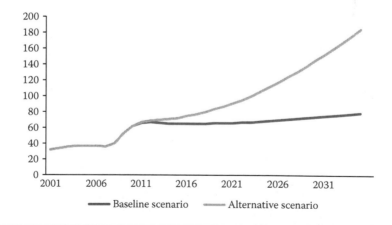

Figure 10.1   Actual and projected U.S. federal debt as a percent of the GDP. (Source: Congressional Budget Office, *The Long-Term Budget Outlook, June 2010,* revised August 2010.)

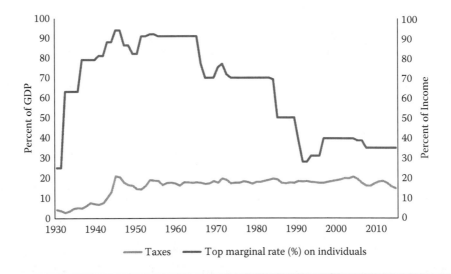

Figure 10.2 Federal taxes as a percent of the GDP versus highest individual marginal tax rate. (Source: De Rugy, Veronique, Reality Isn't Negotiable: The Government Can't Raise More Than 19% in Taxes for Long, 2010, http://mercatus.org/ publication/reality-isnt-negotiable-government-cant-raise-more-19-taxes-long.)

32% of the GDP in 2001 to 37% in 2004, 2005, and 2006. It jumped to 53% in 2009, exceeded 60% in 2010, and continues to escalate under either scenario.

The baseline scenario's total debt burden equal to 79% of the GDP in 2035 is more than double the historical average of 36% over the past 40 years (CBO 2010, i). Yet even this dire projection may be overly optimistic. The baseline assumes federal revenues exceeding 20% of the GDP. Figure 10.2 shows that since 1930, federal tax revenues have rarely exceeded 20% of the GDP, despite substantial changes in marginal income tax rates. It is thus questionable whether the current U.S. tax system could actually generate the amount of revenue assumed in the CBO baseline. This makes CBO's alternative projection, with a debt burden exceeding 100% of the GDP by 2035, much more plausible but no more sustainable.

Some international comparisons shed additional light on the issue. Fully one-third of the Organization for Economic Cooperation and Development (OECD) member countries had a debt-to-GDP ratio exceeding 60% in 2008 or 2009. Sixty percent provides a useful benchmark for fiscal stability, as the European Union's Maastricht Treaty limits general government debt to 60% of the GDP in order to foster economic union (McTigue et al. 2010). Figure 10.3 shows debt-to-GDP ratios for these countries and the United States during 2007, 2008, and 2009. As the comparison with 2007 suggests, many of these countries had significant debt problems before the financial crisis and recession. Several—notably Iceland and the United Kingdom—saw their debt rise above 60% of the GDP only after the financial crisis. At 53% of the GDP in 2009, the U.S. debt is not quite as severe as

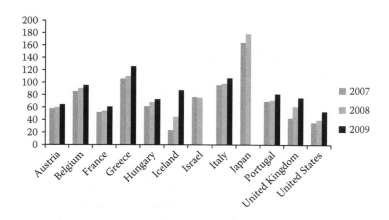

Figure 10.3   U.S. versus OECD members with debt exceeding 60% of the GDP. (Source: Graph created by authors from statistics available at http://stats.oecd. org/Index.aspx?DataSetCode=GOV_DEBT.)

that of the other countries in the graph. However, the CBO estimates that the U.S. debt topped 60% of the GDP in 2010 and will only continue to escalate. If nothing is done, the United States will eventually have as big a debt problem as Belgium, Greece, Italy, or Japan.

Out of the Crisis

The sheer size of the fiscal imbalances in both the United States and other countries suggests that a genuine solution will have to restructure spending programs and reexamine tax expenditures. As the federal government faces increased pressure to do more with less, it will also face temptation to shift more burdens onto individuals, businesses, and other levels of government via regulation. Regulation thus also deserves careful scrutiny to ensure that it accomplishes public purposes at an acceptable cost.

Federal officials could use a variety of criteria to make decisions about the future course of spending programs, tax expenditures, and regulation. Options include across-the-board budget cuts, elimination or retention of programs and activities based on political favoritism, or "faith-based" decisions that hinge on a government activity's stated intentions (accompanied by noble rhetoric about "values" and "priorities" but little information about performance). Or there's the traditional U.S. "budget summit" approach, which declares success when the political wheeling and dealing produces a set of numbers that hits budget or deficit targets, with little consideration of whether federal programs, regulations, and tax expenditures actually achieve their goals at the lowest possible social cost. All of these approaches have been tried in the past, and in many cases they arguably helped create the current problem.

We think GPRA points to a better way. As national leaders, unelected pundits, and the general public debate "what Americans want from their government and how much they are willing to pay for those things," they first need to know what taxpayers should expect and currently receive in exchange for their dollars. Only then can they truly assess what individual interest groups or society as a whole would gain or give up as a result of various spending, tax, and regulatory decisions.

Spending

It is particularly necessary to sort through and prioritize the plethora of seemingly overlapping and duplicative programs that share similar objectives. Surely the programs vary in effectiveness, and the increasingly scarce budget resources available in the future should be allocated to those that produce the best outcomes. To be sure, prioritizing federal spending programs involves subjective value judgments that ultimately must be resolved through the political process. However, political policy judgments should at least be informed by objective performance data. Credible data on performance results should also serve to stimulate rational debate that may bridge ideological divides and move beyond the current gridlock.

A performance-centered approach should apply to entitlement programs as well as discretionary spending. Entitlement programs (particularly social security and Medicare) are a major cause of the projected U.S. fiscal imbalance. Yet the Social Security Administration's current strategic goals, for example, focus on improved service delivery and increasing public trust in the program—as if the ultimate outcome is nothing more than timely and accurate delivery of payments (SSA 2008a). This has been an endemic problem pointed out in numerous editions of the Mercatus Center's *Scorecard*.

Extending performance logic to social security could have significant budgetary effects. The program currently provides an income stream to virtually all retired Americans, regardless of their ability to provide for their own retirement. The appropriate eligibility rules and benefit levels for social security would be very different if its fundamental purpose was to prevent elderly Americans from living in poverty. Similarly, the current debate over the appropriate "retirement age" at which workers qualify for benefits focuses mostly on when it seems fair or desirable for people to retire. The debate would be quite different if the clear purpose of social security was to prevent poverty by providing income when people reach a point in life at which full-time work is not possible. A more carefully defined outcome would also encourage discussion of alternative means of accomplishing the outcome, instead of assuming that the program's current structure is sacred and all policymakers can do is tinker with benefits at the margin. Without a clear consensus on the outcomes social security is supposed to produce, we're likely to see a lot of tinkering on the margin and very little fundamental reexamination. The same logic applies to other government activities.

Tax Expenditures

On the revenue side, Washington appears gridlocked by an ideologically driven impasse over general tax increases. Focusing on tax expenditures, which now total about $1 trillion annually (OMB 2010b, 209–12), may offer a way around this impasse, or at least a means of ameliorating it. As discussed in Chapter 7, tax expenditures largely fly under the radar screen in Washington and thus generate very little scrutiny. However, they clearly deserve to be held to the same level of outcome-oriented performance accountability as budgeted spending programs, since they have the same fiscal impact and often seek to accomplish objectives similar to those of spending programs. One approach (albeit somewhat radical) would be to zero-base tax expenditures. This is largely what New Zealand did when it reformed its tax code in 1986. Specifically, all tax expenditures would be removed from the Internal Revenue Code and made eligible for funding via annual appropriation bills that go through the regular budget process. Those former tax expenditures that could be justified on their merits would be funded as on-budget subsidies to qualified beneficiaries. Their administration would be assigned to relevant executive agencies, just as other spending programs are, and thereby made fully subject to GPRA performance accountability. This is just one idea, but tax expenditures certainly warrant full outcome-oriented scrutiny and accountability in some form.

Regulation

Finally, federal regulations are coming under increasing scrutiny. While effective federal regulation is necessary in many areas, regulations have major economic impacts that can negatively affect economic recovery and job creation. Executive branch agencies have reviewed the prospective benefits and costs of regulations, with varying degrees of thoroughness. As discussed in Chapter 6, though, neither the regulatory agencies nor OMB makes much provision for retrospective analysis of the actual benefits and costs of regulations after they have been adopted. Like the federal government's failure to evaluate tax expenditures, the lack of retrospective evaluation of regulations represents a glaring hole in performance accountability. Since regulations generate hundreds of billions of dollars in social costs that appear nowhere in the federal budget, they should be subject to the same level of outcome-oriented performance scrutiny as other federal programs and activities.

Whether policymakers—particularly legislators—will respond to the debt crisis and public confidence challenges by elevating government performance considerations over blind ideology and partisanship remains to be seen. The problem is clearly too large to ignore. In the 2010 elections, Congress received a large influx of new members who profess hostility to "business as usual." Time will tell whether our elected leaders are up to the task of fundamental reform. If they are, we hope that the tools described in this book will help point the way.

Appendix I: Research Teams and Advisory Panels for the Mercatus Center's *Performance Report Scorecard*

Fiscal Year 1999	
Research Team	*Advisory Panel*
Adolfo Laurenti	John Fund
Daniele Schiffman	Thomas Kessler
	Susan Robinson King
	Thomas McWeeney
	Michael Rosenbaum

Fiscal Year 2000	
Research Team	*Advisory Panel*
Steve Richardson	Mortimer L. Downey III
Adolfo Laurenti	John Kamensky
Gerry Williams	Thomas G. Kessler
Joe Johnson	Donald F. Kettl
Bertin Martens	Susan Robinson King
	Kathryn E. Newcomer
	Michael A. Rosenbaum
	John Sacco
	Virginia L. Thomas
	Christopher Wye
Fiscal Year 2001	
Research Team	*Advisory Panel*
Steve Richardson	Mortimer L. Downey III
Adolfo Laurenti	John Kamensky
Gerry Williams	Thomas G. Kessler
Frank Deal	Patricia A. Kelley
Michelle Bragg	Susan Robinson King
David Mitchell	Kathryn E. Newcomer
	Michael A. Rosenbaum
	John Sacco
	Christopher Wye

Fiscal Year 2002	
Research Team	*Advisory Panel*
Christopher J. Coyne	Jonathan D. Breul
Eric Crampton	Mortimer L. Downey, III
Lawrence P. Grayson	Harry Hatry
Claire D. Kittle	Philip G. Joyce
Adolfo Laurenti	John Kamensky
Peter T. Leeson	Patricia A. Kelley
Myrna V. Malimban	Thomas G. Kessler
Marco Malimban	Michael A. Rosenbaum
Jennifer D. Zambone	John Sacco
	Max Stier
	Henry Wray
	Christopher Wye
Fiscal Year 2003	
Research Team	*Advisory Panel*
Valerie J. Richardson	Jonathan D. Breul
Michael D. Serlin	Veronica Campbell
	Mortimer L. Downey III
	John Kamensky
	Patricia A. Kelley
	Thomas G. Kessler
	Donna McLean
	Sarah E. Nutter
	John M. Palguta
	Michael Rosenbaum
	John Sacco

Fiscal Year 2004	
Research Team	*Advisory Panel*
Valerie J. Richardson	Jonathan D. Breul
Michael D. Serlin	Veronica Campbell
	Mortimer L. Downey III
	John Kamensky
	Patricia A. Kelley
	Thomas G. Kessler
	Sarah E. Nutter
	John M. Palguta
	Michael Rosenbaum
	John Sacco
Fiscal Year 2005	
Research Team	*Advisory Panel*
Valerie J. Richardson	Jonathan D. Breul
Michael D. Serlin	Veronica Campbell
Kyle McKenzie	Mortimer L. Downey III
	John Kamensky
	Patricia A. Kelley
	Thomas G. Kessler
	Sarah E. Nutter
	John M. Palguta
	Michael Rosenbaum
	John Sacco

Fiscal Year 2006	
Research Team	*Advisory Panel*
Valerie J. Richardson	Jonathan D. Breul
Michael D. Serlin	Veronica Campbell
Kyle McKenzie	Mortimer L. Downey III
	John Kamensky
	Patricia A. Kelley
	Thomas G. Kessler
	Sarah E. Nutter
	John M. Palguta
	Paul L. Posner
	John Sacco
Fiscal Year 2007	
Research Team	*Advisory Panel*
Valerie J. Richardson	Jonathan D. Breul
Patricia A. Kelley	Veronica Campbell
Lewis Butler	Mortimer L. Downey III
	John Kamensky
	Thomas G. Kessler
	Sarah E. Nutter
	John M. Palguta
	Paul L. Posner
	Michael Rosenbaum
	John Sacco
	Michael D. Serlin

Fiscal Year 2008	
Research Team	*Advisory Panel*
Patricia A. Kelley	Jonathan D. Breul
Valerie J. Richardson	Veronica Campbell
Christina Forsberg	John Kamensky
Stefanie Haeffele-Balch	Thomas G. Kessler
	Sarah E. Nutter
	John M. Palguta
	Paul L. Posner
	Michael Rosenbaum
	John Sacco
	Michael D. Serlin
	Robert Shea

Appendix II: Mercatus *Scorecard* Scores and the Quality of Regulatory Analysis

This appendix explores whether there is any relationship between the quality of agency GPRA initiatives (as measured by the agency's Mercatus 2008 *Scorecard* score) and the quality of an agency's regulatory analysis (as measured by Ellig and McLaughlin 2010). The Ellig and McLaughlin study assessed the quality of 45 economically significant regulations issued by executive branch agencies in 2008. Each regulation received a score ranging between 0 and 5 on 12 criteria derived from Executive Order 12866 and OMB Circular A-4, which govern regulatory review. The maximum possible score is thus 60 points. All of the econometric analyses below employ ordinary least squares regression, which plots a line that minimizes the sum of the squared distances between each point and the line.

Table A.II.1 shows the results when we use the regulation's total score as the dependent variable. Specification 1, which simply regresses the regulation's score on the agency's *Scorecard* score, conveys the impression that agencies with better GPRA reports do better regulatory analysis. A 1-point increase in the *Scorecard* score is associated with a one-third of a point increase in the quality of the regulatory analysis, and this relationship is statistically significant. However, the correlation disappears once we control for other variables known to affect the quality of regulatory analysis.

Specification 2 adds one control variable: whether the regulation is a budget or transfer regulation. A transfer regulation specifies how the federal government will collect or spend money. The Department of Health and Human Services, for example, issues about ten regulations each year that recalculate the rates the federal government will reimburse medical care providers for services provided under

245

Table A.II.1   Dependent Variable Is the Regulation's Total Score

	(1)	*(2)*	*(3)*
Scorecard score	.323 (2.09**)	.023 (.20)	.025 (.21)
Transfer regulation		−15.53 (−7.39***)	−16.64 (−5.96***)
Midnight regulation			−4.67 (−2.47**)
Judicial deadline			2.73 (.65)
Statutory deadline			.88 (.34)
Review time at OIRA			.007 (.28)
Constant	13.99 (2.15**)	31.67 (6.41***)	33.44 (5.61***)
Adjusted R-squared	.07	.59	.62
Number of observations	45	45	45

Note: T-statistics in parentheses. Statistical significance: ***, 99%; **, 95%; *, 90%.

Medicare and Medicaid. In general, the quality of regulatory analysis accompanying transfer regulations is not nearly as good as the quality of analysis accompanying other regulations (McLaughlin and Ellig 2010). Once we control for whether a regulation is a transfer one, the relationship between the quality of regulatory analysis and the quality of the agency's GPRA report disappears.

Finally, specification 3 adds some other control variables that previous research has found may affect the quality of regulatory analysis: midnight regulation, which indicates whether the Office of Information and Regulatory Affairs had completed its review of the agency's regulation prior to its self-imposed deadline of June 1, 2008; judicial deadline, which indicates whether the agency had a court-imposed deadline to issue the regulation; statutory deadline, which indicates whether the agency had a congressionally mandated deadline to issue the regulation; and review time at OIRA, which measures the number of days the regulation spent under review at the Office of Information and Regulatory Affairs. (For more details on the control variables, see McLaughlin and Ellig 2010.)

**Table A.II.2 Dependent Variable Is the Regulation's Score on Criterion
Assessing the Quality of Goals and Measures the Agency
Adopts to Assess the Regulation's Effects**

	(1)	*(2)*	*(3)*
Scorecard score	−.0004 (−.02)	−.01 (−.70)	−.01 (−.73)
Transfer regulation		−.64 (−1.84*)	−.94 (−2.02**)
Midnight regulation			−.42 (−1.32)
Judicial deadline			.33 (.47)
Statutory deadline			.01 (.03)
Review time at OIRA			−.007 (−1.69*)
Constant	1.38 (1.87*)	2.11 (2.57**)	2.85 (2.86***)
Adjusted R-squared	−.02	.03	.09
Number of observations	45	45	45

Note: T-statistics in parentheses. Statistical significance: ***, 99%; **, 95%; *, 90%.

Ellig and McLaughlin (2010) include two questions that assess whether the agency made any provisions for retrospective analysis at the time it issued the regulation. The dependent variable in Table A.II.2 is the score on a question assessing the quality of any measures and goals the agency adopted to assess the future results of the regulation. This score is not correlated with the *Scorecard* score in any regression specification. Finally, the dependent variable in Table A.II.3 is the score on a question assessing the quality of data the agency indicates it could use to perform retrospective analysis of the regulation in the future. As in the previous table, this score is not correlated with the *Scorecard* score either.

We infer from these results that there is little or no linkage between the quality of an agency's GPRA reporting and the quality of its regulatory analysis.

Table A.II.3 **Dependent Variable Is the Regulation's Score on Criterion Assessing the Quality of Data the Agency Indicates It Could Use to Assess the Regulation's Effects**

	(1)	*(2)*	*(3)*
Scorecard score	.03 (1.41)	.01 (.47)	.02 (.85)
Transfer regulation		−.87 (−2.48**)	−.62 (−1.26)
Midnight regulation			−.47 (−1.42)
Judicial deadline			.03 (.04)
Statutory deadline			−.64 (−1.43)
Review time at OIRA			−.0002 (−.04)
Constant	.69 (.90)	1.69 (2.04**)	1.66 (1.59)
Adjusted R-squared	.02	.13	.12
Number of observations	45	45	45

Note: T-statistics in parentheses. Statistical significance: ***, 99%; **, 95%; *, 90%.

Appendix III: Text of the GPRA Modernization Act of 2010

AUTHENTICATED U.S. GOVERNMENT INFORMATION
GPO
H. R. 2142

One Hundred Eleventh Congress of the United States of America

AT THE SECOND SESSION

Begun and held at the City of Washington on Tuesday, the fifth day of January, two thousand and ten

An Act

To require quarterly performance assessments of Government programs for purposes of assessing agency performance and improvement, and to establish agency performance improvement officers and the Performance Improvement Council.

Be it enacted by the Senate and House of Representatives of the United States of America in Congress assembled,

Sec. 1. Short Title; Table of Contents.

(a) Short Title.—This Act may be cited as the "GPRA Modernization Act of 2010".

(b) Table of Contents.—The table of contents for this Act is as follows:

Sec. 2. Strategic Planning Amendments.

Chapter 3 of title 5, United States Code, is amended by striking section 306 and inserting the following:

"§ 306. Agency strategic plans

"(a) Not later than the first Monday in February of any year following the year in which the term of the President commences under section 101 of title 3, the head of each agency shall make available on the public website of the agency a strategic plan and notify the President and Congress of its availability. Such plan shall contain—

"(1) a comprehensive mission statement covering the major functions and operations of the agency;

"(2) general goals and objectives, including outcome-oriented goals, for the major functions and operations of the agency;

"(3) a description of how any goals and objectives contribute to the Federal Government priority goals required by section 1120(a) of title 31;

"(4) a description of how the goals and objectives are to be achieved, including—

"(A) a description of the operational processes, skills and technology, and the human, capital, information, and other resources required to achieve those goals and objectives; and

"(B) a description of how the agency is working with other agencies to achieve its goals and objectives as well as relevant Federal Government priority goals;

"(5) a description of how the goals and objectives incorporate views and suggestions obtained through congressional consultations required under subsection (d);

"(6) a description of how the performance goals provided in the plan required by section 1115(a) of title 31, including the agency priority goals required by section 1120(b) of title 31, if applicable, contribute to the general goals and objectives in the strategic plan;

"(7) an identification of those key factors external to the agency and beyond its control that could significantly affect the achievement of the general goals and objectives; and

"(8) a description of the program evaluations used in establishing or revising general goals and objectives, with a schedule for future program evaluations to be conducted.

"(9) The strategic plan shall cover a period of not less than 4 years following the fiscal year in which the plan is submitted. As needed, the head of the agency may make adjustments to the strategic plan to reflect significant changes in the environment in which the agency is operating, with appropriate notification of Congress.

"(b) The performance plan required by section 1115(b) of title 31 shall be consistent with the agency's strategic plan. A performance plan may not be submitted for a fiscal year not covered by a current strategic plan under this section.

"(c) When developing or making adjustments to a strategic plan, the agency shall consult periodically with the Congress, including majority and minority views from the appropriate authorizing, appropriations, and oversight committees, and shall solicit and consider the views and suggestions of those entities potentially affected by or interested in such a plan. The agency shall consult with the appropriate committees of Congress at least once every 2 years.

"(d) The functions and activities of this section shall be considered to be inherently governmental functions. The drafting of strategic plans under this section shall be performed only by Federal employees.

"(e) For purposes of this section the term 'agency' means an Executive agency defined under section 105, but does not include the Central Intelligence Agency, the Government Accountability Office, the United States Postal Service, and the Postal Regulatory Commission.".

Sec. 3. Performance Planning Amendments.

Chapter 11 of title 31, United States Code, is amended by striking section 1115 and inserting the following:

"§ 1115. Federal Government and agency performance plans

"(a) Federal Government Performance Plans.—In carrying out the provisions of section 1105(a)(28), the Director of the Office of Management and Budget shall coordinate with agencies to develop the Federal Government performance plan. In addition to the submission of such plan with each budget of the United States Government, the Director of the Office of Management and Budget shall ensure that all information required by this subsection is concurrently made available on the website provided under section 1122 and updated periodically, but no less than annually. The Federal Government performance plan shall—

"(1) establish Federal Government performance goals to define the level of performance to be achieved during the year in which the plan is submitted and the next fiscal year for each of the Federal Government priority goals required under section 1120(a) of this title;

"(2) identify the agencies, organizations, program activities, regulations, tax expenditures, policies, and other activities contributing to each Federal Government performance goal during the current fiscal year;

"(3) for each Federal Government performance goal, identify a lead Government official who shall be responsible for coordinating the efforts to achieve the goal;

"(4) establish common Federal Government performance indicators with quarterly targets to be used in measuring or assessing—

"(A) overall progress toward each Federal Government performance goal; and

"(B) the individual contribution of each agency, organization, program activity, regulation, tax expenditure, policy, and other activity identified under paragraph (2);

"(5) establish clearly defined quarterly milestones; and

"(6) identify major management challenges that are Government-
wide or crosscutting in nature and describe plans to address
such challenges, including relevant performance goals, performance indicators, and milestones.

"(b) Agency Performance Plans.—Not later than the first Monday in
February of each year, the head of each agency shall make available on a public website of the agency, and notify the President
and the Congress of its availability, a performance plan covering each program activity set forth in the budget of such agency.
Such plan shall—

"(1) establish performance goals to define the level of performance
to be achieved during the year in which the plan is submitted
and the next fiscal year;

"(2) express such goals in an objective, quantifiable, and measurable form unless authorized to be in an alternative form under
subsection (c);

"(3) describe how the performance goals contribute to—

"(A) the general goals and objectives established in the agency's strategic plan required by section 306(a)(2) of title
5; and

"(B) any of the Federal Government performance goals
established in the Federal Government performance
plan required by subsection (a)(1);

"(4) identify among the performance goals those which are designated as agency priority goals as required by section 1120(b)
of this title, if applicable;

"(5) provide a description of how the performance goals are to be
achieved, including—

"(A) the operation processes, training, skills and technology, and the human, capital, information, and other
resources and strategies required to meet those performance goals;

"(B) clearly defined milestones;

"(C) an identification of the organizations, program activities, regulations, policies, and other activities that
contribute to each performance goal, both within and
external to the agency;

"(D) a description of how the agency is working with other agencies to achieve its performance goals as well as relevant Federal Government performance goals; and

"(E) an identification of the agency officials responsible for the achievement of each performance goal, who shall be known as goal leaders;

"(6) establish a balanced set of performance indicators to be used in measuring or assessing progress toward each performance goal, including, as appropriate, customer service, efficiency, output, and outcome indicators;

"(7) provide a basis for comparing actual program results with the established performance goals;

"(8) a description of how the agency will ensure the accuracy and reliability of the data used to measure progress towards its performance goals, including an identification of—

"(A) the means to be used to verify and validate measured values;

"(B) the sources for the data;

"(C) the level of accuracy required for the intended use of the data;

"(D) any limitations to the data at the required level of accuracy; and

"(E) how the agency will compensate for such limitations if needed to reach the required level of accuracy;

"(9) describe major management challenges the agency faces and identify—

"(A) planned actions to address such challenges;

"(B) performance goals, performance indicators, and milestones to measure progress toward resolving such challenges; and

"(C) the agency official responsible for resolving such challenges; and

"(10) identify low-priority program activities based on an analysis of their contribution to the mission and goals of the agency and include an evidence-based justification for designating a program activity as low priority.

"(c) Alternative Form.—If an agency, in consultation with the Director of the Office of Management and Budget, determines that it is not feasible to express the performance goals for a particular program activity in an objective, quantifiable, and measurable form, the Director of the Office of Management and Budget may authorize an alternative form. Such alternative form shall—

"(1) include separate descriptive statements of—

"(A) (i) a minimally effective program; and

"(ii) a successful program; or

"(B) such alternative as authorized by the Director of the Office of Management and Budget, with sufficient precision and in such terms that would allow for an accurate, independent determination of whether the program activity's performance meets the criteria of the description; or

"(2) state why it is infeasible or impractical to express a performance goal in any form for the program activity.

"(d) Treatment of Program Activities.—For the purpose of complying with this section, an agency may aggregate, disaggregate, or consolidate program activities, except that any aggregation or consolidation may not omit or minimize the significance of any program activity constituting a major function or operation for the agency.

"(e) Appendix.—An agency may submit with an annual performance plan an appendix covering any portion of the plan that—

"(1) is specifically authorized under criteria established by an Executive order to be kept secret in the interest of national defense or foreign policy; and

"(2) is properly classified pursuant to such Executive order.

"(f) Inherently Governmental Functions.—The functions and activities of this section shall be considered to be inherently governmental functions. The drafting of performance plans under this section shall be performed only by Federal employees.

"(g) Chief Human Capital Officers.—With respect to each agency with a Chief Human Capital Officer, the Chief Human Capital Officer shall prepare that portion of the annual performance plan described under subsection (b)(5)(A).

"(h) Definitions.—For purposes of this section and sections 1116 through 1125, and sections 9703 and 9704, the term—

"(1) 'agency' has the same meaning as such term is defined under section 306(f) of title 5;

"(2) 'crosscutting' means across organizational (such as agency) boundaries;

"(3) 'customer service measure' means an assessment of service delivery to a customer, client, citizen, or other recipient, which can include an assessment of quality, timeliness, and satisfaction among other factors;

"(4) 'efficiency measure' means a ratio of a program activity's inputs (such as costs or hours worked by employees) to its outputs (amount of products or services delivered) or outcomes (the desired results of a program);

"(5) 'major management challenge' means programs or management functions, within or across agencies, that have greater vulnerability to waste, fraud, abuse, and mismanagement (such as issues identified by the Government Accountability Office as high risk or issues identified by an Inspector General) where a failure to perform well could seriously affect the ability of an agency or the Government to achieve its mission or goals;

"(6) 'milestone' means a scheduled event signifying the completion of a major deliverable or a set of related deliverables or a phase of work;

"(7) 'outcome measure' means an assessment of the results of a program activity compared to its intended purpose;

"(8) 'output measure' means the tabulation, calculation, or recording of activity or effort that can be expressed in a quantitative or qualitative manner;

"(9) 'performance goal' means a target level of performance expressed as a tangible, measurable objective, against which actual achievement can be compared, including a goal expressed as a quantitative standard, value, or rate;

"(10) 'performance indicator' means a particular value or characteristic used to measure output or outcome;

"(11) 'program activity' means a specific activity or project as listed in the program and financing schedules of the annual budget of the United States Government; and

"(12) 'program evaluation' means an assessment, through objective measurement and systematic analysis, of the manner and extent to which Federal programs achieve intended objectives.".

Sec. 4. Performance Reporting Amendments.

Chapter 11 of title 31, United States Code, is amended by striking section 1116 and inserting the following:

"§ 1116. Agency performance reporting

"(a) The head of each agency shall make available on a public website of the agency and to the Office of Management and Budget an update on agency performance.

"(b) (1) Each update shall compare actual performance achieved with the performance goals established in the agency performance plan under section 1115(b) and shall occur no less than 150 days after the end of each fiscal year, with more frequent updates of actual performance on indicators that provide data of significant value to the Government, Congress, or program partners at a reasonable level of administrative burden.

"(2) If performance goals are specified in an alternative form under section 1115(c), the results shall be described in relation to such specifications, including whether the performance failed to meet the criteria of a minimally effective or successful program.

"(c) Each update shall—

"(1) review the success of achieving the performance goals and include actual results for the 5 preceding fiscal years;

"(2) evaluate the performance plan for the current fiscal year relative to the performance achieved toward the performance goals during the period covered by the update;

"(3) explain and describe where a performance goal has not been met (including when a program activity's performance is determined not to have met the criteria of a successful program activity under section 1115(c)(1)(A)(ii) or a corresponding level of achievement if another alternative form is used)—

"(A) why the goal was not met;

"(B) those plans and schedules for achieving the established performance goal; and

"(C) if the performance goal is impractical or infeasible, why that is the case and what action is recommended;

"(4) describe the use and assess the effectiveness in achieving performance goals of any waiver under section 9703 of this title;

"(5) include a review of the performance goals and evaluation of the performance plan relative to the agency's strategic human capital management;

"(6) describe how the agency ensures the accuracy and reliability of the data used to measure progress towards its performance goals, including an identification of—

"(A) the means used to verify and validate measured values;

"(B) the sources for the data;

"(C) the level of accuracy required for the intended use of the data;

"(D) any limitations to the data at the required level of accuracy; and

"(E) how the agency has compensated for such limitations if needed to reach the required level of accuracy; and

"(7) include the summary findings of those program evaluations completed during the period covered by the update.

"(d) If an agency performance update includes any program activity or information that is specifically authorized under criteria established by an Executive Order to be kept secret in the interest of national defense or foreign policy and is properly classified pursuant to such Executive Order, the head of the agency shall make such information available in the classified appendix provided under section 1115(e).

"(e) The functions and activities of this section shall be considered to be inherently governmental functions. The drafting of agency performance updates under this section shall be performed only by Federal employees.

"(f) Each fiscal year, the Office of Management and Budget shall determine whether the agency programs or activities meet performance goals and objectives outlined in the agency performance plans and submit a report on unmet goals to—

"(1) the head of the agency;

"(2) the Committee on Homeland Security and Governmental Affairs of the Senate;

"(3) the Committee on Oversight and Governmental Reform of the House of Representatives; and

"(4) the Government Accountability Office.

"(g) If an agency's programs or activities have not met performance goals as determined by the Office of Management and Budget for 1 fiscal year, the head of the agency shall submit a performance improvement plan to the Office of Management and Budget to increase program effectiveness for each unmet goal with measurable milestones. The agency shall designate a senior official who shall oversee the performance improvement strategies for each unmet goal.

"(h) (1) If the Office of Management and Budget determines that agency programs or activities have unmet performance goals for 2 consecutive fiscal years, the head of the agency shall—

"(A) submit to Congress a description of the actions the Administration will take to improve performance, including proposed statutory changes or planned executive actions; and

"(B) describe any additional funding the agency will obligate to achieve the goal, if such an action is determined appropriate in consultation with the Director of the

Office of Management and Budget, for an amount determined appropriate by the Director.

"(2) In providing additional funding described under paragraph (1)(B), the head of the agency shall use any reprogramming or transfer authority available to the agency. If after exercising such authority additional funding is necessary to achieve the level determined appropriate by the Director of the Office of Management and Budget, the head of the agency shall submit a request to Congress for additional reprogramming or transfer authority.

"(i) If an agency's programs or activities have not met performance goals as determined by the Office of Management and Budget for 3 consecutive fiscal years, the Director of the Office of Management and Budget shall submit recommendations to Congress on actions to improve performance not later than 60 days after that determination, including—

"(1) reauthorization proposals for each program or activity that has not met performance goals;

"(2) proposed statutory changes necessary for the program activities to achieve the proposed level of performance on each performance goal; and

"(3) planned executive actions or identification of the program for termination or reduction in the President's budget.".

Sec. 5. Federal Government and Agency Priority Goals.

Chapter 11 of title 31, United States Code, is amended by adding after section 1119 the following:

"§ 1120. Federal Government and agency priority goals

"(a) Federal Government Priority Goals.—

"(1) The Director of the Office of Management and Budget shall coordinate with agencies to develop priority goals to improve the performance and management of the Federal Government. Such Federal Government priority goals shall include—

"(A) outcome-oriented goals covering a limited number of crosscutting policy areas; and

"(B) goals for management improvements needed across the Federal Government, including—

"(i) financial management;

"(ii) human capital management;

        "(iii) information technology management;

        "(iv) procurement and acquisition management; and

        "(v) real property management;

"(2) The Federal Government priority goals shall be long-term in nature. At a minimum, the Federal Government priority goals shall be updated or revised every 4 years and made publicly available concurrently with the submission of the budget of the United States Government made in the first full fiscal year following any year in which the term of the President commences under section 101 of title 3. As needed, the Director of the Office of Management and Budget may make adjustments to the Federal Government priority goals to reflect significant changes in the environment in which the Federal Government is operating, with appropriate notification of Congress.

"(3) When developing or making adjustments to Federal Government priority goals, the Director of the Office of Management and Budget shall consult periodically with the Congress, including obtaining majority and minority views from—

    "(A) the Committees on Appropriations of the Senate and the House of Representatives;

    "(B) the Committees on the Budget of the Senate and the House of Representatives;

    "(C) the Committee on Homeland Security and Governmental Affairs of the Senate;

    "(D) the Committee on Oversight and Government Reform of the House of Representatives;

    "(E) the Committee on Finance of the Senate;

    "(F) the Committee on Ways and Means of the House of Representatives; and

    "(G) any other committees as determined appropriate;

"(4) The Director of the Office of Management and Budget shall consult with the appropriate committees of Congress at least once every 2 years.

"(5) The Director of the Office of Management and Budget shall make information about the Federal Government priority goals available on the website described under section 1122 of this title.

"(6) The Federal Government performance plan required under section 1115(a) of this title shall be consistent with the Federal Government priority goals.

"(b) Agency Priority Goals.—

"(1) Every 2 years, the head of each agency listed in section 901(b) of this title, or as otherwise determined by the Director of the Office of Management and Budget, shall identify agency priority goals from among the performance goals of the agency. The Director of the Office of Management and Budget shall determine the total number of agency priority goals across the Government, and the number to be developed by each agency. The agency priority goals shall—

"(A) reflect the highest priorities of the agency, as determined by the head of the agency and informed by the Federal Government priority goals provided under subsection (a) and the consultations with Congress and other interested parties required by section 306(d) of title 5;

"(B) have ambitious targets that can be achieved within a 2-year period;

"(C) have a clearly identified agency official, known as a goal leader, who is responsible for the achievement of each agency priority goal;

"(D) have interim quarterly targets for performance indicators if more frequent updates of actual performance provides data of significant value to the Government, Congress, or program partners at a reasonable level of administrative burden; and

"(E) have clearly defined quarterly milestones.

"(2) If an agency priority goal includes any program activity or information that is specifically authorized under criteria established by an Executive order to be kept secret in the interest of national defense or foreign policy and is properly classified pursuant to such Executive order, the head of the agency shall make such information available in the classified appendix provided under section 1115(e).

"(c) The functions and activities of this section shall be considered to be inherently governmental functions. The development of Federal Government and agency priority goals shall be performed only by Federal employees.".

Sec. 6. Quarterly Priority Progress Reviews and Use of Performance Information.

Chapter 11 of title 31, United States Code, is amended by adding after section 1120 (as added by section 5 of this Act) the following:

"§ 1121. Quarterly priority progress reviews and use of performance information

"(a) Use of Performance Information To Achieve Federal Government Priority Goals.—Not less than quarterly, the Director of the Office of Management and Budget, with the support of the Performance Improvement Council, shall—

"(1) for each Federal Government priority goal required by section 1120(a) of this title, review with the appropriate lead Government official the progress achieved during the most recent quarter, overall trend data, and the likelihood of meeting the planned level of performance;

"(2) include in such reviews officials from the agencies, organizations, and program activities that contribute to the accomplishment of each Federal Government priority goal;

"(3) assess whether agencies, organizations, program activities, regulations, tax expenditures, policies, and other activities are contributing as planned to each Federal Government priority goal;

"(4) categorize the Federal Government priority goals by risk of not achieving the planned level of performance; and

"(5) for the Federal Government priority goals at greatest risk of not meeting the planned level of performance, identify prospects and strategies for performance improvement, including any needed changes to agencies, organizations, program activities, regulations, tax expenditures, policies or other activities.

"(b) Agency Use of Performance Information To Achieve Agency Priority Goals.—Not less than quarterly, at each agency required to develop agency priority goals required by section 1120(b) of this title, the head of the agency and Chief Operating Officer, with the support of the agency Performance Improvement Officer, shall—

"(1) for each agency priority goal, review with the appropriate goal leader the progress achieved during the most recent quarter, overall trend data, and the likelihood of meeting the planned level of performance;

"(2) coordinate with relevant personnel within and outside the agency who contribute to the accomplishment of each agency priority goal;

"(3) assess whether relevant organizations, program activities, regulations, policies, and other activities are contributing as planned to the agency priority goals;

"(4) categorize agency priority goals by risk of not achieving the planned level of performance; and

"(5) for agency priority goals at greatest risk of not meeting the planned level of performance, identify prospects and strategies for performance improvement, including any needed changes to agency program activities, regulations, policies, or other activities.".

Sec. 7. Transparency of Federal Government Programs, Priority Goals, and Results.

Chapter 11 of title 31, United States Code, is amended by adding after section 1121 (as added by section 6 of this Act) the following:

"§ 1122. Transparency of programs, priority goals, and results

"(a) Transparency of Agency Programs.—

"(1) In general.—Not later than October 1, 2012, the Office of Management and Budget shall—

"(A) ensure the effective operation of a single website;

"(B) at a minimum, update the website on a quarterly basis; and

"(C) include on the website information about each program identified by the agencies.

"(2) Information. Information for each program described under paragraph (1) shall include—

"(A) an identification of how the agency defines the term 'program', consistent with guidance provided by the Director of the Office of Management and Budget, including the program activities that are aggregated, disaggregated, or consolidated to be considered a program by the agency;

"(B) a description of the purposes of the program and the contribution of the program to the mission and goals of the agency; and

"(C) an identification of funding for the current fiscal year and previous 2 fiscal years.

"(b) Transparency of Agency Priority Goals and Results.—The head of each agency required to develop agency priority goals shall make information about each agency priority goal available to the Office of Management and Budget for publication on the website, with the exception of any information covered by section 1120(b)(2) of this title. In addition to an identification of each agency priority goal, the website shall also consolidate information about each agency priority goal, including—

"(1) a description of how the agency incorporated any views and suggestions obtained through congressional consultations about the agency priority goal;

"(2) an identification of key factors external to the agency and beyond its control that could significantly affect the achievement of the agency priority goal;

"(3) a description of how each agency priority goal will be achieved, including—

"(A) the strategies and resources required to meet the priority goal;

"(B) clearly defined milestones;

"(C) the organizations, program activities, regulations, policies, and other activities that contribute to each goal, both within and external to the agency;

"(D) how the agency is working with other agencies to achieve the goal; and

"(E) an identification of the agency official responsible for achieving the priority goal;

"(1) the performance indicators to be used in measuring or assessing progress;

"(2) a description of how the agency ensures the accuracy and reliability of the data used to measure progress towards the priority goal, including an identification of—

"(A) the means used to verify and validate measured values;

"(B) the sources for the data;

"(C) the level of accuracy required for the intended use of the data;

"(D) any limitations to the data at the required level of accuracy; and

"(E) how the agency has compensated for such limitations if needed to reach the required level of accuracy;

"(3) the results achieved during the most recent quarter and overall trend data compared to the planned level of performance;

"(4) an assessment of whether relevant organizations, program activities, regulations, policies, and other activities are contributing as planned;

"(5) an identification of the agency priority goals at risk of not achieving the planned level of performance; and

"(6) any prospects or strategies for performance improvement.

"(c) Transparency of Federal Government Priority Goals and Results.—The Director of the Office of Management and Budget shall also make available on the website—

"(1) a brief description of each of the Federal Government priority goals required by section 1120(a) of this title;

"(2) a description of how the Federal Government priority goals incorporate views and suggestions obtained through congressional consultations;

"(3) the Federal Government performance goals and performance indicators associated with each Federal Government priority goal as required by section 1115(a) of this title;

"(4) an identification of the lead Government official for each Federal Government performance goal;

"(5) the results achieved during the most recent quarter and overall trend data compared to the planned level of performance;

"(6) an identification of the agencies, organizations, program activities, regulations, tax expenditures, policies, and other activities that contribute to each Federal Government priority goal;

"(7) an assessment of whether relevant agencies, organizations, program activities, regulations, tax expenditures, policies, and other activities are contributing as planned;

"(8) an identification of the Federal Government priority goals at risk of not achieving the planned level of performance; and

"(9) any prospects or strategies for performance improvement.

"(d) Information on Website.—The information made available on the website under this section shall be readily accessible and easily found on the Internet by the public and members and committees of Congress. Such information shall also be presented in a searchable, machine-readable format. The Director of the Office of Management and Budget shall issue guidance to ensure that such information is provided in a way that presents a coherent picture of all Federal programs, and the performance of the Federal Government as well as individual agencies.".

Sec. 8. Agency Chief Operating Officers.

Chapter 11 of title 31, United States Code, is amended by adding after section 1122 (as added by section 7 of this Act) the following:

"§ 1123. Chief Operating Officers

"(a) Establishment.—At each agency, the deputy head of agency, or equivalent, shall be the Chief Operating Officer of the agency.

"(b) Function.—Each Chief Operating Officer shall be responsible for improving the management and performance of the agency, and shall—

"(1) provide overall organization management to improve agency performance and achieve the mission and goals of the agency through the use of strategic and performance planning, measurement, analysis, regular assessment of progress, and use of performance information to improve the results achieved;

"(2) advise and assist the head of agency in carrying out the requirements of sections 1115 through 1122 of this title and section 306 of title 5;

"(3) oversee agency-specific efforts to improve management functions within the agency and across Government; and

"(4) coordinate and collaborate with relevant personnel within and external to the agency who have a significant role in contributing to and achieving the mission and goals of the agency, such as the Chief Financial Officer, Chief Human Capital Officer, Chief Acquisition Officer/Senior Procurement Executive, Chief Information Officer, and other line of business chiefs at the agency.".

Sec. 9. Agency Performance Improvement Officers and the Performance Improvement Council.

Chapter 11 of title 31, United States Code, is amended by adding after section 1123 (as added by section 8 of this Act) the following:

"§ 1124. Performance Improvement Officers and the Performance Improvement Council

"(a) Performance Improvement Officers.—

"(1) Establishment.—At each agency, the head of the agency, in consultation with the agency Chief Operating Officer, shall designate a senior executive of the agency as the agency Performance Improvement Officer.

"(2) Function.—Each Performance Improvement Officer shall report directly to the Chief Operating Officer. Subject to the direction of the Chief Operating Officer, each Performance Improvement Officer shall—

"(A) advise and assist the head of the agency and the Chief Operating Officer to ensure that the mission and goals of the agency are achieved through strategic and performance planning, measurement, analysis, regular assessment of progress, and use of performance information to improve the results achieved;

"(B) advise the head of the agency and the Chief Operating Officer on the selection of agency goals, including opportunities to collaborate with other agencies on common goals;

"(C) assist the head of the agency and the Chief Operating Officer in overseeing the implementation of the agency strategic planning, performance planning, and reporting requirements provided under sections 1115 through 1122 of this title and sections 306 of title 5, including the contributions of the agency to the Federal Government priority goals;

"(D) support the head of agency and the Chief Operating Officer in the conduct of regular reviews of agency performance, including at least quarterly reviews of progress achieved toward agency priority goals, if applicable;

"(E) assist the head of the agency and the Chief Operating Officer in the development and use within the agency of performance measures in personnel performance appraisals, and, as appropriate, other agency personnel and planning processes and assessments; and

"(F) ensure that agency progress toward the achievement of all goals is communicated to leaders, managers, and employees in the agency and Congress, and made available on a public website of the agency.

"(b) Performance Improvement Council.—

"(1) Establishment.—There is established a Performance Improvement Council, consisting of—

"(A) the Deputy Director for Management of the Office of Management and Budget, who shall act as chairperson of the Council;

"(B) the Performance Improvement Officer from each agency defined in section 901(b) of this title;

"(C) other Performance Improvement Officers as determined appropriate by the chairperson; and

"(D) other individuals as determined appropriate by the chairperson.

"(2) Function.—The Performance Improvement Council shall—

"(A) be convened by the chairperson or the designee of the chairperson, who shall preside at the meetings of the Performance Improvement Council, determine its agenda, direct its work, and establish and direct subgroups of the Performance Improvement Council, as appropriate, to deal with particular subject matters;

"(B) assist the Director of the Office of Management and Budget to improve the performance of the Federal Government and achieve the Federal Government priority goals;

"(C) assist the Director of the Office of Management and Budget in implementing the planning, reporting, and use of performance information requirements related to the Federal Government priority goals provided under sections 1115, 1120, 1121, and 1122 of this title;

"(D) work to resolve specific Governmentwide or cross-cutting performance issues, as necessary;

"(E) facilitate the exchange among agencies of practices that have led to performance improvements within specific programs, agencies, or across agencies;

"(F) coordinate with other interagency management councils;

"(G) seek advice and information as appropriate from non-member agencies, particularly smaller agencies;

"(H) consider the performance improvement experiences of corporations, nonprofit organizations, foreign, State, and local governments, Government employees, public sector unions, and customers of Government services;

"(I) receive such assistance, information and advice from agencies as the Council may request, which agencies shall provide to the extent permitted by law; and

"(J) develop and submit to the Director of the Office of Management and Budget, or when appropriate to the President through the Director of the Office of Management and Budget, at times and in such formats as the chairperson may specify, recommendations to streamline and improve performance management policies and requirements.

"(3) Support.—

"(A) In general.—The Administrator of General Services shall provide administrative and other support for the Council to implement this section.

"(B) Personnel.—The heads of agencies with Performance Improvement Officers serving on the Council shall, as appropriate and to the extent permitted by law, provide at the request of the chairperson of the Performance Improvement Council up to 2 personnel authorizations to serve at the direction of the chairperson.".

Sec. 10. Format of Performance Plans and Reports.

(a) Searchable, Machine-readable Plans and Reports.—For fiscal year 2012 and each fiscal year thereafter, each agency required to produce strategic plans, performance plans, and performance updates in accordance with the amendments made by this Act shall—

(1) not incur expenses for the printing of strategic plans, performance plans, and performance reports for release external to the agency, except when providing such documents to the Congress;

(2) produce such plans and reports in searchable, machine-readable formats; and

(3) make such plans and reports available on the website described under section 1122 of title 31, United States Code.

(b) Web-based Performance Planning and Reporting.—

(1) In general.—Not later than June 1, 2012, the Director of the Office of Management and Budget shall issue guidance to agencies to provide concise and timely performance information for publication on the website described under section 1122 of title 31, United States Code, including, at a minimum, all requirements of sections 1115 and 1116 of title 31, United States Code, except for section 1115(e).

(2) High-priority goals.—For agencies required to develop agency priority goals under section 1120(b) of title 31, United States Code, the performance information required under this section shall be merged with the existing information required under section 1122 of title 31, United States Code.

(3) Considerations.—In developing guidance under this subsection, the Director of the Office of Management and Budget shall take into consideration the experiences of agencies in making consolidated performance planning and reporting information available on the website as required under section 1122 of title 31, United States Code.

Sec. 11. Reducing Duplicative and Outdated Agency Reporting.

(a) Budget Contents.—Section 1105(a) of title 31, United States Code, is amended—

(1) by redesignating second paragraph (33) as paragraph (35); and

(2) by adding at the end the following:

> "(37) the list of plans and reports, as provided for under section 1125, that agencies identified for elimination or consolidation because the plans and reports are determined outdated or duplicative of other required plans and reports.".

(b) Elimination of Unnecessary Agency Reporting.—Chapter 11 of title 31, United States Code, is further amended by adding after section 1124 (as added by section 9 of this Act) the following:

"§ 1125. Elimination of unnecessary agency reporting

> "(a) Agency Identification of Unnecessary Reports.—Annually, based on guidance provided by the Director of the Office of Management and Budget, the Chief Operating Officer at each agency shall—
>
>> "(1) compile a list that identifies all plans and reports the agency produces for Congress, in accordance with statutory requirements or as directed in congressional reports;
>>
>> "(2) analyze the list compiled under paragraph (1), identify which plans and reports are outdated or duplicative of other required plans and reports, and refine the list to include only the plans and reports identified to be outdated or duplicative;
>>
>> "(3) consult with the congressional committees that receive the plans and reports identified under paragraph (2) to determine whether those plans and reports are no longer useful to the committees and could be eliminated or consolidated with other plans and reports; and
>>
>> "(4) provide a total count of plans and reports compiled under paragraph (1) and the list of outdated and duplicative reports identified under paragraph (2) to the Director of the Office of Management and Budget.
>
> "(b) Plans and Reports.—
>
>> "(1) First year.—During the first year of implementation of this section, the list of plans and reports identified by each agency as outdated or duplicative shall be not less than 10 percent of all plans and reports identified under subsection (a)(1).
>>
>> "(2) Subsequent years.—In each year following the first year described under paragraph (1), the Director of the Office of Management and Budget shall determine the minimum percent of plans and reports to be identified as outdated or duplicative on each list of plans and reports.

"(c) Request for Elimination of Unnecessary Reports.—In addition to including the list of plans and reports determined to be outdated or duplicative by each agency in the budget of the United States Government, as provided by section 1105(a)(37), the Director of the Office of Management and Budget may concurrently submit to Congress legislation to eliminate or consolidate such plans and reports.".

Sec. 12. Performance Management Skills and Competencies.

(a) Performance Management Skills and Competencies.—Not later than 1 year after the date of enactment of this Act, the Director of the Office of Personnel Management, in consultation with the Performance Improvement Council, shall identify the key skills and competencies needed by Federal Government personnel for developing goals, evaluating programs, and analyzing and using performance information for the purpose of improving Government efficiency and effectiveness.

(b) Position Classifications.—Not later than 2 years after the date of enactment of this Act, based on the identifications under subsection (a), the Director of the Office of Personnel Management shall incorporate, as appropriate, such key skills and competencies into relevant position classifications.

(c) Incorporation Into Existing Agency Training.—Not later than 2 years after the enactment of this Act, the Director of the Office of Personnel Management shall work with each agency, as defined under section 306(f) of title 5, United States Code, to incorporate the key skills identified under subsection (a) into training for relevant employees at each agency.

Sec. 13. Technical and Conforming Amendments.

(a) The table of contents for chapter 3 of title 5, United States Code, is amended by striking the item relating to section 306 and inserting the following:

"306. Agency strategic plans.".

(b) The table of contents for chapter 11 of title 31, United States Code, is amended by striking the items relating to section 1115 and 1116 and inserting the following:

"1115. Federal Government and agency performance plans.
"1116. Agency performance reporting.".

(c) The table of contents for chapter 11 of title 31, United States Code, is amended by adding at the end the following:

"1120. Federal Government and agency priority goals.
"1121. Quarterly priority progress reviews and use of performance information.
"1122. Transparency of programs, priority goals, and results.
"1123. Chief Operating Officers.
"1124. Performance Improvement Officers and the Performance Improvement Council.
"1125. Elimination of unnecessary agency reporting.".

Sec. 14. Implementation of This Act.

(a) Interim Planning and Reporting.—

(1) In general.—The Director of the Office of Management and Budget shall coordinate with agencies to develop interim Federal Government priority goals and submit interim Federal Government performance plans consistent with the requirements of this Act beginning with the submission of the fiscal year 2013 Budget of the United States Government.

(2) Requirements.—Each agency shall—

(A) not later than February 6, 2012, make adjustments to its strategic plan to make the plan consistent with the requirements of this Act;

(B) prepare and submit performance plans consistent with the requirements of this Act, including the identification of agency priority goals, beginning with the performance plan for fiscal year 2013; and

(C) make performance reporting updates consistent with the requirements of this Act beginning in fiscal year 2012.

(3) Quarterly Reviews.—The quarterly priority progress reviews required under this Act shall begin—

(A) with the first full quarter beginning on or after the date of enactment of this Act for agencies based on the agency priority goals contained in the Analytical Perspectives volume of the Fiscal Year 2011 Budget of the United States Government; and

(B) with the quarter ending June 30, 2012 for the interim Federal Government priority goals.

(b) Guidance.—The Director of the Office of Management and Budget shall prepare guidance for agencies in carrying out the interim planning and reporting activities required under subsection (a), in addition to other guidance as required for implementation of this Act.

Sec. 15. Congressional Oversight and Legislation.

(a) In General.—Nothing in this Act shall be construed as limiting the ability of Congress to establish, amend, suspend, or annul a goal of the Federal Government or an agency.

(b) GAO Reviews.—

    (1) Interim planning and reporting evaluation.—Not later than June 30, 2013, the Comptroller General shall submit a report to Congress that includes—

        (A) an evaluation of the implementation of the interim planning and reporting activities conducted under section 14 of this Act; and

        (B) any recommendations for improving implementation of this Act as determined appropriate.

    (2) Implementation evaluations.—

        (A) In general.—The Comptroller General shall evaluate the implementation of this Act subsequent to the interim planning and reporting activities evaluated in the report submitted to Congress under paragraph (1).

        (B) Agency implementation.—

            (i) Evaluations.—The Comptroller General shall evaluate how implementation of this Act is affecting performance management at the agencies described in section 901(b) of title 31, United States Code, including whether performance management is being used by those agencies to improve the efficiency and effectiveness of agency programs.

            (ii) Reports.—The Comptroller General shall submit to Congress—

                (I) an initial report on the evaluation under clause (i), not later than September 30, 2015; and

                (II) a subsequent report on the evaluation under clause (i), not later than September 30, 2017.

        (C) Federal government planning and reporting implementation.—

            (i) Evaluations.—The Comptroller General shall evaluate the implementation of the Federal Government priority goals, Federal Government performance plans and related reporting required by this Act.

            (ii) Reports.—The Comptroller General shall submit to Congress—

                (I) an initial report on the evaluation under clause (i), not later than September 30, 2015; and

                (II) subsequent reports on the evaluation under clause (i), not later than September 30, 2017 and every 4 years thereafter.

(D) Recommendations.—The Comptroller General shall include in the reports required by subparagraphs (B) and (C) any recommendations for improving implementation of this Act and for streamlining the planning and reporting requirements of the Government Performance and Results Act of 1993.

Speaker of the House of Representatives.
Vice President of the United States and President of the Senate.

References

Accenture Institute for Public Service Value, Georgetown Public Policy Institute, and OMB Watch. 2009. *Building a Better Government Performance System: Recommendations to the Obama Administration* (June).

Australian Government Department of Infrastructure, Transport, Regional Development and Local Government. 2008. *Annual Report, 2007–08.* www.infrastructure.gov.au/department/annual_report/2007_2008/index.aspx.

Bakija, Jon, and Bradley Heim. 2008. How Does Charitable Giving Respond to Incentives and Income? Paper presented at the NBER conference on the Incentive and Distributional Consequences of Tax Expenditures. http://www.nber.org/chapters/c6792.pdf.

Barbour, Philip L., Ed. 1986. *The Complete Works of Captain John Smith (1580–1631).* Chapel Hill: Published for the Institute of Early American History and Culture, Williamsburg, VA, by the University of North Carolina Press.

Belcore, Jamie, and Jerry Ellig. 2008. Homeland Security and Regulatory Analysis: Are We Safe Yet? *Rutgers Law Journal* 40:1, 1–96.

Berman, Evan M. 1998. *Productivity in Public and Nonprofit Organizations: Strategies and Techniques.* Thousand Oaks, CA: SAGE Publications.

Bipartisan Policy Center Debt Reduction Task Force. 2010. *Restoring America's Future: Reviving the Economy, Cutting Spending and Debt, and Creating a Simple, Pro-Growth Tax System.* http://bipartisanpolicy.org/sites/default/files/FINAL%20DRTF%20REPORT%2011.16.10.pdf.

Blalock, Garrick, Vrinda Kadiyali, and Daniel H. Simon. 2007. The Impact of Post-9/11 Airport Security Measures on the Demand for Air Travel. *Journal of Law & Economics* 50:4, 731–55.

Blanchard, Lloyd A. 2006. *Performance Budgeting: How NASA and SBA Link Costs and Performance.* Washington, DC: IBM Center for the Business of Government.

Brito, Jerry. 2010. Running for Cover: The BRAC Commission as a Model for Federal Spending Reform. Working Paper 10-23. Mercatus Center at George Mason University. http://mercatus.org/sites/default/files/publication/WP1023_The%20BRAC%20Commission%20as%20a%20Model%20for%20Spending%20Reform%20(2).pdf.

Brito, Jerry, and Jerry Ellig. 2009. Toward a More Perfect Union: Regulatory Analysis and Performance Management. *Florida State University Business Review* 8:1, 1–55.

Browning, Edgar K., and Jacqueline M. Browning. 1979. *Public Finance and the Price System.* New York: Macmillan.

275

Buchanan, James M. 1969. *Cost and Choice*. Chicago: University of Chicago Press.

Burman, Leonard E. 2003. Is the Tax Expenditure Concept Still Relevant? *National Tax Journal* 56:3, 613–27.

Carroll, Robert, David Joulfaian, and James Mackie. 2008. Income versus Consumption Tax Baselines for Tax Expenditures. Paper presented at the NBER conference on the Incentive and Distributional Consequences of Tax Expenditures. http://www.nber.org/chapters/c6788.pdf.

Chun, Young Han, and Hal G. Rainey. 2005a. Goal Ambiguity in US Federal Agencies. *Journal of Public Administration Research and Theory* 15, 1–30.

Chun, Young Han, and Hal G. Rainey. 2005b. Goal Ambiguity and Organizational Performance in US Federal Agencies. *Journal of Public Administration Research and Theory* 15, 529–57.

Colorado Department of Transportation. 2009. *Fiscal Year 2008 Annual Performance Report*. www.coloradodot.info/library/AnnualReports/CDOT_2008_lores.pdf/view.

Committee for a Responsible Federal Budget. 2010. *Summary Table of Fiscal Plans*. http://crfb.org/sites/default/files/Table_of_Plans.pdf.

Congressional Budget Office. 2010. *The Long-Term Budget Outlook, June 2010*. Revised August 2010.

Connecticut Department of Transportation. 2009a. *CTDOT Performance Measures 2009 Quarterly Update*. www.ct.gov/dot/lib/dot/documents/dperformancemeasures/pmeasures2009q1.pdf.

Connecticut Department of Transportation. 2009b. *On the Move: Performance Metrics Report, January 2009*. www.ct.gov/dot/lib/dot/documents/dperformancemeasures/pmetrics.pdf.

Crain, Nicole V., and W. Mark Crain. 2010. *The Impact of Regulatory Costs on Small Firms*. Small Business Administration Office of Advocacy report under contract SBAHQ-08-M-0466.

Crandall, Robert W., and Jerry Ellig. 1997. *Economic Deregulation and Customer Choice*. Fairfax, VA: Center for Market Processes. http://mercatus.org/publication/economic-deregulation-and-customer-choice-lessons-electric-industry.

Curristine, Teresa. 2002. Reforming the U.S. Department of Transportation: Challenges and Opportunities of the Government Performance and Results Act for Federal-State Relations. *Publius* 32, 25–44.

De Rugy, Veronique. 2010. Reality Isn't Negotiable: The Government Can't Raise More Than 19% in Taxes for Long. http://mercatus.org/publication/reality-isnt-negotiable-government-cant-raise-more-19-taxes-long.

Desai, Mihir, Dhammika Dharmapala, and Monical Singhal. 2008. Investable Tax Credits: The Case of the Low Income Housing Tax Credit. Paper presented at the NBER conference on the Incentive and Distributional Consequences of Tax Expenditures. http://www.nber.org/chapters/c6794.pdf.

Downs, Anthony. 1967. *Inside Bureaucracy*. Boston: Little, Brown and Co.

Dudley, Susan, and Melinda Warren. 2010. *A Decade of Growth in the Regulators' Budget: 2011 Annual Report*. Washington, DC: Regulatory Studies Center, George Washington University; St. Louis, MO: Weidenbaum Center, Washington University. http://www.gwu.edu/~regstudies/Reg%20Budget%202010-05-18.pdf.

Dull, Matthew. 2009. Results-Model Reform Leadership: Questions of Credible Commitment. *Journal of Public Administration Research and Theory* 19, 255–84.

Eissa, Nada, and Hilary Hoynes. 2008. Redistribution and Tax Expenditures: The Earned Income Tax Credit. Paper presented at the NBER conference on the Incentive and Distributional Consequences of Tax Expenditures. http://www.nber.org/chapters/c6795.pdf.

Ellig, Jerry. 2010. Has GPRA Improved the Availability and Use of Performance Information? Working paper. Mercatus Center at George Mason University. http://mercatus.org/publication/has-gpra-increased-availability-and-use-performance-information.

Ellig, Jerry. 2002. Railroad Deregulation and Consumer Welfare. *Journal of Regulatory Economics* 21:2, 143–67.

Ellig, Jerry, Amos Guiora, and Kyle McKenzie. 2006. *A Framework for Evaluating Counterterrorism Regulations*. Arlington, VA: Mercatus Center at George Mason University.

Ellig, Jerry, and Patrick McLaughlin. 2010. The Quality and Use of Regulatory Analysis in 2008. Working paper. Mercatus Center at George Mason University. http://mercatus.org/publication/quality-and-use-regulatory-analysis-2008.

Ellig, Jerry, Maurice McTigue, and Steve Richardson. 2000. Putting a Price on Performance: A Demonstration Study of Outcome-Based Scrutiny. Mercatus Center at George Mason University. http://mercatus.org/sites/default/files/publication/MC_GAP_PriceonPerformance_001201.pdf.

European Commission. 2009. *Impact Assessment Guidelines*. http://ec.europa.eu/governance/impact/commission_guidelines/docs/iag_2009_en.pdf.

Executive Order 12866. 1993. *Federal Register* 58:190, 51,735–44.

Federal Communications Commission. 2005. *In the Matter of Comprehensive Review of Universal Service Fund Management, Administration, and Oversight, Notice of Proposed Rulemaking and Further Notice of Proposed Rulemaking*. WC Docket 05-195 et al. Adopted June 9.

Federal Reserve. 2010. *Flow of Funds*, Table B.100 (June 10).

Florida Department of Transportation. 2009. *2025 Florida Transportation Plan: Performance Report, December 2009*. www.dot.state.fl.us/planning/performance/Performance-Report.pdf.

Florida Department of Transportation, Office of Inspector General. 2008. *Advisory Memorandum 08P-0001: 2007 Performance Measures Assessment*. www.dot.state.fl.us/inspectorgeneral/Reports/08P-0001.pdf.

Florida Transportation Commission. 2008. *Annual Performance and Production Review of the Department of Transportation, Fiscal Year 2007/2008*. www.ftc.state.fl.us/PDF/Reports/PPR/Performance_&_Production_Review_of_the_Department_of_Transportation_-_FY_2007-2008.pdf.

Frederickson, D. G., and H. G. Frederickson. 2006. *Measuring the Performance of the Hollow State*. Washington, DC: Georgetown University Press.

Frisco, Velda, and Odd J. Stalebrink. 2008. Congressional Use of the Program Assessment Rating Tool. *Public Budgeting and Finance* 28:2, 1–19.

Galston, Bill, and Maya MacGuineas. 2010. *The Future Is Now: A Balanced Plan to Stabilize Public Debt and Promote Economic Growth*. http://crfb.org/sites/default/files/Galston-MacGuineas_Plan.pdf.

Gandhi, Sima J. 2010. *Audit the Tax Code*. Center for American Progress.

Gilmour, John B., and David E. Lewis. 2006a. Does Performance Budgeting Work? An Examination of the Office of Management and Budget's PART Scores. *Public Administration Review* 66:5, 742–52.

Gilmour, John B., and David E. Lewis. 2006b. Assessing Performance Assessment for Budgeting: The Influence of Politics, Performance, and Program Size in Fiscal Year 2005. *Journal of Public Administration Research and Theory* 16:2, 169–87.

Glaeser, Edward L., and Jesse M. Shapiro. 2003. The Benefits of the Home Mortgage Interest Deduction. In James Poterba (Ed.), *Tax Policy and the Economy* 17, 37–82.

Government Performance and Results Act of 1993, Public Law 103–62.

Graham, John D. 2008. Saving Lives through Administrative Law and Economics. *University of Pennsylvania Law Review* 157, 395–540.

Hall, Joshua. 1999. *Tax Expenditures: A Review and Analysis*. Joint Economic Committee Staff Report.

Harrington, Winston. 2006. Grading the Estimates of the Benefits and Costs of Federal Regulation. Resources for the Future Discussion Paper 06-39. http://www.rff.org/RFF/Documents/RFF-DP-06-39.pdf.

Harrington, Winston, Richard D. Morgenstern, and Peter Nelson. 2000. On the Accuracy of Regulatory Cost Estimates. *Journal of Policy Analysis and Management* 19:2, 297–322.

Hatry, Harry P., E. Morley, S. B. Rossman, and J. S. Wholey. 2005. How Federal Programs Use Outcome Information: Opportunities for Federal Managers. In John M. Kamensky and Albert Morales (Eds.), *Managing for Results 2005*. New York: Rowman & Littlefield Publishers, 197–274.

Hawke, Lewis. 2007. Performance Budgeting in Australia. *OECD Journal on Budgeting* 7:3, 1–15.

Heckman, James, Carolyn Heinrich, and Jeffrey Smith. 1997. Assessing the Performance of Performance Standards in Public Bureaucracies. *American Economic Review* 87:2, 389–95.

Heinrich, Carolyn. 2002. Outcomes-Based Performance Management in the Public Sector: Implications for Government Accountability and Effectiveness. *Public Administration Review* 62:6, 712–25.

Heinrich, Carolyn, and Gerald Marschke. 2010. Incentives and Their Dynamics in Public Sector Performance Management Systems. *Journal of Policy Analysis and Management* 29:1, 183–208.

Hendershott, Patric H., and James D. Shilling. 1982. The Economics of Tenure Choice, 1955–79. *Research in Real Estate* 1, 105–33.

Hughes, Adam, and J. Robert Shull. 2005. PART Backgrounder. *OMB Watch* (April).

Ingraham, Patricia W., Philip K. Joyce, and Amy Kneedler Donahue. 2003. *Government Performance: Why Management Matters*. Baltimore: Johns Hopkins University Press.

Joint Committee on Taxation. 2008. *A Reconsideration of Tax Expenditure Analysis*. Staff Report JCX-37-08 (May 12).

Joyce, Philip G. 2007. Linking Performance and Budgeting: Opportunities in the Federal Budget Process. In Jonathan D. Breul and Carl Moravitz (Eds.), *Integrating Performance and Budgets*. Lanham, MD: Rowman & Littlefield, 19–70.

Kamensky, John M., Albert Morales, and Mark A. Abramson. 2005. From "Useful Measures" to "Measures Used." In John M. Kamensky and Albert Morales (Eds.), *Managing for Results 2005*. Lanham, MD: Rowman and Littlefield.

Kettl, Donald F. 1997. The Global Revolution in Public Management: Driving Themes, Missing Links. *Journal of Policy Analysis and Management* 16:3 (Summer), 446–62.

Key, V. O. 1940. The Lack of a Budgetary Theory. *American Political Science Review* 34:6, 1137–44.

Lewis, Verne B. 1952. Toward a Theory of Budgeting. *Public Administration Review* 12:1, 42–54.

Light, Paul Charles. 1997. *The Tides of Reform: Making Government Work, 1945–1995*. New Haven, CT: Yale University Press.

Manchester, Patrick, and E. Norcross. 2008. Politics and Performance in the Bush Administration's Program Assessment Rating Tool. Unpublished manuscript.

McLaughlin, Patrick, and Jerry Ellig. 2010. Does Haste Make Waste in Regulatory Analysis? Working paper. Mercatus Center at George Mason University. http://mercatus.org/sites/default/files/publication/wp1057-does-haste-make-waste-in-federal-regulations.pdf.

McTigue, Maurice P., Jerry Ellig, and Steve Richardson. 2001. *2nd Annual Performance Report Scorecard: Which Federal Agencies Inform the Public?* Arlington, VA: Mercatus Center at George Mason University. http://mercatus.org/sites/default/files/publication/2nd_annual_performance_report_scorecard.pdf.

McTigue, Maurice P., Christina Forsberg, and Stefanie Haeffele-Balch. 2010. The Factors and Motivations of Fiscal Stability: A Comparative Analysis of 26 Countries. Working paper. Mercatus Center at George Mason University. http://mercatus.org/sites/default/files/publication/The%20Factors%20and%20Motivations%20of%20Fiscal%20Stability.pdf.

McTigue, Maurice P., Sarah E. Nutter, and Jennifer Zambone. 2003. *4th Annual Performance Report Scorecard: Which Federal Agencies Inform the Public?* Arlington, VA: Mercatus Center at George Mason University. http://mercatus.org/sites/default/files/publication/4th_annual_performance_report_scorecard.pdf.

McTigue, Maurice, Henry Wray, and Jerry Ellig. 2009. *10th Annual Performance Report Scorecard: Which Federal Agencies Best Inform the Public?* Arlington, VA: Mercatus Center at George Mason University. http://mercatus.org/publication/10th-annual-performance-report-scorecard-which-federal-agencies-best-inform-public.

McTigue, Maurice, Henry Wray, and Jerry Ellig. 2008. *9th Annual Performance Report Scorecard: Which Federal Agencies Best Inform the Public?* Arlington, VA: Mercatus Center at George Mason University. http://mercatus.org/sites/default/files/publication/20080506_9th_Annual_Performance_Report_Scorecard.pdf.

McTigue, Maurice, Henry Wray, and Jerry Ellig. 2004. *5th Annual Performance Report Scorecard: Which Federal Agencies Best Inform the Public?* Arlington, VA: Mercatus Center at George Mason University. http://mercatus.org/sites/default/files/publication/5th_annual_performance_report_scoreacre.pdf.

Melkers, J., and K. Willoughby. 2007. Staying the Course: The Use of Performance Measurement in State Governments. In Jonathan D. Breul and Carl Moravitz (Eds.), *Integrating Performance and Budgets*. Lanham, MD: Rowman & Littlefield, 71–106.

Metcalf, Gilbert E. 2008. Assessing the Federal Deduction for State and Local Tax Payments. Paper presented at the NBER conference on the Incentive and Distributional Consequences of Tax Expenditures. http://www.nber.org/chapters/c6796.pdf.

Metzenbaum, Shelley H. 2009. *Performance Management Recommendations for the New Administration*. Washington, DC: IBM Center for the Business of Government.

Morrall, John F., III. 2003. Saving Lives: A Review of the Record. *Journal of Risk and Uncertainty* 27:3, 221–37.

Morrall, John F., III. 1986. A Review of the Record. *Regulation* 19, 25–34.

Morrison, Steven, and Clifford Winston. 1995. *The Evolution of the Airline Industry*. Washington, DC: Brookings Institution.

Morrison, Steven, and Clifford Winston. 1985. *The Economic Effects of Airline Deregulation*. Washington, DC: Brookings Institution.

Moynihan, Donald P. 2008. *The Dynamics of Performance Management*. Washington, DC: Georgetown University Press.

National Commission on Fiscal Responsibility and Reform. 2010. *The Moment of Truth: Report of the National Commission on Fiscal Responsibility and Reform*. http://www.fiscalcommission.gov/sites/fiscalcommission.gov/files/documents/TheMomentofTruth12_1_2010.pdf.

New Zealand Ministry of Transport. 2009. *New Zealand Transport Statistics, July 2009*. www.
    transport.govt.nz/topic/Walking/Documents/NZ%20Transport%20Statistics%20
    Final%20august%2011.pdf.
New Zealand Ministry of Transport. 2008. *Annual Report 2007/08: Report of the Ministry of
    Transport for the Year Ended 30 June 2008*. www.transport.govt.nz/about/publications/
    Documents/Annual%20Report%202008.pdf.
New Zealand Ministry of Transport. 2007. *Statement of Intent 2007–2010*.
Niskanen, William A., Jr. 1994a. *Bureaucracy and Public Economics*. Brookfield, VT:
    Edward Elgar.
Niskanen, William A., Jr. 1994b. *Bureaucracy and Representative Government*. Reprinted in
    William A. Niskanen, Jr., *Bureaucracy and Public Economics*. Brookfield, VT: Edward Elgar.
Niskanen, William A., Jr. 1994c. Bureaucrats and Politicians. Reprinted in William A.
    Niskanen, Jr., *Bureaucracy and Public Economics*. Brookfield, VT: Edward Elgar.
Noman, Zafar. 2008. Performance Budgeting in the United Kingdom. *OECD Journal on
    Budgeting* 8:1, 1–16.
Norcross, Eileen. 2005. An Analysis of the Office of Management and Budget's Program As-
    sessment Rating Tool. Working paper. Mercatus Center at George Mason University.
    http://mercatus.org/publication analysis-office-management-and-budgets-program-
    assessment-rating-tool-fy06.
Norcross, Eileen, and Joseph Adamson. 2007. An Analysis of the Office of Management
    and Budget's Program Assessment Rating Tool for Fiscal Year 2008. Working paper.
    Mercatus Center at George Mason University. http://mercatus.org/publication/
    analysis-office-management-and-budgets-program-assessment-rating-tool-fy-2008.
Norcross, Eileen, and Kyle McKenzie. 2006. An Analysis of the Office of Management
    and Budget's Program Assessment Rating Tool for Fiscal Year 2007. Working paper.
    Mercatus Center at George Mason University. http://mercatus.org/publication/
    analysis-office-management-and-budgets-program-assessment-rating-tool-fy-2007.
Nozick, Robert. 1974. *Anarchy, State, and Utopia*. New York: Basic Books.
OECD. 2009a. *Indicators of Regulatory Management Systems*. http://www.oecd.org/datao-
    ecd/44/37/44294427.pdf.
OECD. 2009b. *Measuring Government Activity*.
Olson, Mancur. 1965. *The Logic of Collective Action*. Cambridge, MA: Harvard University Press.
Osborne, David, and Ted Gaebler. 1992. *Reinventing Government*. New York: Penguin Books.
Pennsylvania Independent Regulatory Review Commission. 2008. The Regulatory
    Review Process in Pennsylvania. http://www.irrc.state.pa.us/Documents/Misc/PA_
    Regulatory_Review_Process_January_2008.PDF.
Perrin, B. 2007. Moving from Outputs to Outcomes: Practical Advice from Governments
    around the World. In Jonathan D. Breul and Carl Moravitz (Eds.), *Integrating
    Performance and Budgets*. Lanham, MD: Rowman & Littlefield, 107–68.
Poterba, James. 1992. Taxation and Housing: Old Questions, New Answers. *American
    Economic Review* 8:2, 237–42.
Poterba, James, and Todd Sinai. 2008. Income Tax Provisions Affecting Owner-Occupied
    Housing: Revenue Costs and Incentive Effects. Paper presented at the NBER confer-
    ence on the Incentive and Distributional Consequences of Tax Expenditures. http://
    www.nber.org/chapters/c6793.pdf.
Primo, David M. 2010. Making Budget Rules Work. Working Paper 10-62. Mercatus
    Center at George Mason University. http://mercatus.org/sites/default/files/publica-
    tion/Making%20Budget%20Rules%20Work.Primo_.9.28.10.pdf.

Primo, David M. 2007. *Rules and Restraint: Government Spending and the Design of Institutions.* Chicago: University of Chicago Press.

Radin, Beryl. 2006. *Challenging the Performance Movement.* Washington, DC: Georgetown University Press.

Radin, Beryl. 2000. Intergovernmental Relationships and the Federal Performance Movement. *Publius* 30:1, 143–58.

Rawls, John. 1971. *A Theory of Justice.* Cambridge, MA: Harvard University Press.

Richardson, Steven O. 2010. *The Political Economy of Bureaucracy.* London: Routledge.

Rosen, Harvey S. 1979. Housing Decisions and the US Income Tax. *Journal of Public Economics* 11, 1–23.

Rosen, Harvey S., and Kenneth T. Rosen. 1980. Federal Taxes and Homeownership: Evidence from Time Series. *Journal of Political Economy* 88:1, 59–75.

Rosen, Harvey S., Kenneth T. Rosen, and Douglas Holtz-Eakin. 1984. Housing Tenure, Uncertainty, and Taxation. *Review of Economics and Statistics* 66:3, 405–16.

Scott, Graham. 1996. *Government Reform in New Zealand.* Washington, DC: International Monetary Fund.

Scott, Graham, Ian Ball, and Tony Dale. 1997. New Zealand's Public Sector Management Reform: Implications for the United States. *Journal of Policy Analysis and Management* 16:3, 257–81.

Tengs, Tammy, Miriam E. Adams, Joseph S. Pliskin, Dana Gelb Safran, Joanna E. Siegel, Milton C. Weinstein, and John D. Graham. 1995. Five Hundred Life-Saving Interventions and Their Cost-Effectiveness. *Risk Analysis* 15:3, 369–90.

Tullock, Gordon. 2005. *The Politics of Bureaucracy.* Reprinted in Charles K. Rowley (Ed.), *The Selected Works of Gordon Tullock.* Indianapolis, IN: Liberty Fund.

United Kingdom Department for Transport. 2008a. *2008 Annual Report.* http://webarchive.nationalarchives.gov.uk/+/http://www.dft.gov.uk/about/publications/apr/ar2008.

United Kingdom Department for Transport. 2008b. *Autumn Performance Report 2008.* http://webarchive.nationalarchives.gov.uk/+/http://www.dft.gov.uk/about/publications/apr/ap/autumnperformance08.pdf.

U.S. Department of Agriculture. 2008. *Performance and Accountability Report, FY 2008.* www.ocfo.usda.gov/usdarpt/par2008/pdf/par2008.pdf.

U.S. Department of Commerce. 2008. *Performance and Accountability Report, FY 2008.* www.osec.doc.gov/bmi/BUDGET/FY08PAR/DOC_PAR_FY08_508version.pdf.

U.S. Department of Education. 2008. *Performance and Accountability Report, FY 2008.* www2.ed.gov/about/reports/annual/2008report/report.pdf.

U.S. Department of Energy. 2009. *Citizens' Report, FY 2008.* www.cfo.doe.gov/CF1-2/2008CR.pdf.

U.S. Department of Health and Human Services. 2009. *Citizens' Report, FY 2008.* www.hhs.gov/asrt/ob/docbudget/citizensreport.pdf.

U.S. Department of Homeland Security. 2009. *Citizens' Report, FY 2008.* www.dhs.gov/xlibrary/assets/cfo_citizensfy2008.pdf.

U.S. Department of Homeland Security. 2007. *Highlights Report, FY 2007.* www.dhs.gov/xlibrary/assets/cfo_highlightsfy2007.pdf.

U.S. Department of Homeland Security. 2006. *Performance and Accountability Report, FY 2006.* www.dhs.gov/xlibrary/assets/cfo_par2006_fullreport.pdf.

U.S. Department of Housing and Urban Development. 2010. US Housing Market Conditions, Historical Data, Exhibit 9, http://www.huduser.org/portal/periodicals/ushmc/summer10/hist_data.pdf.

U.S. Department of Housing and Urban Development. 2008. *Performance and Accountability Report, FY 2008*. www.hud.gov/offices/cfo/reports/hudpar-fy2008.pdf.

U.S. Department of the Interior. 2008. *Performance and Accountability Report, FY 2008*. www.doi.gov/pfm/par/par2008/par08_final.pdf.

U.S. Department of Justice. 2009. *Citizens' Report, FY 2008*. www.justice.gov/archive/jmd/2008citizens-report.pdf.

U.S. Department of Justice. 2008. *Performance and Accountability Report, FY 2008*. www.justice.gov/ag/annualreports/pr2008/2008par.pdf.

U.S. Department of Labor. 2009. *Citizens' Report, FY 2008*. www.dol.gov/_sec/media/reports/Citizens2008/CitizensReport.pdf.

U.S. Department of Labor. 2008. *Performance and Accountability Report, FY 2008*. www.dol.gov/_sec/media/reports/annual2008/2008annualreport.pdf.

U.S. Department of State. 2009. *Citizens' Report, FY 2008*. www.state.gov/documents/organization/114171.pdf.

U.S. Department of Transportation. 2008. *Performance and Accountability Report, FY 2008*. www.dot.gov/par/2008/pdf/DOT_PAR_2008.pdf.

U.S. Department of Transportation, Research and Innovative Technology Administration. 2009. *State Transportation Statistics.*

U.S. Department of the Treasury. 2008. *Performance and Accountability Report, FY 2008*. www.ustreas.gov/offices/management/dcfo/accountability-reports/2008-par/Full_Version.pdf.

U.S. Department of Veterans Affairs. 2008. *Performance and Accountability Report, FY 2008*. www4.va.gov/budget/report/.

U.S. Environmental Protection Agency. 2008. *Performance and Accountability Report, FY 2008*. www.epa.gov/ocfo/par/2008par/par08report.pdf.

U.S. General Services Administration. 2008. *Performance and Accountability Report, FY 2008*. www.gsa.gov/graphics/staffoffices/GSAFY2008PAR.pdf.

U.S. Government Accountability Office. 2009a. High-Risk Series: An Update. GAO-09-271. www.gao.gov/new.items/d09271.pdf.

U.S. Government Accountability Office. 2009b. Government Performance: Strategies for Building a Results-Oriented and Collaborative Culture in the Federal Government. GAO-09-1011T. www.gao.gov/new.items/d091011t.pdf.

U.S. Government Accountability Office. 2008. Government Performance: Lessons Learned for the Next Administration on Using Performance Information to Improve Results. Statement of Bernice Steinhardt, Report GAO-08-1026T.

U.S. Government Accountability Office. 2007. Re-Examining Regulations: Opportunities Exist to Improve Effectiveness and Transparency of Retrospective Reviews. Report GAO-07-791.

U.S. Government Accountability Office. 2005a. Performance Budgeting: Efforts to Restructure Budgets to Better Align Resources with Performance. Report GAO-05-117SP.

U.S. Government Accountability Office. 2005b. Performance Budgeting: PART Focuses Attention on Program Performance, but More Can Be Done to Engage Congress. Report GAO-06-28.

U.S. Government Accountability Office. 2005c. Government Performance and Accountability: Tax Expenditures Represent a Substantial Federal Commitment and Need to Be Reexamined. Report GAO-05-690.

U.S. Government Accountability Office. 2005e. Managing for Results: Enhancing Agency Use of Performance Information for Management Decision-Making. Report GAO-05-927.

U.S. Government Accountability Office. 2004a. Results-Oriented Government: GPRA Has Established a Solid Foundation for Achieving Greater Results. Report GAO-04-38.

U.S. Government Accountability Office. 2004b. Performance Budgeting: Observations on the Use of OMB's Program Assessment Rating Tool for the Fiscal Year 2004 Budget. Report GAO-04-174.

U.S. Government Accountability Office. 2003. Results-Oriented Cultures: Creating a Clear Linkage between Individual Performance and Organizational Success. Report GAO-03-488.

U.S. Government Accountability Office. 2001. Managing for Results: Federal Managers' Views on Key Management Issues Vary Widely Across Agencies. Report GAO-01-592.

U.S. Government Accountability Office. 1997a. The Government Performance and Results Act: 1997 Implementation Will be Uneven. Report GAO/GGD-97-019.

U.S. Government Accountability Office. 1997b. Proprietary Schools: Millions Spent to Train Students for Oversupplied Occupations. GAO/HEHS-97-104.

U.S. Government Accountability Office. 1996. Executive Guide: Effectively Implementing the Government Performance and Results Act. Report GAO/GGD-96-118.

U.S. Government Accountability Office. 1992. Program Performance Measures: Federal Agency Collection and Use of Performance Data. Report GAO/GGD-92-65.

U.S. National Aeronautics and Space Administration. 2008. *Performance and Accountability Report, FY 2008.* www.nasa.gov/pdf/291255main_NASA_FY08_Performance_and_Accountability_Report.pdf.

U.S. National Science Foundation. 2009. *Citizens' Report, 2008.* http://www.nsf.gov/pubs/2009/nsf0903/nsf0903.pdf.

U.S. Nuclear Regulatory Commission. 2009. *Citizens' Report, FY 2008.* http://www.nrc.gov/reading-rm/doc-collections/nuregs/staff/sr1542/v14/s1/sr1542v14s1.pdf.

U.S. Nuclear Regulatory Commission. 2008. *Performance and Accountability Report, FY 2008.* www.nrc.gov/reading-rm/doc-collections/nuregs/staff/sr1542/v14/s1/sr1542v14s1.pdf.

U.S. Office of Management and Budget. 2010a. *2009 Report to Congress on the Benefits and Costs of Federal Regulations and Unfunded Mandates on State, Local and Tribal Entities.*

U.S. Office of Management and Budget. 2010b. *Budget of the United States Government, Fiscal Year 2011, Analytical Perspectives.*

U.S. Office of Management and Budget. 2010c. *Budget of the United States Government, Fiscal Year 2011, Historical Tables.*

U.S. Office of Management and Budget. 2009a. *Budget of the United States Government, Fiscal Year 2010, Historical Tables.*

U.S. Office of Management and Budget. 2009b. *Budget of the United States Government, Fiscal Year 2010, Analytical Perspectives.*

U.S. Office of Management and Budget. 2009c. *The FY 2008 Performance Report of the Federal Government* (January).

U.S. Office of Management and Budget. 2008a. *Budget of the United States Government, Fiscal Year 2009, Historical Tables.*

U.S. Office of Management and Budget. 2008b. Executive Branch Management Scorecard.

U.S. Office of Management and Budget. 2008c. *Budget of the United States Government, Fiscal Year 2009, Analytical Perspectives.*

U.S. Office of Management and Budget. 2008d. Program Assessment Rating Tool Guidance 2008-01 (January 29). http://www.whitehouse.gov/omb/part/fy2008/part_guid_2008.pdf.

U.S. Office of Management and Budget. 2007a. *Budget of the United States Government, Fiscal Year 2008, Analytical Perspectives.*

U.S. Office of Management and Budget. 2007c. *Financial Reporting Requirements.* Circular A-136.

U.S. Office of Management and Budget. 2006. *Budget of the United States Government, Fiscal Year 2007, Analytical Perspectives.*

U.S. Office of Management and Budget. 2005a. *Validating Regulatory Analysis: 2005 Report to Congress on the Benefits and Costs of Federal Regulations and Unfunded Mandates on State, Local, and Tribal Entities.*

U.S. Office of Management and Budget. 2005b. *Budget of the United States Government, Fiscal Year 2006, Analytical Perspectives.*

U.S. Office of Management and Budget. 2004. *Budget of the United States Government, Fiscal Year 2005, Analytical Perspectives.*

U.S. Office of Management and Budget. 2003a. *Regulatory Analysis.* Circular A-4.

U.S. Office of Management and Budget. 2003b. *Budget of the United States Government, Fiscal Year 2004, Analytical Perspectives.*

U.S. Office of Management and Budget. 2002a. *Budget of the United States Government, Fiscal Year 2003, Analytical Perspectives.*

U.S. Office of Management and Budget. 2002b. Memorandum for Chief Financial Officers and Inspectors General (October 18). http://www.whitehouse.gov/omb/rewrite/financial/final_yr_end_memo2002.html.

U.S. Office of Management and Budget. 2001a. *The President's Management Agenda, Fiscal Year 2002.* http://www.whitehouse.gov/omb/assets/omb/budget/fy2002/mgmt.pdf.

U.S. Office of Management and Budget. 2001b. Executive Branch Management Scorecard Baseline.

U.S. Office of Management and Budget. 2001c. *Budget of the United States Government, Fiscal Year 2002, Analytical Perspectives.*

U.S. Office of Management and Budget. 2000. *Budget of the United States Government, Fiscal Year 2001, Analytical Perspectives.*

U.S. Office of Management and Budget. 1999. *Budget of the United States Government, Fiscal Year 2000, Analytical Perspectives.*

U.S. Office of Management and Budget. 1998. *Budget of the United States Government, Fiscal Year 1999, Analytical Perspectives.*

U.S. Office of Management and Budget. 1997. *Budget of the United States Government, Fiscal Year 1998, Analytical Perspectives.*

U.S. Office of Management and Budget. 1996. *Budget of the United States Government, Fiscal Year 1997, Analytical Perspectives.*

U.S. Office of Personnel Management. 2009. *Citizens' Report, FY 2008.* http://www.opm.gov/gpra/opmgpra/performance_report2008.pdf.

U.S. Office of Personnel Management. 2008. *Performance and Accountability Report, FY 2008.* www.opm.gov/gpra/opmgpra/performance_report2008.pdf.

U.S. Office of Personnel Management. 2007. *Alternative Personnel Systems in the Federal Government.*

U.S. Office of Personnel Management. 2006. *Performance and Accountability Report, FY 2006.* www.opm.gov/account/gpra/opmgpra/par2006/PAR06-Complete.pdf.

U.S. Senate, Committee on Governmental Affairs. 1993. Government Performance and Results Act of 1993, Report to Accompany S. 20. 103rd Congress, 1st Session, Report No. 103-58. http://www.whitehouse.gov/omb/mgmt-gpra/gprptm#h1.

U.S. Small Business Administration. 2009. *Annual Performance Report, FY 2008*. www.sba. gov/idc/groups/public/documents/sba_homepage/serv_abtsba_2008_apr_001-040. pdf.

U.S. Small Business Administration. 2008. *Agency Financial Report. FY 2008*. www.sba.gov/ aboutsba/budgetsplans/SERV_ABTSBA_BUDGET_2008AFR.html.

U.S. Small Business Administration. 2004. *Performance and Accountability Report, Fiscal Year 2004*. http://www.sba.gov/aboutsba/budgetsplans/serv_bud_2004par.html.

U.S. Small Business Administration. 2003. *Performance and Accountability Report, Fiscal Year 2003*. http://www.sba.gov/idc/groups/public/documents/sba_homepage/sba_010475.pdf.

U.S. Social Security Administration. 2008a. *Performance and Accountability Report, FY 2008*. www.ssa.gov/finance/2008/Full%20PAR.pdf.

Viscusi, W. Kip, Joseph E. Harrington, Jr., and John M. Vernon. 2005. *Economics of Regulation and Antitrust*. 4th ed. Cambridge, MA: MIT Press.

von Mises, Ludwig. 1946. *Bureaucracy*. New Haven, CT: Yale University Press.

Walker, David M. 2005. *21st Century Challenges: Reexamining the Base of the Federal Government*. Statement of David M. Walker, Comptroller General of the United States, before the Senate Committee on Homeland Security and Governmental Affairs, GAO-05-352-T.

Wildavsky, Aaron. 1992. Political Implications of Budget Reform: A Retrospective. *Public Administration Review* 52:6, 594–99.

Wilson, James Q. 1989. *Bureaucracy: What Government Agencies Do and Why They Do It*. New York: Basic Books.

Winston, Clifford. 1998. U.S. Industry Adjustment to Economic Deregulation. *Journal of Economic Perspectives* 12:3, 89–110.

Winston, Clifford. 1993. Economic Deregulation: Days of Reckoning for Microeconomists. *Journal of Economic Literature* 31:3, 1263–89.

Winston, Clifford, Thomas M. Corsi, Curtis M. Grimm, and Carol A. Evans. 1990. *The Economic Effects of Surface Freight Deregulation*. Washington, DC: Brookings Institution.

Wiseman, Alan E., and Jerry Ellig. 2007. The Politics of Wine: Trade Barriers, Interest Groups, and the Commerce Clause. *Journal of Politics* 69:3, 859–75.

Wray, Henry. 2009. Performance Accountability for Regulations. In Richard Williams (Ed.), *21st Century Regulation: Discovering Better Solutions for Enduring Problems*. Arlington, VA: Mercatus Center at George Mason University, 20–33. http://mercatus.org/ publication/21st-century-regulation-discovering-better-solutions-enduring-problems.

Zerbe, Richard O., and Allen S. Bellas. 2006. *A Primer for Benefit-Cost Analysis*. Cheltenham, UK: Edward Elgar.

Zerbe, Richard O., Jr., and Dwight D. Dively. 1994. *Benefit-Cost Analysis in Theory and Practice*. New York: HarperCollins.

Index